Pentecostal Catholics

POWER, CHARISMA, AND ORDER IN A RELIGIOUS MOVEMENT

TEMPLE
UNIVERSITY
PRESS
Philadelphia

Pentecostal Catholics

Power,
Charisma,
and Order
in a
Religious
Movement

MEREDITH B.
McGUIRE

Temple University Press, Philadelphia 19122
© 1982 by Temple University. All rights reserved
Published 1982
Printed in the United States of America

Library of Congress Cataloging in Publication Data

McGuire, Meredith B.
  Pentecostal Catholics.

  Includes bibliographical references and index.
  1. Pentecostalism—Catholic Church. 2. Catholic
Church—United States. I. Title.
BX2350.57.M39   306'.6   81-14434
ISBN 0-87722-235-5   AACR2

To my parents,
Virginia and George Black

Contents

Acknowledgments

In writing this book, I have received help from many people whose assistance I gratefully acknowledge: Deborah Offenbacher and Thomas Luckmann, for their helpful suggestions in the preliminary stages of research; and Jim Beckford, Tom Bridges, Peter Freund, Harriet Klein, David McGuire, Jim Richardson, and Len Rubin, for their thoughtful comments on earlier drafts. Thanks also to Joleen Benedict, Barbara Garrison, Ursula Gilbert, and Linda Mai for their assistance in parts of the data gathering, and to Pat Brown, Sue Goscinski, Debra Kantor, Matt Krautheim, Kathy Landrigan, and Valerie Simpson for their care in the preparation of the manuscript. The advice and encouragement of my editor, Kenneth Arnold, and reviewers, Karen Fasano and Sharon Hollie are greatly appreciated.

Partial funding for the "healing" portion of the research was received from the Society for the Scientific Study of Religion and from Sigma Xi. The research and writing were also aided by grants of released time and a sabbatical leave from Montclair State College.

I want to express my special gratitude to Laura Gordon for her thoughtful advice, sustained encouragement and collegial support in my work. Thanks also to my family for their patience and good humor. Daniel and Rachel witnessed my efforts on this project from their pre-school to their junior-high-school years, and Kieran was born shortly before data collection ended. I appreciate their wonderful ways of helping me keep an extensive project in perspective.

Pentecostal Catholics

POWER, CHARISMA, AND ORDER IN A RELIGIOUS MOVEMENT

One—
Introduction

In 1969 a young couple, speaking for the emerging Catholic pentecostal movement, wrote:

> The rapid spread of what is usually termed "secularity" among men in contemporary society is by now a fact. It is alarming to some, understandable to many. Its cause is debated quite regularly in academic circles. But one thing seems clear: There has been a remarkable failure on the part of institutional Christianity, Catholic and Protestant alike, to speak a relevant word of salvation to modern man. A God may indeed be worshipped here, but he is faceless and abstract. . . . We believe the baptism in the Holy Spirit with these dynamic gifts and fruit speaks radically to the secular man.[1]

The movement has continued to spread and develop, and members continue to see its message as a confrontation with the forces for secularization of society.

Sociologists, too, are interested in the process of secularization,[2] primarily because of its implications for the role of religion in the larger society, and the place of meaning for individual members of that society. Writing in the same year, in a book subtitled "Modern Society and the Rediscovery of the Supernatural," sociologist Peter Berger summarized sociological observation of the situation: "Today the supernatural as a meaningful reality is absent or remote from the horizons of everyday life of large numbers, very probably of the majority, of people in modern societies, who seem to manage to get along without it quite well."[3] The secularization of modern society is the result of sociologically understandable processes that are not readily reversible.

How, then, can one explain the recent development of numerous religious and quasi-religious movements in America and elsewhere? Standard sociological theories provide little understanding because the contemporary religious revival—unlike most earlier enthusiastic religious movements—seems to be primarily among the middle classes. Do these contemporary religious movements suggest that the trend toward secularization may be slowing or stopped? Do they point to a resacralization of society? Studying the Catholic pentecostal movement is especially useful for examining these questions, because this movement is widespread, middle-class, and not specifically a product of youth culture. This book examines research data on this and related movements for an understanding of the place of religion in contemporary society. By extension, this analysis of the case of Catholic pentecostalism also illuminates the relationship of the individual to the larger society and sources of meaning and identity.

The Nature and Scope of the Catholic Pentecostal Movement

The pentecostal movement began in the early part of the twentieth century and has spread worldwide.[4] Its early practice was not amenable to Catholic or mainline Protestant affiliation; in fact, a strong anti-Catholic strain in classical pentecostalism still exists and hinders efforts for "ecumenical" pentecostal activities. In the second half of the century, however, a modified form of pentecostalism ("neo-pentecostalism")[5] began to spread among some members of mainline Protestant denominations (for example, Episcopalians, Lutherans, Presbyterians) and later among Roman Catholics. The term "pentecostalism" refers to the expectation that the Holy Spirit (Holy Ghost) bestows powerful spiritual gifts upon believers just as at the time of Pentecost in the New Testament. Some gifts of the Spirit include, for example, speaking in tongues (glossolalia), prophecy, discernment of spirits, and healing.

In the early stages of development of the Catholic pentecostal movement, members unabashedly referred to themselves as "Catholic pentecostals" or "pentecostal Catholics," emphasizing their dual commitment to both pentecostalism and Catholicism. As the movement gained broader membership, however, many members were uncomfortable with the social connotations of the term "pentecostals," as denoting a style of religious expression not compatible with their middle-class behavior and disparaged as "cultural baggage." The term "Catholic charismatics" was coined to refer to those who had received the gifts (charismata) of the Spirit. Eventually, the emphasis shifted from the concept of a "charismatic movement" to a "charismatic renewal," implying that the process was one of thorough renewal of the Catholic church, thus mitigating the members' fear of disloyalty. The term "Catholic pentecostal movement" is employed herein for consistency; the term "charismatic renewal" may, however, be used interchangeably.

The development of the pentecostal movement within Catholicism began in the spring of 1967. Some Catholic laymen, faculty members at Duquesne University, had been praying together and, after reading Wilkerson's *The Cross and the Switchblade*, they decided to seek out Protestant pentecostals to learn more about their experiences. They received the baptism of the Holy Spirit and began to spread their newfound faith and enthusiasm. Through a network of friends, the idea spread to students and faculty members at the University of Notre Dame, who also sought the assistance of local Protestant pentecostals. The Notre Dame group then met with students from Michigan State University (M.S.U.) for a prayer weekend, and by these and similar contacts the movement began to spread.[6] Although the initial appeal was to college and graduate students, by the early 1970s the membership could be characterized mainly as middle-aged. In subsequent years the movement appears to have had decreasing appeal to college-age students and increasing appeal to older persons.

Catholic pentecostalism reached the attention of the national news media in May 1967, and was described sympathetically in a Catholic magazine the following month. By mid-1971, the movement had developed a pastoral newsletter, *The New Covenant*. By 1977 this publication had a circulation of approximately 65,000, and was only one of several activities under the organization of the Charismatic Renewal Services, an extensive operation supplying music, books, cassette-lectures, speakers, and conferences for the national movement.[7] The growth of the movement was also reflected in the estimated attendance at national and international conferences:[8]

1967	60–90 (essentially only groups from Notre Dam and M.S.U.)
1968	150
1969	450 (the first real national conference)
1970	1,400
1971	4,500–5,000
1972	10,000–11,000
1973	20,000
1974	25,000
1975	10,000 (held in Rome)
1976	30,000
1977	45,000 (the first ecumenical conference; approximately half were Catholics)

1978   20,000 (held in Dublin)
1980   10,000 (since 1977 the movement has de-emphasized
        national gatherings and encouraged regional
        conferences)

Similarly, a regional rally in the New York Metropolitan area attracted an estimated 35,000 in 1977, and an ecumenical pentecostal rally was attended by approximately 55,000, of which at least half were Catholics.[9] Estimates of actual membership are difficult, since few groups keep accurate membership lists and many groups have overlapping membership. In 1974, the *New York Times* cited the figure of 350,000 members, and in 1975, *Newsweek* gave the estimate of 500,000.[10] These figures seem reasonable, based upon the number of prayer groups around the country, as listed in the movement directory.[11] If the growth of national membership has been comparable to that of the region studied in this research, a reasonable estimate for 1978 is about 600,000 members. There is evidence that membership peaked in 1977 or 1978 and may have declined somewhat since then.

The movement has developed in another significant way: it has gained acceptance by some clergy and, especially, some members of the church hierarchy. Movement leaders were particularly pleased with the strong support of Cardinal Suenens of Belgium and with the public expression of acceptance by Archbishop Bernardin, recent president of the Conference of American Bishops.[12] At the local level numerous priests and nuns have been attracted, and entire parishes, schools, and monasteries are now organized as pentecostal prayer communities.[13] The movement has also spawned numerous "covenant communities," most members of which live and work communally.

The Catholic pentecostal movement is interesting, not only because of its size, scope, and growth, but also because of its appeal to middle-class and middle-aged persons. The "enthusiastic" religious expression has been adapted to a style comfortable to the middle-class; for example, mildly altered states of consciousness are valued, but are carefully controlled and moderated. The appeal of the movement to middle-aged and elderly persons is also interesting. The pentecostal style of religiosity is often compatible with the devotions of, for example, an elderly lady who still says her daily rosary, attends Mass faithfully each Sunday, and makes regular Novenas for her "fallen-away" grandchildren. The Catholic pentecostal movement has numerous characteristics which differ dramatically from the values and practices of the dominant culture in America. These include its reaffirmation of the relevance and meaning of religion in daily life, and its strong emphasis on the family and the prayer community—a community based on shared beliefs and religious experience, together with a concomitant non- (or anti-) rationality.

Catholic pentecostalism is essentially a lay movement, although priests and nuns figure prominently in its membership and often provide leadership for prayer groups. Many members believe the movement makes religious power and experience available to ordinary people, not just to the hierarchy. At the same time, movement leaders have (more or less successfully) legitimated the pentecostal practices as consistent with Catholic loyalties. Issues, such as the stance of the movement toward hierarchical exercise of authority, liturgical worship and the sacraments, and the place of Scripture and tradition in informing contemporary religious thinking, have been addressed by movement intellectuals.

The attraction of Catholics to pentecostalism is not new. There have been pentecostal churches for Italian and Puerto Rican immigrants for many years prior to the neo-pentecostal movement, but until recently, becoming pentecostal meant leaving the Catholic church.[14] This alternative may have been plausible to an immigrant aspiring to upward mobility but is less attractive to a comfortable middle-class church member. It is interesting how the Catholic pentecostal movement has adapted pentecostal piety to a middle-class style of expression and legitimated its place within Catholicism.

At the same time, however, the acceptance of this movement within the Catholic church is largely due to the loss of power of the church itself. Methods of controlling, encapsulating, or eradicating dissenting movements within the church which were historically successful are not very effective in modern pluralistic societies; the Catholic church represents, in America at least, merely one competing world view among many. For many members, it is no longer (in comedian Lenny Bruce's words) "the only The Church"; in fact, many respondents in this study referred to it as "my denomination." Furthermore, pluralistic interpretations within the church itself have reduced its capacity to control dissenting movements; dissenting members can say correctly, "I want to remain a Catholic—but on my terms—and you can't make me leave." Under such conditions the church authorities are moved to greater tolerance of such movements and constrained to effecting controls by more subtle means such as co-optation and routinization. For example, the creation of the office of "diocesan director for the charismatic renewal" (a term Weber would have appreciated) both acknowledges and routinizes the effects of the movement.

Details about the movement's belief system and practices are presented in subsequent chapters; four qualities of the movement are particularly relevant for understanding its stance against secular society. The key analytical concept unifying all of these qualities is "power." From a sociological perspective, then, these qualities are (1) a belief that the power of God is given directly to ordinary humans (through the "gifts of the Holy Spirit"), (2) that, as a result, members have the power to see the relevance of religion in their everyday lives, and prayer groups experience a power which serves as the basis for meaning and moral norms, (3) this power has a strong experiential component, and (4) all these beliefs and experiences compel members to seek out a community of fellow believers—a community which both produces and is the product of power. Although these qualities have important theological implications, their significance for this volume is primarily sociological.

The concept of power is significant for a discussion of theories of secularization, that propose that major changes have occurred in the social location and significance of religion in Western society over the last several centuries. The secularization thesis is an interpretive paradigm that tries to "make sense" of historical processes. Four general themes are emphasized: institutional differentiation, competing sources of legitimacy, rationalization, and privatization (developed further in Chapter 9).[15] The processes of institutional specialization, and the rationalization of the public spheres of big business, law, government, and education have resulted in a social world over which many individuals feel they have no control.[16]

The world has become too large to handle. Traditional religious meaning systems provided believers with, among other things, a sense of borrowed power; they could understand their world and even have some control over it. Thus, the "discovery" of new sources of power by various religious movements can be understood as an attempt to restore a sense of order and meaning. Catholic pentecostalism gives members an experience of being empowered to handle their world and to function in it more effectively. The sociologist needs to understand how this experience of power affects individual relationships and identities.

The Organization of This Volume

After describing the groups studied and methods of this research, we explore, in Chapter Two, the central beliefs, values, and meanings promulgated by the movement, with particular attention to the beliefs and attitudes of ordinary members. Chapter Three is an analysis of the processes of conversion, commitment and socialization into the Catholic pentecostal prayer group, and specifically focuses on social processes that serve to draw the new member into full commitment to the group and its distinctive beliefs and practices.

Chapters Four and Five contain a detailed analysis of ritual and the use of language within the prayer group; ritual and language figure importantly in the establishment of social and personal power. Chapter Four gives an ethnographic description of the central ritual expression of the movement—the prayer meeting. It notes the extent to which the emerging patterns of language in the prayer group are resolutions of conflicting strains in the movement itself—egalitarianism versus appeals to authority, spontaneity versus order, freedom versus control. Chapter Four also analyzes the use of specific "word gifts" of the Spirit, especially prophecy. The social functions of these word gifts within the prayer group demonstrate the structure and exercise of authority in the group. Mechanisms for social control and routinization of charisma are developed to manage the ambiguity inherent in the use of some word gifts. Chapter Five includes a theoretical discussion of the implications of Catholic pentecostals' alternate world view for "religious speaking" and "religious hearing." The belief that God frequently communicates with people through the medium of ordinary human speech (for example, gifts of prophecy, wisdom, or interpretation of tongues) results in a dramatically different mode and normative structure for speaking and hearing in the prayer group.

Chapters Six and Seven examine Catholic pentecostal beliefs about illness, health, and healing. Their specific healing practices are discussed and related to other aspects of the prayer ministries of the groups. The social functions of pentecostal healing are discussed in terms of four themes: illness as deviance and healing as social control, healing the metaphorical body, illness as disorder and healing as restoration of order, healing, and power. Chapter Eight discusses some aspects of the interface between Catholic pentecostal beliefs and the social structure and norms of their groups. Cultic and sectarian aspects of the movement are analyzed, with special reference to communitarian arrangements within the movement (for example, covenant communities). Included in this discussion are group attitudes toward authority, hierarchy within the movement, roles of women, idealization of family structure, relationships with secular authorities, and the implication of these beliefs and attitudes for the social structure of prayer communities. The concluding Chapter Nine locates the Catholic pentecostal movement in a socio-historical framework with the major interpretive question: What does this movement imply about the location and significance of religion in contemporary society?

Research Methodology

To establish the empirical base of the interpretations presented in this volume, it would probably be sufficient to say that I conducted a total of 184 interviews, acted as participant-observer in 138 prayer meetings, and 47 other meetings, gathered 93 verbatim records of speech acts, etcetera, in nine different groups over a period of six years (1971–1977). This volume of data is impressive, but does not accurately describe the research process. Discussing one's methodology at the completion of a study usually results in a nice, neat package, implying that the work was all thoroughly mapped out and each detail anticipated in advance. In practice, most research—even survey research—is very rarely that neat.

This field-research approach (sometimes called "qualitative research methods") is highly flexible, allowing the research setting itself to suggest subsequent steps. In other words, first I developed ways to get data to answer my initial questions; then, while gathering these data, I found myself asking further questions. I frequently had to try different ways of getting information or to add more groups to the sample. Even while pursuing a single question, I often found it helpful to try several different approaches because even if I discovered that my findings did not really address the issues as I wished to frame them, they often led to further insights that, in turn, evoked further research questions. I value the flexibility of this process; it leads to more depth and breadth than would the rigid application of a more limited research methodology. On the other hand, there are drawbacks. One limitation is that these data are not strictly comparable. For example, I did not ask exactly the same questions of persons interviewed early in the research as I did of those interviewed in a later phase. Similarly, I did not discover the significance of some beliefs and actions until later in the study. I could not then readily retrieve comparative data from early notes, since the data were not initially perceived to be significant enough to record. Also, after completing a detailed analysis of one aspect (for example, witnessing in prayer meetings), I often heard or saw further examples that would have been valuable additions to my body of data, but could not pursue these in detail because I was too busy recording some other aspect. I had to be content with letting these further data form something of an unfocused background sense of the situation, while recording only those new aspects which deviated from the previously observed patterns.

The foremost reason for choosing field research methods, such as participant-observation and intensive interviewing, is that these methodological approaches are best suited to trying to grasp the meanings of a situation for the participants themselves. Furthermore, they yield firsthand insights into the ongoing life of the groups studied. The advantages and limitations of these research methods are developed further at the end of this chapter.

Groups Studied

The study began in 1971 with five groups, only one of which had been in existence as a pentecostal group for more than one year. Another had been meeting for several years as an "underground church"[17] and had only just become pentecostal. In 1973 two more were included in the study in order to balance the sample with more large and medium-sized groups. The two additional groups had been functioning about as long as the first five. Data from these seven groups are the basis of most of this study. Because few of the seven groups had highly developed healing ministries, however, another two groups were included in 1976 and 1977 in order to gather more data on healing practices. Only the chapters on healing and community reflect specific data from these two groups, although observations in these groups generally corroborated previously gathered information.

The methodological problem of whom to study is serious; even a research project of this scope cannot achieve the perfect solution. Ideally the entire relevant population would include not only firm members of a Catholic pentecostal prayer group at any given time, but also those who participate at a lower level of commitment, those who once participated but are no longer part of the group, those who decided not to join, those who have similar background experiences to members but who have not joined, non-Catholic neo-pentecostals, and so on. Even such an ambitious research project as this cannot approximate the methodological ideal. Rather, it has focused on several specific groups of believers; comparisons with others of different experiences can be only inferred from other sources of data.

The groups studied were selected for accessibility and do not represent a formal sample, although they do include various size and age ranges. It is interesting, however, that only one of the groups resembled the moderation, the theological focus and the use of Scripture and tradition that are described as characteristic of the movement in the national literature.[18] This contrast raises the problem of representativeness; that is, were all of the groups studied atypical? On the contrary, the version of pentecostalism presented in the literature of the national movement should be considered as an idealization, not necessarily representative of what actually happens in the ordinary prayer group. The findings of this research suggest that the differences between the groups studied and the idealizations described in the literature are due to sociological variables. One variable is the membership itself. For example, the national movement is centered around universities with theologians as contributing members or critical colleagues; the local groups studied are relatively isolated (although much less so in the last two years of the study) and the membership consists mainly of housewives, businessmen, blue-collar workers, and the like. The most important factor, however, is that the very nature of the pentecostal movement is to be open to all kinds of possibilities for the influence of the Holy Spirit. With this kind of highly individualized openness, it is difficult to put a fence about the phenomenon and say: "This is valid Catholic pentecostalism," or "That is not valid" (although regional and national leaders are attempting greater definition and control with considerable success). Nevertheless, a person becomes a Catholic pentecostal by joining the local prayer group, not the national movement. Thus the local prayer group is an appropriate focus for research. A variety of types of groups consider themselves members of the same movement. All of the groups studied considered themselves "Catholic pentecostals," and all have been listed in the movement's *Directory* (published by Charismatic Renewal Services of Notre Dame). For the purposes of this study, that definition of membership was sufficient.

These questions highlight the methodological difficulties of trying to "capture" a movement, especially one that is relatively diffuse. Not only is there a problem of how representative the local groups are, but also of how representative are data gathered at any one point in the movement's development. Groups change and the movement changes over time. This also means that data are not strictly comparable. For example, prophecies recorded in Group A's second year are not totally comparable with those drawn from Group B's seventh year. Nor would Group A's second and fifth years be exactly comparable. The researcher can be attentive to the influences for change in each group; for example, when core members attended annual national or regional charismatic conferences there were often substantial changes in prayer meeting practices immediately afterwards. Nevertheless, the recorded profiles of each group remain limited—pale reflections of the dynamic, multifaceted, and complex human interaction that was observed over the six years.

There were seven groups studied in the main body of this research of which only capsule descriptions are given. Identifying details have been disguised or omitted to protect the anonymity of the groups. As of 1973, when the main part of this research began, two groups were relatively large (over 100 members); two were of average size (twenty-five to sixty members); and three were relatively small (three to twenty members). Of the two groups added to the study in 1976, one was large and one was middle-sized. Since 1973, most of the groups have grown steadily by moderate increments (for example, from thirty-five to fifty-five members). One small group ceased to exist, and one of medium size was absorbed by a larger group, resulting in the loss of about one-third of the original members. One of the large groups had a noticeable decrease in attendance, but claims not to have lost members. The overall trend between 1971 and 1977, however, was one of moderate growth among the groups.

One of the large and one of the small groups had a considerable number of college-student members at the outset of the study; the other seven groups studied had few, if any, student members. The non-student pentecostals were much older than the students, with most members between thirty-five and fifty-five years of age. In student prayer meetings, students comprised about sixty to ninety percent of those attending; non-students were mainly teachers or other professionals, often recent graduates themselves. These groups underwent more changes in membership over the six years than did the non-student groups. This is partly because students come and go from a college community, but also reflects decreasing numbers of college-age recruits. As of 1977, most new student members were of high-school age, and the college-student groups had become more like the non-student groups in their general membership.

There was a heavy predominance of women attending both student and non-student groups (a ratio of about 2:1), although male members were conspicuous in leadership roles. In six of the groups, all prayer meetings observed were led by men; in another group a priest and a layman shared leadership with a nun; in the other two groups some women were in leadership roles—about one for every three men. Most groups were socio-economically homogeneous and many of the members of the non-student groups had known each other for several years. Two groups had a few non-white participants, but these members were of generally the same age and social class background as other members. Non-student groups consisted mainly of housewives (roughly 60 percent), white-collar workers and small business operators (about 20 percent), blue-collar and service-trade workers (another 15 percent) and lower professions (about 5 percent, including numerous priests and nuns). Most participants, especially in non-student groups, were recruited from active parish members. A large number of priests and nuns were active in three of the nine groups; the others were primarily lay groups.

Phases of the Study

The initial research undertook to determine Catholic pentecostals' social attitudes, involvement, and beliefs, and to compare and contrast these with findings from a previous study of the underground church movement among American Catholics. This exploratory study entailed participant-observation in twenty-four prayer meetings, forty-one focused interviews, and approximately fifty informal interviews. These informal interviews included chatting before and after meetings with participants, being witnessed to, and casual conversations while giving rides home. Additional data were gathered from books, cassette tapes, and periodicals distributed by the national movement.

The second phase of research began with an ethnographic approach to the prayer meeting itself. Participant-observation provided most of the data in this phase. In three groups where leaders permitted, tape recordings of prayer meetings were made (seventeen sessions). These were analyzed for content, structure, tempo, and other patterns; these same indicators were examined in other prayer meetings (twenty-seven sessions), but results were less complete and less reliable because they had to be reconstructed from memory and scant notes. Next, individual speech events in the prayer meeting were examined in greater detail. In particular, prophecy, witnessing, and speaking in tongues were each in turn the focus of attention during participant-observation in the groups. Because of their brevity, seventy-two of the prophecies could be recorded verbatim even without taping. Complete witnessing tales were obtained only in those groups which permitted use of the tape recorder, but others were reconstructed from memory and notes (twenty-one verbatim, thirty-seven reconstructed). Although numerous instances of glossolalia were recorded, these were not transcribed; rather, factors surrounding the use of glossolalia were of primary interest and could be noted adequately from simple observation. An additional twenty-nine formal interviews were conducted during this phase, and many more informal interviews were noted.

The third phase of research entailed studying recruitment and commitment mechanisms in the groups. Of the seven groups being studied at that point, three offered formal Life in the Spirit seminars for recruits. Five groups held an Introductory Session to introduce newcomers (in one group, attendance at this session was required before the newcomer could attend the prayer meeting). Introductory sessions in these five groups were attended (as were similar sessions in the two groups added later in the study). The entire induction process was observed in three of the groups—two large and one middle-sized; later in the study, I also attended the Life in the Spirit seminars of another group.

The induction processes observed occurred in the most closed group, the most open group, and a third group which was identified as being roughly in the middle of the continuum; the group observed much later was toward the open end of the continuum (see Chapter 5 for details of this typological continuum). The relatively closed group and the middle group ran formal Life in the Spirit seminars, attended by sixteen and seven persons, respectively. The open group had a more informal induction process, beginning whenever a newcomer began to show interest. Two new members were received during this phase of the study. In addition to participant-observation, the methods used include interviewing five seminar leaders and twenty-one out of twenty-three participants. An additional thirty prayer meetings were attended during this phase. Other valuable sources include the handbook for seminar leaders and a series of Life in the Spirit seminar tape cassettes issued by the national movement.

The final phase of the research focused on the healing practices which developed later in the groups' existence. While all of the groups made some mention of healing, only two had highly developed "healing ministries," so it was necessary to seek additional groups for data on this later development. These groups were studied by participant-observation for several weeks prior to interviewing (forty-seven meetings attended altogether). In addition to those engaged in the healing ministries of these groups (twenty-two interviews), six other persons were interviewed who were identified as knowledgeable about the healing ministry in the region. Subsequently, participants in three prayer groups were interviewed; these included both those who felt they had experienced a healing and those who did not. I also attended healing workshops, healing Masses, and other relevant group sessions.

Almost all of the data were gathered in social situations readily accessible to non-members. The research is, therefore, primarily an analysis of that interaction about which the average prayer-group participant could have knowledge and experience. Certain situations are less apparent to the group's general membership (for example, processes of deliberation within the core group, interaction within communal households, and spectacular exorcisms). Reticence about these aspects is understandable for many reasons, such as preservation of privacy, likelihood of misunderstanding, and protection of power. Therefore, this research does not focus on these aspects, and descriptions of these less overt activities are from knowledgeable informants.

This distinction points to a methodological problem in all research of this kind. Where there are numerous levels of belonging but no formal acknowledgment of these differences, how does the researcher decide whom to interview? Is there a distinction between "participants" and "members"? Is there a clear dividing line between "core member" and "member"? Is there a different quality to the membership of one who lives in a communal household compared with one who lives elsewhere? In several sections of this study I have tried to show the distinctions discovered in the course of the research. Initially I employed a very rough and deliberately broad definition of "participants": any person whom I had observed attending two or more prayer meetings.

Additional data were gathered by the analysis of themes of hymns chosen during prayer meetings, Scripture selections, and use of non-scriptural references in prayer meetings. Issues of the movement's first magazine, *New Covenant*, were analyzed for several themes, including dualistic imagery, body symbolism, and sex role-specific language. This yielded a volume of supporting data, but the results seemed superficial compared with the depth of data from interviews. These sources of data also raise the problem of the relationship between the national movement and the local groups. In the last two years of the study the regional leaders developed a newsletter for the area, but before that almost all movement media came from the national leadership. Since many members read and respected the *New Covenant* (and its later companion/competitor *Catholic Charismatic*), we can assume that the publications did have some influence on them. On the other hand, local groups studied had many attitudes, beliefs, and practices that were inconsistent with official views of the national leadership.

The magazines may have been responsible for certain elements of cultural diffusion. For example, members interviewed after a 1977 article on "resting in the Spirit" (the Catholic pentecostals' term for what classical pentecostals call "slaying in the Spirit") had never heard of the practice before reading the article. In sum, it is difficult to know what methodological use to make of media from the national leadership, since it is not actually expressive of the local prayer meeting, except indirectly. For example, the hymnals in use in recent years are edited by the national movement, but the hymn selection is frequently highly expressive.

This relationship with the national movement points to a larger methodological problem: What is the actual unit of study? Of greatest interest sociologically is the entire movement, but it is not possible to analyze that movement in any depth because of the diversity among groups that consider themselves Catholic pentecostals. Fichter's 1975 study[19] comes the closest to giving an overview, incorporating a large number of questionnaire responses from members from all over America. The characterization of the movement which arises from his study is corroborated by data from groups studied in this research.

My research has aimed for depth and more of a microsociological understanding of what is occurring in the movement. Data at this level of analysis have value, not only for descriptive interpretation of one religious movement, but also for a theoretical approach to interpersonal relations. The section on "religious speaking and hearing," for example, analyzes assumptions about communication in special religious contexts. While it helps to explain certain forms of pentecostal behavior, this discussion addressed primarily broader theories of interpersonal communication. As such, much of this study should be understood as using these data as a springboard for theorizing about relationships in certain social contexts. That this theorizing explains certain pentecostal behavior is helpful, but the broader theoretical task is central.

I have generalized from these findings to statements about Catholic pentecostals, the Catholic pentecostal movement, and new religious movements in general. There are serious limitations in generalizing from a study of only nine groups; for example, there may be groups of Catholic pentecostals that do not resemble those described in this report. The chief responsibilities of the researcher in the face of such problems are to be attentive to factors that are likely to account for major variations (such as age and socioeconomic status), and to report and try to correct for factors which might introduce bias in results. Some distortions due to the methodological process are inevitable; they are inherent in all research. Nevertheless, from my reading of national literature, visits in prayer groups around the country, corroboration from many other studies such as Fichter's, and discussions with researchers studying groups in other parts of the country, I am confident that the beliefs, attitudes, behaviors, and group structures described here are typical of a large portion of the national membership. Other researchers may wish to document, for comparative purposes, groups that differ sufficiently as to constitute another "type" of Catholic pentecostal prayer group.

Furthermore, findings and interpretations applicable to Catholic pentecostalism in American culture may not be generalizable to other countries to which the movement has spread. While cross-cultural comparisons are made in this volume, the interpretations apply mainly to the movement in the United States and, with important qualifications, to other modern Western cultures. They do not necessarily apply to non-Western or developing lands.[20]

Methodological Issues

A major methodological focus of this research has been upon language and ritual behavior in the groups studied. The analyses of these elements have been more fruitful than the use of a sociological survey or formal questionnaire. Standard survey-type techniques are useful for a limited set of research tasks, but may be even counterproductive when applied to researching a dynamic and not-clearly-defined phenomenon such as a new religious movement. As Luckmann points out, while surveys can provide information on the distribution of well-structured, identifiable, separate, and stable items of opinion, belief, and attitude, they are based upon the premise of isomorphy between individual religiosity and some identifiable official model. This premise may not hold in describing the "subjective systems of 'ultimate meaning'" held by many persons in modern society. What is needed, according to Luckman, is some methodological way of analyzing these "subjective relevance structures" in the actual situation in the individual's life where these are acted out:

> To the extent that such structures are fully articulated they are probably modeled on social definitions of "ultimate meaning" (the normal traditional situation) or are reflectively constructed and verbalized by presumably highly articulate "religious seekers". . . . To the extent that these subjective relevance structures are not well articulated (not even in the conventional language of "official" models or counter-models) the problem is that of the analysis of latent (but very real) structures generally.[21]

How is it possible to discover what is subjectively relevant to people? One obvious way is to have people name what is important to them. In this study, informal interviews (where persons were not self-conscious about formulating "official" answers to formally posed questions) were very valuable. Less satisfactory were formal interviews. The specific religious beliefs of the members interviewed were sometimes critical in shaping the interaction of the interview itself. For example, due to the length of the formal interviews, it was necessary to schedule them in advance. This not only put respondents "on notice" (such that some of them tried to read about what they should say), but also considerably increased the anxiety of some over being interviewed. The typical response was to pray intensely beforehand; sometimes respondents resorted to prayer even during the interview. In some groups respondents were reassured by the prayers of others. While there is little indication of collusion in the content of responses, it is interesting to reflect on the methodological implications of having responses so intensely prayed over.

Similarly, consonant with the movement's belief system, individuals frequently witnessed to each other and to me as an individual nonmember. These witnessing events were highly expressive of subjective meaning systems, even though they were stylized in a limited form. Witnessing yielded some understanding of what was personally meaningful to members and how they individually interpreted their everyday experiences. It should be emphasized that these subjective meaning constructions often differed significantly from those officially promulgated by the movement's leadership and the Catholic church. For a sociologist to point out these discrepancies is not to say, "Aha! heretics!" It is rather a recognition that the effective religious reality of the individual believer has no necessary connection with the official model by which one may name one's beliefs. These diversities of belief and practice point to the difficulty of discussing deviant religious belief systems when there is scant documentation of the real subjective meaning systems of seemingly orthodox believers.

A further method for trying to capture subjective meaning systems is the observation of a group's ritual behavior and the documentation of its special uses of language and particular speech events.[22] These methodological approaches can provide data for understanding the images that organize behavior and inform the individual's meaning-construction.[23] The analysis of ritual and language is especially useful when the group is developing, and in the process of collectively defining reality. This is because the group's language and ritual behavior both *express* and *inform* the individual's interpretation of reality. Because the religious group is striving to establish a basis of intersubjectivity—the sharing of experiences through communication—the researcher, too, has greater access to those shared subjective meanings.[24] I have used this analysis of language and ritual primarily as a methodological device to describe and interpret a developing religious movement, and specifically to understand the nexus between the social power experienced in the group and the personal power derived by many members—especially the leaders.

Clarifying Participant-Observation

It is not sufficient to say merely that these nine groups were studied by participant-observation; as a method, participant-observation needs clarification. In other words, exactly how are empirical data generated by this method and what is the quality of these data? A fundamental goal of this study is an understanding of believers' actions from their point of view; this involves seeking their "definition of the situations." It means trying to take the role of the other, seeing things as believers see them and using their categories of thought in the organization of experience. It means developing a personal stance of empathy.[25]

Methodological empathy differs from sympathy in that it is not necessary to agree with a perspective in order to understand it. Douglas's distinction between "empathy" and "sympathy" is applicable: "Empathy is the ability to feel with, to see things from the standpoint or perspective of the individual being studied rather than to identify with or to act from this standpoint."[26] Such an empathic stance leads logically and naturally to a specific style of participant-observation and interviewing (discussed more fully below). There is a tendency in sociology and psychology to treat a subject such as pentecostalism as a study of "weirdos." Methodological empathy is a useful antidote to this. All, or most, seemingly weird behavior is perfectly rational and highly meaningful—within that believer's frame of reference. For example, pentecostals' use of glossolalia, healing rituals, and testimonies, makes considerable sense within the framework of their meaning system.

There is a fundamental difference of perspective, however, between a sociologist and a believer, in that the sociologist *as* sociologist does not accept the believer's taken-for-granted meanings as a given, but rather as an object of study. This perspective sometimes implies that the reason members believe is not only because of the truth value of the belief system. Also, the more action the believers attribute to supernatural sources, the less their viewpoint can be reconciled with a sociological one. The very fact of treating certain interactions, such as prophecy, as purely human behavior—and therefore as objects for sociological study—is often incompatible with the basic beliefs of many Catholic pentecostals. Furthermore, sociology must necessarily bracket the crucial religious question—to what extent is this action *also* from God? The more important the supernatural base is to the believer as a legitimation, the more upsetting a sociological interpretation will be to that person. For example, when I showed my earlier article on prophecy[27] to leaders in one of the groups studied, they thought it an accurate description and evidence that God was using human vessels for His work in this world. Another group of leaders, however, was horrified and angered that I had treated one of their most valued gifts as human (read, "merely human") action. So let me reiterate: I am not saying that the behavior described in this study is merely human. I am saying that, whatever else it may be, it is *also* human—and as such, amenable to sociological interpretation.

One easy way out of this fundamental clash of perspectives would be to simply describe behavior, using as many "emic," or indigenous, categories of description as possible. This approach may lead to elaborate taxonomies, but it avoids the important sociological task of interpretation which is valuable, not merely to explain the course of one interesting movement, but also because an understanding of the development of that movement may increase our knowledge about the larger society and participants' responses to larger societal situations. Since the assertion of linkages with broader situations, especially causal ones, is sometimes necessarily speculative, I have tried to be cautious.

Yet, there is a value in pushing beyond the data toward a broader theoretical perspective.

Very early in this research I found it necessary to clarify for myself—and often for members of the groups—exactly what my personal stance was. The research was not disguised, but neither did I call specific attention to my research purpose. As a result, everybody except a few highly cautious leaders treated me as one more potential recruit—even sociologists can be converted! And, methodologically speaking, they were right. In other words, it is a poor participant-observer who remains aloof from the action and never experiences the moods of the group, the periods of fervor, the moments of awe. The difference between pure "observation" and "participant-observation" is that the latter requires encountering the group on its own terms and (in anthropological terms) the risk of "going native." In the sociology of religion this means deliberately exposing oneself to the ideas and experiences which lead many other participants to be converted. Nevertheless, the participant-observer is also in the other sphere: recording observations, analyzing actions, and asking questions from a sociological perspective. This kind of marginality means that the sociologist is not likely to be converted, because the sociological perspective does not assume precisely those beliefs and actions which must be taken for granted by the believer. In other words, by definition, the participant-observer lacks "faith."

In my interactions with members of the groups I have studied, I have presented myself openly as a spiritually concerned person with respect for their intentions and feelings. As Richardson points out, there is considerable methodological difficulty in conducting this kind of research with such "loving subjects." He points out the considerable strain this poses for the subject-object dichotomy so often used in research.[28] Thus, not only the stance of the researcher, but also the stance of the subjects, contributes to the framework within which these data must be considered.

I have participated in these groups as far as my personal beliefs would let me, but I did not consider it ethical to represent myself as more committed than I really was. For example, leaders of several groups invited me to attend their Life in the Spirit seminars. I was delighted with this opportunity, but found it methodologically and personally awkward to continue in the seminars past the session in which the participants received their baptism in the Spirit. I could not, in good faith, request this baptism for myself and was forthright about this. In the last few sessions, therefore, I was clearly no longer a participant-observer but a somewhat obtrusive observer.

The problem of commitment highlights a research dilemma—the

problematic interaction between research and believers. The dilemma is well described by Schwartz:

> This kind of empathic rapport creates its own problems as well as bestowing its obvious benefits on the student of religious sects. Once the members of the small Pentecostal group discovered that I sympathized with their religious aims and that I could also empathize with their distinctive religious experience, they could not understand why I did not take the next 'natural' step and become a full-fledged member of their group. They simply could not understand how anyone who perceived the 'truth,' however remotely, could resist the 'innate' desire to participate in it with his whole being.[29]

Robbins and Anthony point out that an empathic stance on the part of the researcher is likely to create problems especially for members of groups which are highly conversionist, maintain an exclusivist definition of religious truth, and hold a dichotomized conception of humankind (for example, "saved" versus "damned," "good" versus "evil").[30] While the Catholic pentecostals studied were not as extreme on these criteria as were the Jesus People studied by Robbins and Anthony or the classical pentecostals studied by Schwartz, they were nevertheless disturbed by the presence of a researcher who appeared to understand, yet was not compelled by that understanding to believe. This appearance of understanding is largely due to methodological techniques and to the function of language in establishing group identity. The technique of using people's own words back to them, in conversations and probes, was interpreted as evidence of some level of "belonging." The more accurate I became in using their terms and empathizing with the experiences referred to, the more the members assumed that I "really" understood, and, therefore, should believe.

The orientation of the average believer that I encountered in Catholic pentecostal prayer groups can, in fact, be characterized as conversionist, exclusivist, and dichotomous (with themselves viewed as among the "saved"). At the same time, however, there were some believers who were not so exclusivist (and, by extension, not so conversionist). Because I was less threatening to and, consequently, less threatened by, members with this less dogmatic stance, I found it sorely tempting to spend most of my research energies on them. This would have been a serious mistake, because the less dogmatic members accounted for only a small number (0 to 20 percent) of the members of the groups studied, and the dogmatic stance is probably central to the appeal of the movement for many of its members.

What should the attitude of the participant-observer be? How should the participant-observer relate to the ongoing interaction? How does one gather relevant data while also participating in an event? The answer to these questions depends upon the research task (that is, the kind of data needed). I found it useful to discipline myself to applying several different attitudes or stances during the same event. By using various approaches at different times I was able to gather different kinds of information about what was observed. The disadvantage is, of course, that while viewing the event from one stance, one misses information that could be gathered from the other possible stances. This dilemma can be dealt with by constant awareness of one's research objectives in the choice of stance for any one moment.

One stance is that of full participant. The participant-observer in this role participates as fully as possible in the moods of the group; one actually experiences enthusiasm, the joyous singing with swaying or other movements, the awe-filled or uncomfortable silences. One useful technique was to close my eyes occasionally and try to describe the emotional atmosphere being created and exactly how that was being effected. This was an easy device, since closed eyes are normatively approved in the prayer meetings. A sociologist attending a number of these prayer meetings, who would not admit to having on occasion literally felt the moods created by the group, would strike me as being too defensive to be objective. These feelings which one experiences are not merely subjective reactions but empirical data; it is the researcher's task to clarify what aspects of the experience account for these feelings.

Most of the data gathered for this study was the result of one persons's observations. At two brief junctures, however, I had the benefit of second observers. On the latter occasion, a graduate student research assistant accompanied me to prayer meetings and wrote independent observations. Her observations in this research stance of "participant" differed considerably from my own and provided a useful counterpoint to my experiences. She came from a traditional Catholic upbringing and had no previous exposure to pentecostalism or any similar enthusiastic religiosity. This background is more like that of newcomers to Catholic pentecostalism than is my own, so her reactions to the prayer groups were valuable data. How much is the "shock" that she experienced actually part of the conversion process for many members? Her observations made clear how much of my own lack of surprise with elements of the movement may have been due to my relatively cosmopolitan background, including experiences of everything from Quaker prayer meetings to Tennessee tent revivals, from solemn Greek Orthodox rituals to free-wheeling "underground church" Masses.

This example raises the research problem of the accuracy of observation conducted by one person alone. There are certainly limitations to these findings due to the unique background of my personal perceptions. While I have tried to overcome these limitations as much as possible by learning about the perceptions of other participants, the basic limitation is inherent in all research of this type.

A second stance is that of critical observer. A sociologist who is too busy *feeling* the interaction of a prayer meeting will miss much other relevant data. For example, if the participants are praying intensely with closed eyes and uplifted heads, and the observer is doing the same, how are eye-cues between leaders to be noticed, or subtle shifts in body posture, or which participant begins speaking a prophecy? In other words, to accomplish the research task, the observer cannot be merely a participant, but sometimes must observe critically.

Similarly, it is sometimes useful to take the attitude of the non-critical observer. For example, it might be helpful to imagine how the behavior would look to someone accidentally off the street, or from a very different culture. That is, in taking the "stranger" stance, one should start from no cultural assumptions—even about the religious nature of the gathering.

Another possible attitude would be that of a newcomer-who-wants-to-be-part-of-the-event. It is useful to ask oneself: What would a newcomer need to know in order to participate effectively? An objective of this stance would be to discover the operant norms of this group and the roles open to the various levels of committed persons. One technique employed by some researchers is intrusion into the event. There are serious ethical problems with researcher-intrusion. Furthermore, my limited experience with this technique persuaded me that the results were not worth the risks. Nevertheless, intrusion deserves mention, because in some cases it is the only way to discover the operative norms of a group. Data about the newcomer-who-wants-to-be-part-of-the-event could be gathered more effectively and with fewer ethical problems from interviewing and observing newcomers in various stages of participation, if only the researcher could find ways of identifying these people early enough.

A fifth perspective to be taken is that of the leader-participant. The participant-observer, in this stance, could try to experience the prayer meeting from the point of view of the leader. The leader's participation is likely to be very different from that of ordinary members, because he or she participates on several different levels. A leader who is too wrapped up in personal participation is not likely to be sensitive enough to the group's needs to be effective. The participant-observer taking the leader stance can focus on meeting dynamics, seeking the leader's definition of what is a successful prayer meeting and anticipating which actions contribute to or detract from that outcome.

In sum, the use of sociological field methods has limitations in that data produced are not neat, easily quantifiable, or strictly comparable.

Nevertheless, these methods are well-suited to this research task because they are highly flexible, oriented to discovering meanings embedded in the social situations studied, and enable the researcher to address numerous research objectives.

Two—
Beliefs
and
Practices

The image of Catholics engaged in enthusiastic pentecostal religious styles seems anomalous. Only a few years earlier, staid Sodalities and Altar and Rosary societies, silent weekend retreats, and clergy-led devotionals such as Benediction, characterized the religious life of those lay persons who sought more than Sunday Mass gatherings. In sharp contrast, the pentecostal prayer meeting, usually held in church basements or private homes, features rousing hymns sung to the accompaniment of guitars and tambourines, members witnessing to each other, prophesying and praying in tongues. As the movement developed, some groups adopted other pentecostal practices, such as healing, "resting in the Spirit," and singing in tongues.

Pentecostal religiosity differs from traditional Catholic religiosity, not only in its overt manifestations such as the prayer meeting, but also in its belief system and in the characteristic patterns of commitment of its members. Although some of these beliefs, practices, and relationships are not as discontinuous with traditional Catholic religiosity as they first appear, the development and rapid spread of a pentecostal movement among Catholics invites sociological interpretation.

What do Catholic pentecostals believe? This chapter explores some complex answers to this apparently simple question. On one hand, there are the formal beliefs of the movement, including statements promulgated by movement leaders and publications, and ideas taught to new members during induction into local prayer groups. A hierarchy of beliefs exists even within this formal system. It is more important, for example, for a member to assent to basic beliefs about baptism in the Spirit than to hold a particular belief about the gift of wisdom. Catholic pentecostals differ from non-pentecostal Catholics in the relative importance given to ordinary Catholic doctrine and practices. For example, the catechisms used in the religious instruction of most Catholics who are now adults taught about the existence of the Devil and his powers. These beliefs are greatly emphasized and expanded among Catholic pentecostals, whereas many non-pentecostal Catholics either do not believe them or find them irrelevant for everyday life.[1] Nevertheless, in addition to their special pentecostal beliefs and practices, Catholic pentecostals presumably also believe Catholic doctrines in proportions comparable to non-pentecostal Catholics of similar levels of commitment and activity.

Catholic pentecostals consider experiential religiosity to be more important than assent to faith-propositions. Knowing God is more important than knowing about God. Thus they would downplay any body of formal beliefs as mere teaching devices to bring believers to the crucial experience of commitment to God and baptism in the Spirit. Nevertheless, the formal belief system is extensive and very important and, with greater concern for orthodoxy within the movement, the promulgation of an official version of Catholic pentecostalism is taking on even greater significance. The leadership of the movement has increasingly consolidated its authority as "teaching-ministers" through its control over the Communications Center, national and regional conferences of the movement, the movement magazine *New Covenant*, an extensive series of movement books and tape-cassettes, and unified programs of induction and resocialization seminars.

Another aspect of the belief system includes personal convictions that members find meaningful—often even more so than the formal beliefs—but which are not taught as essential beliefs. For example, a large number of Catholic pentecostals believe that they can be sure they are already "saved"[2] and, in fact, this notion figures importantly in the appeal of the movement, but few leaders are officially teaching this belief.

A further aspect is the existence of a disbelief system, by means of which members clarify what they believe by focusing on items they do *not* believe. Many of these disbeliefs are manifest in pentecostals' criticisms of the religiosity of the rest of Christianity or of the condition of the larger society. Other disbeliefs crystallize only when a specific issue develops. For example, one group became increasingly biased against full freedom of the press after a local paper gave unfavorable coverage to a program they promoted. Only when this issue developed did a flood of other views crystallize: "The press is often the medium of evil forces in the world," "The press only communicates the mess the society is in, but does not side with the only One who could change it," "Newspapers are not sufficiently respectful of order in society," and so on. The informal belief system also includes a series of "beliefs about people who hold beliefs."[3] Especially important are their views about non-pentecostals and their strong condemnation of competing new religious movements, such as Transcendental Meditation (TM), the Unification Church, the Hare Krishna movement, and occult groups.

While this chapter focuses especially upon some elements of movement ideology, the selection of which beliefs to emphasize is based on what is sociologically significant, not necessarily what is theologically important. For example, some Catholic pentecostals have produced several volumes of careful theological explanations of glossolalia, but the theological implications of tongues-speaking are only peripherally important to sociological understanding. Furthermore, the analysis below is interpretive, rather than purely descriptive. As such, it is necessarily a transformation of the belief system itself; that is, the analysis represents what a sociologist thinks is important about what pentecostals think is important.

Gifts of the Spirit

One foremost characteristic of the belief system of Catholic pentecostals is the literal interpretation of biblical accounts of Pentecost, together with a view that the same experiences hold true for Christians today. Thus many beliefs focus on the "baptism in the Holy Spirit."[4] This baptism is distinguished from the sacrament of Baptism. The sacrament of Baptism is believed to be necessary for salvation, whereas baptism in the Spirit is an interior, transformative experience of God's power. Although the official Catholic pentecostal position holds that baptism in the Spirit is not necessary for salvation, many members persist in the belief that it is necessary and is even a sure sign that they are already saved.

Baptism in the Spirit is characterized as "an *experience* of the working of the Holy Spirit (that) may not be conscious . . . but at least the effects of the Spirit's actions are perceptible."[5] In addition to an inner experience (for example, a sense of peace, joy, love), the baptism in the Spirit is believed to be often manifested by the reception of *charism* (or "gift" of the Holy Spirit). These charisms are discussed more fully in Chapters 4 and 5. The most frequent charism is the "gift of tongues," although less spectacular gifts such as wisdom, faith, or love are also believed to be given. Baptism in the Spirit and accompanying charisms are thought to be available to those who desire the baptism, repent of those aspects of their lives which impede the Spirit, and commit themselves to Christ.

The idea that the Holy Spirit is powerful and that this power is available to the individual through baptism in the Holy Spirit is related to beliefs about specific effects of this baptism for the individual and for the pentecostal group. For the individual, the foremost effects are believed to be increased personal spiritual growth, aided by new power to pray, and new appreciation of Scripture, "deliverance" and/or healing, and personal "transformation." The belief system holds that the Holy Spirit gives specific powers for spiritual growth (for example, glossolalia as a prayer-gift, enabling the individual to pray better). The belief system encourages a renewed attention to Scripture and holds that baptism in the Spirit often enables members to find personal meaning in the Bible rather than merely to study it. This attention to Scripture is often converted to a fundamentalist-literalist approach to the words of the Bible. A common practice is "finding a text," in which individuals open the Bible at random, expecting that God will guide them to a specific passage that will be the answer to their particular problems.

"Deliverance" refers to belief that the Holy Spirit can break "bonds" of serious sin, and also psychological bonds such as anxiety or depression. Similarly, physical, psychological, and spiritual healings are attributed to the power of the Holy Spirit. The Spirit, it is believed, also effects the power for individuals to be transformed because when believers' interior, spiritual lives are changed by the power of the Spirit, they are enabled to change their behavior and to practice various Christian virtues also given by power of the Holy Spirit.

At the same time, the belief system holds that certain gifts of the Spirit are specifically directed toward developing the movement and the local prayer community. Practices such as prophecy and discernment, associated with prayer meetings, are examples of these Spirit-given communal powers. The belief system also teaches that the Spirit gives authority to specific members of the prayer community over other members and will communicate direction for the entire group through these authorities. Especially important is the underlying belief that belonging to a community of charismatic Christians is necessary for further growth in the Spirit.

This explanation of basic beliefs of the movement is necessarily greatly simplified. Although some pentecostal thinkers have developed detailed theological expositions of the entire formal belief system, the version presented here is an appropriate starting point for sociological analysis because it incorporates the basics learned by new Catholic pentecostals themselves. Full theological explication of the formal belief system is a function of a relatively small movement elite and the average believer may never even be exposed to the intricacies of the larger theology of Catholic pentecostalism. The version of Catholic pentecostalism presented in Life in the Spirit seminars, in which neophytes are prepared for baptism in the Spirit, is deliberately very simple and clear-cut.

Indeed part of the initial appeal of the movement is probably the very simplicity of its basic teachings. Recruits appear to have been attracted by a new sense of order, a better answer to the complex problems of their lives and society. A belief system which, at least initially, presents a simple explanation of what is responsible for these problems, as well as a simple solution, is likely to be highly appealing. The clarity, simplicity, and somewhat dogmatic approach of Catholic pentecostal beliefs may be important factors in motivating believers to pursue the course of personal change the movement necessitates.[6]

Order and Power

Other beliefs revolve around two basic themes: order and power. These beliefs are not necessarily officially promulgated by movement leadership, but they occur frequently in much movement literature and are very common in personal and public witnessing by ordinary members.

The themes of order and power are part of the movement's ideology which expands the group's basic theological ideas into teachings about the appropriate ideas, attitudes, values, and behavior of those who are committed to the movement's position. The ideology legitimates the movement and its claims to authority.[7] The true believer in the movement needs to accept both the obviously theological doctrines and the broader ideology. Several sets of beliefs, exemplifying the emphasis on order and power include: God's influence and direct action in everyday life, mystery and miracle, dualism, the coming of the Millennium, and the nature of charisma and authority.

God's Influence

Belief in the immediacy of God's presence and influence in everyday life derives from ideas about baptism in the Holy Spirit. Further logical extension is the belief that God is in control of events and nothing happens without His having a purpose for that occurrence. These beliefs are important parts of the ideology, and they appeal to those who feel that their lives and their society are "out of control," lacking a sense of order. To believe that there is an order, a purpose, for events—even if humans cannot know what—is a very reassuring attitude. Believers are confident that meaning exists, even if they cannot comprehend it.

This belief in God's control produces a distinct image of human volition. If God has a purpose for every occurrence, then what is the believer's role in the course of events? The recommended response is "submission," to "let it happen," simply allowing events to occur, since God is in control. For example, one respondent said, "I used to struggle over making decisions—even little choices were agonizing for me, but now I just let God go ahead and do what He likes in my life, and I know it must be for the good." Another woman explained, "Before baptism in the Spirit I used to worry over whether I should quit my job (it paid well, but I hated it), but now I am given the strength to adjust and realize that it must have been God's will that I stay on the job." Members used this belief to explain many seemingly bad events as "God's will" (for example, miscarriages, loss of jobs, illnesses, and even failure to receive certain gifts of the Spirit).

By contrast, another attitude of submission encourages the believer to actively seek God's will in prayer, Scripture, or through the advice of one of the Shepherds (spiritual leaders) of the group. This very different approach often produces dramatic changes in the direction of the individual's life, interpreting them as God's will. For example, one young member testified:

> "I prayed fervently to God that He should show me the way He wanted my life to go and what He wanted me to do in my future. And He showed me how so many of my career plans and school and all were part of an ego-trip I had been on, and I knew that I didn't have to stay on that path anymore. So now I'm living here in the [prayer community's] house and working a little job that I don't much care about one way or the other and putting all my energies into the ministry efforts of the house. I've never been happier.

Sometimes, of course, the question of authority arises and the individual faces the difficult decision of whether to obey a human authority (such obedience is strongly advocated by the movement) or to obey the Spirit's promptings. For example, a nun took a leave of absence from her religious congregation in order to do the work she felt God wanted her to do. She explained, "I recognized that . . . they were asking me more than I could say yes to, because they couldn't see the direction of the Spirit when I could see it. And I felt that I was not bound to give obedience there, when the Spirit was leading me."[8]

Concomitant with this emphasis on God's power and control is a view of humans as being virtually powerless. One man stated, "It was when I acknowledged my own total powerlessness, nothingness, that God gave me all the power of His Holy Spirit." There are two prevalent notions about how human reception of God's power occurs. One view holds that God gives little "doses" of power to believers as they grow to be able to use them. The individual's appropriate response, according to this view, is to be open and receptive to these gifts at the right moments. The other notion is that God has already given all the gifts of power and that all the believer need do is claim and use them. This latter conception implies that individuals are responsible for their own charismatic shortcomings.

Mystery and Miracle

Modern society is, as Berger points out, characterized by a general "disenchantment of the world"—a world view stripped of mystery, miracle, and magic.[9] Historically, Protestantism has largely divested itself of these three elements, and recent changes in Roman Catholicism may have had a similar effect. Although the Catholic church has retained all its sacraments, their content and atmosphere may have been divested of some of their awe-inspiring qualities; they are less able to produce a "sense" of the Holy. Using the vernacular instead of an obscure language in worship may have reduced the feeling of mystery. Likewise, new emphasis upon understanding what is happening in the Mass may have diminished the belief that some of the effects such as the "production of grace" are magical. And thirdly, although the idea of the Mass as a miracle has been retained, it is de-emphasized—as are the lesser miracles and the influence of the saints. All of these developments are part of the entire post-Conciliar Catholic milieu, not just the experience of Catholic pentecostals. The situation is not merely a matter of a "cultic void"[10] but indeed the demise of a whole view of the world. The scope of the sacred is dramatically diminished. The Catholic pentecostal view of the world, however, represents a renewed sense of mystery, miracle, and magic.

Whereas changing the language of worship to the vernacular demystified the Mass, pentecostals' emphasis upon glossolalia represents a re-mystification of worship. In fact, praying in tongues is even more dramatically mysterious than praying in Latin because *no one* understands the "tongue." Prophecy is also mysterious and awesome, because it is believed to be God speaking directly, in the first person, through the voice of the human speaker. This renewed emphasis on the possibility of human mediation of the sacred may be related to the post-Vatican II decline in other mediators (for example, the de-mystification of the power of priests, saints, or other intercessors to mediate between the human and divine realm). Similarly, pentecostals' interest in religious experience and de-emphasis of rational explanations of experience heighten the mystery element. The re-mystification of the world produces a sense of awe, wonder, and appreciation of the powers manifest in it.

At the same time, everyday life becomes mystified, resulting in a sense of the miraculous, particularly unlike that of most contemporary Christians. Pentecostals strongly believe in miraculous healing, exorcisms of evil spirits, and other miraculous interventions. For example, in a testimony before the prayer group, one woman described how she had gone from room to room in her house exorcising the influence of the Evil One which had been manifesting itself in the unpleasant attitudes of her sister, an unbeliever. The typical pentecostal's approach is quite mechanistic and simplistic, asking God's intervention in getting jobs, finding lost articles, curing colds and more serious ailments, granting good weather for desired events, and so on.

Not only do Catholic pentecostals regularly ask for miraculous intervention in everyday life, but also they see evidence of such intervention. Real events occur which confirm their belief in miracles; real experiences are interpreted as miraculous. Many of these events may be interpreted as "holy coincidences."[11] Whereas secularized consciousness would identify the connection between these events as mere coincidence, believers see the connection as meaningful, evidence of God's power in the world. For example, one prayer group feared it would lose use of the church hall due to a shortage of heating oil that winter. The group prayed fervently that the Lord would provide for their needs, and the day before the next meeting the weather turned warm and pleasant. For believers, the providence of God was amply demonstrated. The ultimate evaluation of whether "holy coincidence" does, in fact, involve causally unrelated events, rests on an assumption about the non-existence of divine intervention—an assumption which sociologists cannot legitimately make.

The leadership of the movement does not especially encourage the element of magic in the belief system. Magical belief is an outgrowth of a conception of the Spirit as some kind of impersonal Power. Believers consider themselves able to invoke this Power when needed, and the results are perceived as "produced" by invocation of the Power. This invocation is exemplified by prayers of exorcism, commanding evil spirits to depart. Similarly, use of glossolalia frequently borders on the magical.[12] For example, several groups believed prayers in tongues to be more efficacious in "working a healing" than vernacular prayers. The following testimony illustrates a quasi-magical approach to tongues:

> It is really important to be open to the action of God in our lives, and it is particularly important for us to accept the idea of tongues and other gifts from the Holy Spirit. We have to be open to his gifts and not resist them. These gifts are a very important weapon against Satan. For example, last week, my husband was very grouchy and he started a fight. I saw that

it wasn't any good to try and argue back with him, so I started praying in tongues, and immediately he shrugged and gave up.

Miracle and magic are closely related to the idea of controlling aspects of human existence which seem humanly uncontrollable—raising the dead, healing the incurable, and taking charge over a whole array of spirits otherwise outside of human management (for example, demons, angels, and the like). There are additional areas of human existence which may be peculiarly modern "uncontrollable" situations. The fact of large, anonymous organizations and massive, seemingly autonomous institutions in government, military, and economic spheres has created a new sense of diminished control. The rediscovery of mystery, miracle, and magic at this time in history may represent believers' attempts to regain a sense of power and control over their lives and social world.[13] Thus individuals suffering from a sense of powerlessness (or alienation from sources of power which they may objectively have) are able to gain a new sense of power by aligning themselves with the omnipotent forces for Good.

Dualism

A dualistic world view holds that reality consists of two irreducible modes or opposing principles—one Good and the other Evil. This form of dualistic perspective is central in the ideology of Catholic pentecostals. O'Connor states:

> It is characteristic of the Pentecostal movement that, along with renewed faith in the Holy Spirit, there comes a greater awareness of the evil spirit . . . experience has taught people in the Pentecostal movement to take very seriously that aspect of the Christian life that has to do with warring against the evil one . . . it has been a common practice within the movement to exorcise Satan any time there seems to be reason to fear his influence.[14]

Typically, prayer meetings and baptisms in the Holy Spirit are preceded by an exorcism. Some sick persons are also believed to require exorcism to end their harassment by evil spirits. Members use exorcism in response to disruptive influences in the prayer group and in private lives. Just as the world is re-mystified by the presence of God's spirit, so too it is re-mystified by the presence of Satan in numerous forms. Not only is God influential in the world, but so too is Satan immediate and active. For example, during the petitions in one prayer meeting, the following set of prayers were offered:

> Lord, we ask you to use your power to overcome evil in this world.

Yes, Lord, we ask you to protect us and our loved ones from the influence of Satan.

Keep us all free from the taint of all that filth, that pornography, that ugly sex stuff, those violent shows on TV, and all that materialistic advertising.

Yes, Lord, and protect our little ones from the influence of all the evil in the world.

Blessed Jesus, guide our youth from all the snares of Satan —away from all those weird religions, like Maharaji something, and witchcraft, and Transcendental Meditation, and show them the path away from the evils of easy sex and drugs. Give them the strength to stand up against the power of the Evil One who has his way so much of the time in this world.

Members identify and personify the forces of evil in movements, issues, or personages that threaten their values (for example, "my sister, who brings Satan's influence into our house," pro-abortionists, or those who want to take religion out of the schools). Furthermore, they attribute numerous maladies and troubles to the Devil's influence. For example, one member had been suffering much anxiety that was considered by her group to be the direct influence of the Devil. More frequently, however, Satan is identified with vague forces which counter the commitments and efforts of the group. A strong sense of opposition often enhances a social movement's strength and effectiveness.[15] Cosmic dualism creates a sense of ultimate opposition for Catholic pentecostalism.

Interest and concern over the influence of evil spirits appear to be increasing in the movement.[16] Although there is some disagreement among the movement leadership about the degree to which this element of belief should be emphasized, it appears to be very significant in all prayer groups studied. Dualism is such a strong and pervasive element of the belief system that it may indeed be central to the movement's appeal. Nor is it coincidental that other new religious movements of recent years have also emphasized a dualistic view of the world. For example, the Jesus Movement and Reverend Moon's Unification Church also focus on dualistic perspectives of the universe.[17] Such interpretations serve important functions for both the group and the individual.

Dualism is closely related to the issues of order and power. Catholic pentecostals view the moral order of society as decayed and nearly defunct. They consider the Church to be weak and tainted by the very ills of society it should be addressing. In the face of this disorder, they posit a new framework of order and a new source of power to fight the evils of the decadent social order.

A dualistic world view serves especially well both as a framework for the construction of a new social and moral order and as a legitimation-support for that order's maintenance. Religious dualism is particularly effective in such re-ordering, because it posits that a transcendent realm is the source of all "problems" and all "real" solutions.[18] The believer is enabled to name sources of anxieties, fears, and problems; this identification alone is an important source of the believer's newfound sense of order and control. Furthermore, identifying the Devil as the source of all problems and difficulties implies a clearcut course of action. Believers locate their personal direction within a cosmic struggle, as part of a continual battle between the forces of Good and the forces of Evil. This identification explains all events, good or bad, and give a sense of meaning to daily existence. The dualistic world view interprets even trivial aspects of everyday life as part of the larger order.

This ordering potential of dualism is partly responsible for a characteristic which might be called "religious paranoia." The everyday world becomes re–mystified; believers constantly perceive evidence of the immediacy and influence of both good and evil spirits. This evidence, it should be emphasized, is usually in the form of real events, real happenings in everyday life. There is an inherent tendency to ascribe all good events to God and all bad ones to the Devil. Some movement leaders discourage such a simplistic interpretation.[19] The simplistic view continues, however, not merely because believers are too theologically naive to understand, but rather because the tidiness and order of its dualistic interpretation of the world are part of the basic appeal of the movement.

Religious paranoia is a useful motivation to "fight" the "enemy"; in facing the opposition, even symbolically, the group gains cohesion and strength. Furthermore, religious paranoia constitutes a valuable theodicy for maintaining the group's new framework of order, because it enables believers to see order in subsequent events—including events which would otherwise threaten their new beliefs. Those who hold a dualistic world view consider the Opposition to be in a conspiracy against them and their group.[20] For example, in one group a leader testified:

> We became aware at the [leaders'] meeting of how Satan is really alive today. He is trying to get at the leaders of the movement, trying to disintegrate our unity. He's really powerful, and he's working hard to hurt our movement. One of the ways he's working is trying to disunite the leaders' families. He is really alive today. Bind him! Bind him in Jesus' precious blood.

To see the parallels between dualism and a specifically religious paranoia, however, is not to suggest that Catholic pentecostals have emotional problems. On the contrary, the dualism and the religious paranoia are resolutions to their previous problems of ambiguity and meaninglessness. There are two sides to the believers' religious paranoia. The negative side is a sense of fearsome powers, bent on a conspiratorial attack on believers and all they hold dear. On the positive side, the dualistic perspective provides the believer with a sense of order, harmony, and symmetry. Both aspects of religious paranoia are pattern-forming tendencies.[21] Because believers expect that everything is ordered, they subsequently perceive order and patterns in the world. The positive side of religious paranoia is illustrated by the believer's constant discovery of "holy coincidences," "providence," and other evidences of the pattern of God's work in everyday life. The dualistic world view gives form and a scripturally derived cast of characters to the patterns that Catholic pentecostals perceive in the world around them.

Not only does dualism provide form and order for experiencing the world, but it also offers the believer an explanatory system for interpreting and reinterpreting order-threatening events. As such, it functions as a theodicy, a special form of legitimation which allows the believer to integrate threatening personal experiences (such as suffering, poverty, death of a loved one, or loss of a job) into a socially constructed framework of order.[22] A theodicy provides meaning but not necessarily happiness, informing the believer, "You may be in misery, but be comforted that there is, at least, meaning to your suffering."

Dualism is a particularly effective form of theodicy, because it is a closed system of legitimation. In other words, built into the legitimating system is an explanation of every argument against the system. Thus the theodicy simultaneously explains both good and bad events, both opposition and confirmation. It also provides a basis for moral self-justification and condemnation of others.[23]

Catholic pentecostals frequently use the dualistic theodicy to explain the doubts and uncertainties experienced by new believers. For example, a pamphlet for members of the Life in the Spirit (induction) seminars tells members who have recently been baptized in the Holy Spirit, "Satan is also concerned with you in a new way. Since you now have more spiritual power, you are more dangerous to him, and he would like to stop you. . . . Satan will try to make you think it was not real or that it did not happen to you. . . . Resist all doubts and anxieties. . . . You can count on Satan to try to confuse you. . . ."[24] This theodicy explains the natural doubts and sense of uncertainty they encounter in the resocialization process. Concrete identification of the source of their difficulties gives believers a greater sense of power with which to face such problems.

This theodicy is especially important for handling doubts about the crucial experience of baptism in the Spirit. Many individuals are baptized in the Spirit, but have no spectacular experience such as speaking in tongues. For example, one woman explained privately, "I'm afraid mine didn't take. Nothing seemed to happen." Since the baptism is defined by the group as a crucial experience, these fears are very serious ones. The most frequent legitimation offered for such apparent failure is that the baptism did indeed occur and that fears and doubts are put into the new member's mind by Satan. Similarly, many new members expressed the fear that perhaps the experiences they had were humanly fabricated, rather than gifts of the Spirit. This doubt is also effectively dealt with by the dualistic theodicy.

Dualism reshapes members' interpretations of events of everyday life —including their own roles—and it gives significance to events that formerly seemed meaningless. Dualism assigns meaning to human failure, suffering, social problems, personal difficulties, and death. Events that once appeared to be random, haphazard, or disorderly, now are seen as part of a clear pattern. Believers' sense of ambiguity and insecurity is resolved by seeing their role as part of "something big"— a cosmic struggle in which one gains power and purpose by siding with the forces of Good. Dualism creates order out of chaos. The external chaos of the disordered social world is not the only source of threat; intra-group problems also constitute a threat. Problems of disorder are inherent in the establishment of the prayer group itself, because there is much ambiguity during the early development of a movement, especially when members perceive their new belief system to be a departure from their previous religious tradition. The participants resolve problems of uncertainty and ambiguity by emphasizing their role in a cosmic dualistic order.[25]

The dualistic theodicy supports the biographical security of individual believers. One of the fundamental concerns expressed by recruits to the Catholic pentecostal movement is a strong desire to know for sure where they "stand" before God. This desire for certainty is fulfilled by a secure framework of order positing a distinct duality between the forces of Good and Evil and showing a clear-cut path for the believer who would side with Good. Such simplified course of action informs the member that one is safe and secure by siding with the Good. This personal sense of security is expressed in the belief that "I am saved already." Fichter's survey found that over 50 percent of the Catholic pentecostal respondents believe that they are already saved.[26] This assuredness is not merely a peculiar characteristic, accidentally borrowed from Protestant pentecostals; rather, it is very important as an appeal to Catholic pentecostals.

This discussion of the movement's emphasis on dualistic interpretations of reality has focused on the foundation of a new order. It should be noted, however, that the old framework of order of pre-Vatican II Catholicism was, for many believers, essentially a dualistic scheme as well. The imagery and concreteness of the pentecostal dualism is more potent than that of pre-Vatican II Catholic dualism, but many members of the movement were probably exposed to a number of dualistic interpretations in early religious socialization. For example, the Baltimore Catechism taught the following ideas, among others, about angels and devils:

> 95. Not all the angels remained faithful to God; some of them sinned.
> 101. The good angels help us by praying for us, by acting as messengers from God to us, and by serving as our guardian angels.
> 103. Our guardian angels help us by praying for us, by protecting us from harm, and by inspiring us to do good.
> 107. The chief way in which the bad angels try to harm us is by tempting us to sin.
> 111. Besides tempting us, the devils are sometimes permitted by God to plague persons from without, and this is called obsession, or even to dwell in them and exercise power over their faculties and this is called possession.
> 112. Sometimes God permits obsession and possession to punish wicked persons; and sometimes He permits these attacks of the devil in the case of good persons to afford them an opportunity of practicing virtue.
> 114. The commands used by the Church against the attacks of the devils are called exorcisms.[27]

In the years immediately preceding Vatican II, as well as during and after the Council, the salience of these images appears to have declined. For example, O'Connor notes, "Even more than the doctrine of the Holy Spirit, the doctrine of the evil spirit has been discarded by the sophisticated theology that has sprung from the Enlightenment and demythologizing."[28] A renewed emphasis on a dualistic world view, therefore, may have had the functions both of positing a strong new framework of order while relating that new order to elements of the lost one, and of providing a sense of continuity with tradition.

The Imminence of the Millennium

A dualistic theodicy is especially forceful combined with a millenarian theodicy. The millenarian dream that the perfect New Order is imminent is also a response to problems of order and power.

When the old order is seen as nearly defunct, the new order surely must be near. The view of this society as badly out-of-order, concomitant with the evaluation of the Church as impotent to do anything about the "problems," leads to an understandable desire for a dramatic change. The coming of the Millennium will not only destroy the old problematic order, but it will also vindicate the faith of the believers. Catholic pentecostal millenarian themes bear considerable resemblance to the messages of judgment and impending damnation that characterized mission sermons of pre-World War II Catholic revivalism.[29] Like mission preachers, Catholic pentecostal leaders portray the world as a dangerous place, full of moral decay. They attack television, clothing styles, liberal laws and legislators, gay rights and women's rights, and changing family patterns, as sources of corruption and evidence of a rotten society. Unlike earlier Catholic revivalists, however, Catholic pentecostals consider the church to be seduced by, and in complicity with, the evils of the modern world. At the 1980 national conference, a movement spokesperson read this prophecy, "My people, my church is desperately in need of this judgment. They have continued in an adulterous relationship with the spirit of the world. They are not only infected with sin, but they teach sin, embrace sin, dismiss sin. . . ."[30]

Belief in the imminence of the Millennium is widespread among Catholic pentecostals. Fichter's study showed that 53 percent of the "liberals" (N = 155), 72 percent of the "moderates" (N = 370), and 83 percent of the "conservatives" (N = 219) believe that the Second Coming of Christ is near. The conservatives' stronger belief in the Millennium is predictable in the framework developed above; conservatives are more likely than liberals to evaluate negatively recent changes in the society and the church.[31]

While most of the leadership of the movement would not consider millenarianism to be a crucial belief, many leaders expect the Second Coming soon. For example, one national figure cites a number of prophecies in which the Lord said, "I am coming very soon."[32] Similarly, the themes of several prophecies at the 1975 Charismatic Conference (held in Rome) were of millenarian inspiration.[33] Although the millenarian theme has been present in movement teachings for many years, it has become increasingly prominent and claims of God's coming wrath are more strident.[34] Such beliefs are not merely incidental items but are a potent response to problems of order. Millenarianism posits a new order for the present and points to a future re-ordering which will reintegrate all the problematic aspects of the present situation into an all-encompassing, ultimate meaningful order.

Thus the millenarian vision is also a theodicy for the apparent discrepancies of the new framework of order espoused by the movement. For example, even after coming to a new life in the Spirit, Catholic pentecostals are likely to have difficulties—friends and relatives "not understanding," prayers seemingly not answered, doubts and uncertainties, and the society and Church still not on the "right track." The belief in the coming of the Millennium relativizes the problems and opposition of the present by affirming that all of these will be overcome in a glorious future.[35]

The millennial expectation gives a stronger sense of order and security to individual believers who not only locate themselves in the new framework of order, but also interpret their past, present, and future personal identities within its terms. Without the millenarian dream the future is one of terror—society appears to be collapsing, the unknown is amplified by rampant and uncontrolled social change, and the sources of safety and security of the past are increasingly helpless to protect the individual. Belief in the imminence of the Millennium enables individuals to feel that although "things" are really bad now and probably will get worse, they are not personally threatened by disorder and ambiguity because they are allied in the present with the ultimate Source of order and will have a privileged position in the unknown glorious future.

The millennial vision of Catholic pentecostals, combined with their ideological emphasis on voluntarism, results in a non-activist (often anti-activist) stance on social problems. Voluntarism, in this context, refers to the belief that all change must proceed from changing individuals—especially oneself.[36] Fichter observes that "the charismatic renewal movement tends to withdraw its members from the struggle for social justice and to blunt their zeal for social reform."[37] He notes that many members have relatively liberal opinions on social issues, but are not activists; furthermore, the movement is attracting a less and less activist membership. Fichter suggests that these findings show that members may retain their social attitudes even after becoming pentecostal, and that the movement does not necessarily neutralize strongly held social views.[38]

Fichter's interpretation does not take into account the fact that the movement ideology effectively reduces these liberal views to the status of mere opinions, and the issues are frequently considered virtually irrelevant to all which is meaningful in the pentecostal context. Members can afford to be tolerant about beliefs that have little significance for action. Prayer meetings and other pentecostal gatherings are typically arranged to avoid social issues and clashes of socio-political belief. The result, intentional or not, is the reduction of these areas of belief and action to the realm of irrelevance. Some authors have pointed out that millenarian movements are frequently pre-political revitalization forces that often result in engaging members in efforts for social change.[39] The Catholic pentecostal movement does not appear to fit this model. It is, if anything, anti-political, denying the validity of social and political modes of action.

Two elements of belief contribute to the non-activism of Catholic pentecostals: voluntarism and an ideal of civil obedience. Emphasis on personal sanctification reduces all world problems to a voluntaristic scope. Accordingly, all social and personal problems would be solved if only the individuals involved would turn to God and change their lives. Such an emphasis removes these larger problems from the responsibility of believers; there is no need to do anything about any of this except to pray and proselytize. This voluntaristic stance may be related to dualism as a form of rigid personal privatization in which the sense of social conflict is withdrawn from the social sphere and isolated in the private sphere where it can be resolved to the satisfaction of the believer.[40]

Emphasis on voluntaristic solutions may also be related to a sense of powerlessness, in which believers feel themselves lacking any control or power in the face of the massive disorder of society. It is important to note, however, that the Catholic pentecostal movement recruits very few members who were formerly social activists and "gave up." The voluntaristic solution may appeal especially to persons who held beliefs that social change was desirable, but never quite mobilized their personal resources into activism.

The ideal of civil obedience held by many Catholic pentecostals proposes that believers should be submissive to all due authority in the family, prayer group, church, and nation. Thus they consider any social activism which engages in conflict with civil authorities to be wrong and against God's will. This ideal is widespread in the movement, but some members argue against it. One national leader criticized the movement for encouraging an over-literal notion of obedience to human authority on the grounds that uncritical obedience does not promote Christian freedom.[41]

Finally theodicies of voluntarism and millenarianism are related to the appeal of the Catholic pentecostal movement. Many observers have wondered why a middle-class group would adopt beliefs formerly identified with underprivileged religious groups. These observers fail to recognize the considerable potency of these theodicies to serve as legitimations for the situation of both the relatively privileged and the unprivileged, the powerful and the powerless. A voluntaristic-millenarian stance on social change informs unprivileged members that individual sanctification will gain them a more privileged status in the new order, and that prayer and proselytizing will hasten that order. The same belief informs relatively well-off persons that they are justified in enjoying their privileged status, because they can most effectively help the underprivileged by prayer and proselytizing. The theodicy has the dual potential to justify the status of both the underprivileged and privileged. It also justifies their non-involvement in activism for social change.

Catholic pentecostals do sometimes get involved in what they call "social action," although this is seldom more than an individual effort. Respondents in this study indicated strong distaste for activist movements, almost to the point of being against them on principle. Even very mild forms of activism, such as signing petitions or supporting the United Farm Workers' boycott of lettuce received little support among the groups studied.[42] The only unified action taken during the several years of this study was that one group sponsored an inmate of a prison in a distant part of the country by praying for him each week and sending him monthly letters. It appears that he was singled out for the group's attention simply because one member kept mentioning his name at each prayer meeting's petition period.

Respondents cited other examples of social concern: visiting the sick, praying for sick or unhappy friends and relatives, praying for problems (for example, American hostages in Iran), giving food to the needy, and participating in neighborhood cleanup campaigns. Most social concern is directed at members' immediate families, friends, and neighbors. Other prayers are directed to such highly abstract issues and problems as "the problems of the government," "conflict in society," and the like. In many respects the "social action" of members is co-extensive with proselytizing. For example, a member might visit a sick relative in the hospital, witness to her, and then offer to pray for her. These privatized forms of social concern, together with the time and energy required for increased devotional practices, attendance at prayer meetings, and other religious practices, effectively remove Catholic pentecostals from even the potential for concerted activism in social reform.

Charisma and Authority

The movement describes itself as "charismatic" because of the centrality of the "gifts of the Spirit." The concept of "charisma" (gift) implies different things to Catholic pentecostals, to the public and mass media, and to sociologists. This array of meanings has resulted in some misunderstanding; the term is indiscriminately applied. Exploration of the term's sociological usages relative to the Catholic pentecostal usages leads to some interesting interpretations of the nature of charisma, power and authority. Specifically, charisma may be understood as the empowerment of individuals by drawing upon the social power of the group. Charismatic authority is but one type of personal empowerment—itself the result of a process of negotiation between the would-be leader and followers. Ordinary members, too, can experience a sense of empowerment, and group interactions can heighten the social power that members experience.

Catholic pentecostals speak of charisma as a special gift of power from the Holy Spirit to believers who have received the Spirit's baptism. They believe that there are many different gifts, and that individuals may receive one or several. Charisma empowers individuals to pray or witness better, to exert themselves more effectively toward ideal Christian living, and to participate more fervently in prayer meetings. This charismatic quality is diffused throughout the prayer group. Most members have some charisma, in their sense of the word.

In the mass media and popular imagery, "charisma" refers to a peculiar quality of only a few individuals, persons who stand out by virtue of a special aspect of their personalities. It is a somewhat psychologized and mystified concept: a quality of certain personalities that makes them seem awesome and have magnetic appeal to others. The media dub certain politicians, entertainers, athletes, and other public figures as "charismatic."

Sociological use of the concept of "charisma" stems from Weber's characterization of charismatic authority. Charisma refers to "a certain quality of an individual personality by virtue of which he is set apart from ordinary men and treated as endowed with . . . specifically exceptional powers or qualities . . . not accessible to the ordinary person."[43] Thus the authority of the charismatic leader is based upon a set of *social* interactions with followers in which the would-be leader asserts authority and the followers accept her or his claims. The concept of "charisma" is, therefore, not a psychological notion of the personalities of leaders, but a sociological idea describing social interaction. Charismatic authority, according to Weber, is a source of innovation, because the charismatic leader can proclaim new meanings and new obligations, superseding the teaching of traditional or official authorities. The charismatic leader announces, in effect, "You have heard it said . . . but I say to you . . ."

Based upon this sociological interpretation of charisma, the Catholic pentecostal movement is not a charismatic movement. There are some movement leaders whose leadership is based partly on charismatic appeal (for example, national leaders such as Ralph Martin and Francis MacNutt, and some local leaders, especially in relatively closed groups). The movement itself, however, exemplifies "revolution by tradition."[44]

The changes sought by the Catholic pentecostal movement are essentially changes *back* to an earlier model, an image of pristine Christianity. It is a movement of religious *virtuosi* (persons within a religious tradition who are trying for the highest spiritual level).[45]

Although the movement is not "charismatic" in the Weberian sense, there are elements of personal dynamism, effervescence, and empowerment in the experience of individual members that suggest the usefulness of distinguishing between charismatic empowerment as the basis of authority of leaders and charismatic empowerment in the commitment of individual members. The experience of charisma may be understood as the result of a process by which the social power of the group is transformed into personal power.

The idea that a social group produces a force or power that can be experienced by members is central in Durkheim's interpretation of religion. Durkheim made the collective basis of religious force the definitive characteristic of religion. Although the symbols by which this force is expressed are imperfect, the force—the power that people experience—is real—it is society. Durkheim described religion as a system of shared meanings by which individuals represent to themselves their society and their relations to that society.[46] He adds that, through participating in religious rituals, members both experience that power and internalize it in their consciousness. Members gain strength from the collective force.[47] Durkheim's observations about the relationship between individual and collective effervescence are borne out particularly in relatively small social groups, such as pentecostal prayer groups. The individual's experience of an immediate group, rather than an entire large society, is the foremost source of this collective force. Although the experience of power may also have a transcendent source, it is at least partly a product of the group's unity and integration. Prayer group leaders often recognize the importance of group unity for the "successful" reception of charismatic gifts.[48]

Charisma may, thus, be understood as the empowerment of individuals drawing on the collective force of the group. It could be in the form of individuals successfully claiming authority ("charismatic authority" in Weber's usage) by drawing upon this force, but charisma is not necessarily extra-ordinary. Ordinary members could, likewise, draw upon this collective force for a sense of power in their everyday lives, such as the power to overcome alcoholism or the power to witness to friends. Charisma is not a property of the individual but of the collectivity; individual members who draw on it experience it as something outside themselves—a power they do not have of themselves, a "gift."[49]

The sense of empowerment that individuals have in the group setting is real, whether or not members think of the group as the source of that power. The group may enhance the individual's sense of personal power in the face of opposition, such as the real or imagined opposition of competing groups or even ambiguous forces (for example, changing mores). The group or individual members may draw upon the collective power in the attempt to disempower others. Individuals may use this sense of power to assert dominance over other members, or the group may use it against non-members. The sense of empowerment gained from a collective force need not be explicitly religious. The sense of empowerment may be experienced in political terms (the unionized factory worker who feels a renewed sense of control in life), in psychological terms (the depressed housewife who feels a new basis of hope), or in physical terms (the cancer patient who feels a sense of power to fight the illness).

Individual commitment to the group is both a source and a product of the social power of the group. Zablocki, in his study of communes, made this feature definitive. He states, "We wish to define charisma as a collective state resulting from an objective pattern of relationships in a specific collectivity that allows the selves of the participants to be fully or partially absorbed into a collective self."[50] Interaction with others in the group enhances the individual's sense of personal empowerment by shaping the believer's world, providing a coherent world view and thus enabling action. The relationship between empowerment and the production of meaning is especially strong in the role of charismatic leader—one whose authority is based upon group acceptance of claims of empowerment.

Charismatic authority may be understood as a result of negotiation between a would-be leader and followers, in which the leader proffers an order which may appeal to followers and communicates this meaningful order through symbols which may produce a sense of that leader's power.[51] The charismatic leader gains power by the manipulation of symbols such that order is produced in one sphere of reality by linking it with the order of another sphere of reality through symbols (such as language or ritual action). Thus, for example, the religious leader who enables members to interpret concrete physical suffering through reference to metaphorical suffering actually produces a sense of order for believers. It is this production of order, through linkage of everyday reality to a transcendent reality, that is the basis of the leader's power. Indeed, Fabian suggests that "charismatic authority is based on the perception and formulation (and . . . in a sense 'creation') of meaning for human action."[52] He notes that the charismatic leader has impact because he or she offers an all-encompassing message; that is, meaning is total.[53]

The authority of the charismatic leader is not based only upon what the leader does, however; it also depends upon validation by followers. That validation consists in the willingness of members of the group to take seriously the leadership of a person thus empowered. The potential leader must symbolize reception of charisma in forms the group understands and respects. The ability to arouse in the group a sense of that power is, therefore, one sign of the effectiveness of these symbols. The particular symbols of empowerment vary from group to group, but micro-sociological analysis would enable us to specify them for each case.[54] Participant observation is helpful but somewhat too crude a methodological tool to detail this interaction, but it does point to some ways pentecostal leaders symbolize their power (for example, body language of dramatic gestures, forms of eye contact, and proficient use of potent gifts of the Spirit like prophecy and discernment).

Specific actions of the leader or group may produce a heightened sense of power; the development of certain ideologies, group structures, leadership patterns, norms and rituals, create a sense of awe, mystery, and potency. One fundamental source of collective power is the creation of a group ideology explaining broad areas of members' lives and legitimating their surrender and commitment to the group and its way of life. Especially effective ideologies (including that of Catholic pentecostals) specify awe-inspiring qualities, such as prophecy and discernment, expected of individuals who assume leadership roles. Certain leadership structures heighten the sense of power and awe; groups in which the final decision-making process is remote from ordinary members experience greater awe of those decisions. For example, a prayer group in which the direction of the whole group is "received" in a closed meeting of the core group feels in greater awe of that decision than another group in which all members rationally discuss and actively try to reach a joint decision.[55]

Hierarchy and stratification within the group also promote a sense of power and awe. Several prayer groups had highly stratified decision-making processes, but incorporated ordinary members so actively in non-powerful roles that the actual stratification was minimized in the eyes of most members. A sense of power and awe is further enhanced by mysteriousness.[56] Catholic pentecostals' beliefs about the gifts of the Spirit allowed for much mystery in every aspect of their group or individual lives: "The Lord works in mysterious ways." Providence and divine coincidence lent an atmosphere of mystery to everyday occurrences. Glossolalia, by its very incomprehensibility, was mysterious. The direction of individual lives and the prayer group as a whole could be determined by mysterious processes of prophecy and discernment. Healings and exorcisms mysteriously effected changes in peoples' lives, even if the nature of the changes could not be known by the persons involved.

The idea that powerful persons within the group mediated spiritual powers to other members further promoted a sense of awe and power. The existence of very real social control mechanisms in the prayer group both consolidated the power of leaders and further enhanced the experience of power within the group. For example, preventing an "inappropriate" prophecy from being given in a prayer meeting controls a powerful and potentially challenging event and, simultaneously, guarantees that the overall effect of the prayer meeting will be "successful" and "uplifting" to participants. The prayer meeting "comes off" because it is controlled to achieve a desired effect of power and mystery; this same control also enhances the power of the leaders who exercise it. The prayer meeting, as a ritual of unity, can actually produce greater power. Thus, charisma is not a byproduct of social power which exists uniformly in a group; rather it may be heightened or diminished by group interaction.

Catholic pentecostal emphasis on charisma—gifts of power available to both leaders and ordinary members—suggests clarifications of a sociological interpretation of charisma. Charisma may be understood as personal empowerment derived from the social power of a group. Charismatic authority is, thus, only one form of this empowerment; it is the result of a process of negotiation in which a would-be leader evokes symbols of power and order and the potential followers respond to those claims. Nor is charisma static. The group's social power (and, by extension, the member's experience of power) can be heightened or diminished by specific changes in group organization, leadership styles, norms, and rituals.

Three—
Sharing
Life
in the Spirit:
Conversion
and Commitment

Understanding a movement's ideology and practices helps to explain its appeal, but it does not adequately explain how or why individual members become converted and committed to the movement's distinctive perspective and way of life. This chapter focuses on the processes of conversion and commitment, with special emphasis on the functions of "witnessing" for Catholic pentecostals.

The use of the term "conversion" to describe the Catholic pentecostal's new way of thinking, believing, and behaving is appropriate but needs qualification. In common parlance, religious conversion refers to a dramatic shift from one religious stance to another (for instance, Catholic-turned-Baptist) or from non-believing to believing. Most Catholic pentecostals do not undergo this kind of change. Most were Catholics both before and after beginning their "new life"; many were active members of their local churches, and many have increased participation in Catholic liturgies and devotions.[1]

"Conversion," here, means a transformation of one's self concurrent with a transformation of one's central meaning system.[2] In this sense of the word, most Catholic pentecostals do experience a conversion. The important shift of meaning system means more than adopting a new set of beliefs; rather, it means a whole new way of experiencing the world and oneself. This new mode of experiencing is, then, a basis for subsequent alterations in behavior. The individual comes to "see" the world with a whole new perspective. Indeed, the new believer may say, "I once was blind, but now I see." This phrase is both metaphorical and actual, because the new perspective causes the individual to perceive the world differently—literally a new "world" "view."[3] That which was marginal in the field of consciousness becomes central, and that which once was focal becomes peripheral.[4] Every world view entails the selective perception of events and objects according to its meaning system. Conversion means adopting new criteria for selecting.

Perceptions of the past, present, and future are changed. Converts reconstruct their biographies to incorporate their new world view.[5] They reinterpret their past experiences in relation to their new system of meaning. Basically this is a re-ordering, fitting personal experience into a new framework of order. It involves a reconstruction of identity in the context of the new meaning system and new relationships with fellow believers. Jones emphasizes that the "conversion experience is not simply . . . some specific 'internal' experience, but a reorganization of the 'world' in a *transformative* manner with a concomitant plausibility structure to maintain the new reality."[6]

Such transformations usually include both a reversal of the previous sense of order (for example, "He who is first shall be last") and a reinforcement of the familiar (that is, retaining and reinterpreting elements of the former world view).[7] It is difficult, however, to demonstrate empirically whether these aspects of conversion are part of the conversion process or are simply legitimations of the results. Several "rhetorics" (socially available plausible explanations), may be used to explain the transformation: rhetorics of choice, rhetorics of change, and rhetorics of continuity. Rhetorics of choice emphasize how much the change was the result of a personal, even "agonizing" decision. Rhetorics of change highlight the dramatic nature of personal change in the conversion (as in before-and-after stories). Rhetorics of continuity focus on the extent to which one's new world view is the logical extension of earlier beliefs and experience (that is, reconstruction of biography).[8] Different cultures emphasize different rhetorics; thus rhetorics of choice are prominent in American society. Also, different ideologies emphasize one rhetoric over another. For example, Catholic pentecostals generally encourage new believers to interpret their conversion as continuous with their former belief system; but Jesus People typically encourage recruits to view their conversion as dramatic change.

Since most of the evidence about the subjective meaning of those transformations is, however, in the form of already "interpreted" testimonies, it is not possible to distinguish which aspects describe the process of conversion itself and which are essentially aspects of the individual's reconstruction of personal biography—including a conversion story. All such conversion stories are, in their very nature, transformations of the subjective experience to which they refer.[9] Catholic pentecostal "witnessing" (analyzed below) illustrates this transformative process.

Kinds of Conversion

Conversions among Catholic pentecostals may be distinguished by the degree of transformation necessary to become a committed member of the movement. How different is the new member's pentecostal identity from the former identity? Generally, the more dramatic the difference between the former way of life and the new one, the more extreme the social processes leading to conversion need to be.

A radical transformation of self and meaning system characterizes the conversions of, for example, an atheist or a Jewish person to Catholic pentecostalism. Instances of this kind of conversion were observed in three of the groups studied, but such extreme conversions are relatively rare. They are also seldom as dramatic as popular imagery implies. Radical transformations of self and world view occur by essentially the same kinds of social processes as less extreme conversions.[10]

A somewhat more common type of conversion among Catholic pentecostals (especially young adult recruits) may be characterized as identity consolidation. Many of these persons had been raised as Catholics (typically in pre-Vatican II modes of religious education), had rejected their religion and were uninterested in returning to the Catholicism they had known. Subsequently some of them had tried alternative world views, such as Esalen, TM, Silva Mind Control, or *est*. Becoming Catholic pentecostal was not a return to their former Catholicism, because their pentecostal meaning system and new selves were dramatically different. Yet the beliefs and practices of Catholic pentecostalism enabled these members to consolidate elements of both former identities into a new, "superior" self. Similar identity consolidation occurs in many conversions to the Jesus People, the Meher Baba cult, and Orthodox Jewish ba'ale teshuvot.[11]

An even less extreme type of conversion is a transformation of self and meaning system representing a reaffirmation of elements of one's previous identity. These conversions involve no change in religious affiliation yet entail real changes in one's personal meaning system and sense of identity. Most conversions of older adults who become Catholic pentecostals are of this type. These persons change their personal meaning systems and selves, but they interpret these changes as consistent with their former meaning system. They consider their former Catholic religiosity to be a vague groping for the truth, which they now have found. This type of conversion does not necessarily involve a complete rejection of the previous meaning system. Converts' interpretations of continuity, however, belie the very real changes in their identities and perspectives.

By contrast, some conversion experiences involve little or no change in meaning system and sense of self. As the Catholic pentecostal movement becomes increasingly routinized, this kind of quasi-conversion is more common, especially among youths whose parents are already involved in the movement. In several of the groups observed, the proportion of converts, twelve to seventeen years of age, has greatly increased, while the numbers of college age and young adult recruits has dropped considerably. Like their Protestant counterparts, Catholic pentecostals expect their young members to make personal faith decisions and to undergo a conversion experience as they approach adulthood. Thus the conversion experience functions as a rite of passage to religious adulthood. As Catholic pentecostal conversion becomes increasingly routinized, Life in the Spirit seminars and special pentecostal youth retreats become the carefully managed and appropriate social settings for the expected conversion experience to occur.[12] These experiences, while meaningful to participants, are generally not conversions but rather merely affirm the identity and meaning system into which the person had already been socialized.

Accounting for Conversion

Several events lead to conversion and several further events are necessary to sustain it. Most religious groups (in our society) and recruits define a moment of decision and commitment as a crucial event; however, it is not so dramatic as it may seem, since usually many preparatory measures have been taken to make it successful. In fact, the heightened expectations of the neophyte, together with the fact that the event is considered crucial, are part of these measures. It is far more difficult for the new believer to sustain the new world view.[13] For this reason, both sociologists and religionists emphasize that there is more to religious commitment than merely deciding to believe. The following description examines the sequence of events in conversion, none of which is, however, sufficient in itself to "cause" conversion.[14] Also, the process seldom occurs in such clearly identifiable steps, and frequently one interaction fulfills several functions in the process. Among Catholic pentecostals, for example, the first meeting of a Life in the Spirit seminar simultaneously functions to raise recruits' sense of need for change, to resocialize them in Catholic pentecostal ways of thinking and acting, and as a minor commitment event. Often, steps in conversion seem to be discrete and identifiable because of the legitimating rhetorics used by participants. Thus the element of individual decision is heightened by rhetorics of choice. In a culture in which individual decision is less significant (or even negatively viewed), the element of personal decision would have a less prominent place in conversion stories; indeed, it might not even be experienced.[15]

Predisposition to Conversion

Personal and situational factors can predispose people to conversion by sensitizing them to the inadequacy of their prior meaning system to explain or give meaning to experiences and events. Persons whose meaning systems adequately "handle" experiences and events have no particular reason to seek any alternative meanings for their lives. Persons who experience a tension, malaise, or crisis that is not manageable within the former meaning system are particularly predisposed to conversion. Three characteristics of this tension make it especially problematic: a sense of powerlessness, a sense of disorder (making it impossible to project expectations into the future), and a sense of hopelessness (leaving no end in sight to this situation).[16]

Sometimes individuals who feel acutely the need for a new meaning system become "seekers"—persons who actively look for a satisfactory alternative meaning system, often trying several different alternatives.[17] Some recruits to Catholic pentecostalism had been seekers. For example, one woman in her mid-thirties had previously tried Spiritualism, astrology, Silva Mind Control, Transcendental Meditation, and Subud. Members who had been seekers characteristically had a different kind of commitment to the group. They tended to be more tentative in their commitment and more eclectic in their beliefs, often retaining some of the beliefs and practices of previously tried alternatives (see Chapter 8 on cultic mode of adherence).

The more typical convert to Catholic pentecostalism had not sought out the group with any conscious intention of changing to a new meaning system. Some of these persons had previously experienced only a vague tension or malaise. Others described an acute sense of crisis in their lives. Some such crises were purely personal as in the death of a spouse, or the loss of a job. Generally, however, most recruits were predisposed to convert because of events and social situations that (1) raised their religious expectations and/or (2) promoted their dissatisfaction with their prior meaning system and its ability to manage everyday experiences.

The Religious Situation

Several events undermined satisfaction with the Catholic world view into which recruits had been socialized, especially: emergence from the ethno-religious ghetto, religious pluralism, social activism in the churches, and extensive post-Vatican II "changing the rules."

Ethno-religious communities had initially served to protect immigrant Catholics from the not-altogether-hospitable American society, while easing the transition in world view, language, and everyday behavior into the mainstream of American life. The ethno-religious ghetto not only protected its members but also often provided services that eventually, in effect, pushed them out of the ghetto community. Catholic schools (especially secondary and college level) prepared members for possible achievement in the larger society. A great reduction of anti-Catholic prejudice was hastened by experiences during the Second World War and culminated in the election of a Catholic president. Catholics moved out of the ethnic ghettoes, literally, as suburban housing came within their economic reach, and figuratively, as they began to attend non-Catholic schools and colleges, join non-Catholic voluntary organizations, find acceptance by previously non-Catholic professional organizations, and so on.

While these moves were the desired goals of most upwardly mobile Catholics, they often resulted in social-psychological losses, especially loss of a strong source of identification with a community.[18] The ethno-religious community not only represented an identifiable and coherent way of life, but also taught and enforced a relatively unambiguous package of norms and values. By contrast, the person who emerged into the larger society met with norms that conflicted with those of the ghetto community and often were internally inconsistent or ambiguous. Emergence from the Catholic ghetto meant leaving a stable—although perhaps constricting and narrow—way of life.

Most Catholics who were adults by the 1960s had been taught that the Roman Catholic church possessed "The Truth," that its Sacraments were the only way to salvation, and that other religions were at best misguided. Pre-Vatican II efforts at dialogue between Catholic and non-Catholic Christians were mincing and tenuous, supported mainly by intellectuals. Thus for the Catholic church to break suddenly into regular interaction with non-Catholic churches, to openly acknowledge respect for the Jewish faith, and to show some openness to non-Western religions, represented a dramatic change for the average believer. As Berger has shown, however, pluralization and the ecumenical model have the built-in potential for undermining the certainty of the believer's original world view. They reduce the taken-for-granted quality of the belief system and, by the very "peaceful coexistence" of competing interpretations of reality, the given-ness of any one interpretation is put into doubt.[19] Thus while ecumenism and a pluralistic ideal helped to reduce prejudices and intolerance between Catholics and their non-Catholic neighbors, these same movements may have been deeply confusing to persons who were socialized into an earlier triumphalistic Catholicism.

After Vatican II, the increasing call to social and political activism resulted in Catholic prominence in the civil rights movement of the 1960s and in the anti-war movement of the 1960s and 1970s. Less conspicuous, but just as significant, was their local involvement in urban renewal, open housing, child care and education reforms, legal aid, draft counselling and welfare rights. Out of this period of social activism grew the "underground church"—a largely, but not exclusively, Catholic movement dedicated to political and social dissent and activism.[20] While only a small percentage of American Catholics was ever involved in such activism, average members were confronted with the idea of Christian dissent and involvement in social change. They were compelled to resolve their own stance on issues of social and political concern and felt some pressure to explain themselves if they opted out of such involvement.[21] Some commentators had suggested that Catholic pentecostalism was a response to the futility of social activism, but interviews conducted early in this research found that very few Catholic pentecostals had ever been involved in activist movements and that increasingly smaller percentages of new recruits were ever so-involved. Nevertheless, the presence of social and political activists among the ranks of Catholics—especially priests and nuns—was disturbing to many.

Finally, the rapid change in religious norms and practices produced by the Vatican II "changing of rules" created a sense of ambiguity for many Catholics.[22] This ambiguity was not merely a problem of *which* rules to follow; rather, it was an issue of *why* one should follow rules. Previous Catholic norms had been legitimated by a strong appeal to supernatural bases of authority. The typical layperson had learned that infractions, such as eating meat on Friday, breaking the pre-Communion fast, or touching the Communion host with one's hands, were so serious as to endanger one's soul. The very fact of rapid change resulted in humanizing these rules. An infraction was a mortal sin one day and no longer sinful the next; certain actions were absolutely forbidden in one diocese and not in the next, and so on. Regardless of whether the individual favored or disliked the substance of change, the fact of change revealed the human source of the whole system of rules. The suprahuman legitimation of the entire system was debunked, and the authority supporting the revised norms and practices was undermined.

Such ambiguity produced greater malaise for Catholics than similar change might have for other religious groups, because the pre-Vatican II Catholic socialization emphasized neat, orderly, enduring categories of "good" and "bad." When this sense of order was undermined, it was thoroughly disrupted. Catholics, as a group, had been taught to be less tolerant of ambiguity. The presence of a sense of malaise among movement recruits is corroborated by Mawn's study, which found that 45 percent of the Catholic pentecostals studied (N = 455) said that before becoming charismatic, "I was uncertain as to the values to pursue"; 39 percent agreed that they had, "no clear answers as to how to conduct my life"; 31 percent felt, "My life was without meaning or purpose"; and 47 percent had experienced a personal crisis shortly before joining.[23] The shattering of the nice, neat categories and clear-cut prescriptions for behavior had a further effect on many Catholics; it brought into doubt the security of personal salvation. It seems that for many Catholics there used to be security in the belief that following certain practices would provide some guarantee of getting to heaven. This assuredness, while not in keeping with official theology, was probably very important for many Catholics. The fact of change destroyed the old assuredness, and simply positing new rules could not overcome the ambiguity. Who could say that the new rules would not change, too?

The events following Vatican II may have simultaneously raised many Catholics' religious expectations because possibilities for a more meaningful liturgy, for lay participation in church decision-making, for a greater sense of community in parishes, for new lifestyles for members of religious orders, and so on, were opened. Dissatisfaction with the former mode of Catholic religiosity was thus as much a product of raised expectations as it was the shortcomings of Church and Society.

The Social Situation

Broad social conditions in American society disturbed many potential converts. They asserted the need for a religious response to the "decay" of the society. The mere opening-to-question of large spheres of private morality has been experienced by many Americans as a highly threatening change. These changes, ranging from big issues such as divorce and homosexuality, to such seemingly minor issues as long hair and mini-skirts, are significant, mainly because they create an uncertainty about what to expect and what is expected of one. The profound discomfort experienced by Catholic pentecostal recruits over these areas of change can be seen in their before-and-after witnessing tales, as well as in their fervent prayers against the influence of Satan in forms of pornography, drugs, cults, materialism, and television.

The various liberation movements, especially women's liberation, have also had an effect on the norms of private and public life. Challenges to traditional gender roles of both men and women are profoundly disturbing to many who feel they no longer have a sense of exactly what is expected of them. A certain satisfaction could be gained by fulfilling these norms, and there was security in knowing one's place. Such assuredness did not necessarily produce happiness in one's assigned role, but it did result in a modicum of meaning and purpose.

Catholic pentecostal teachings reassert gender norms of chaste behavior and dress, traditional sexual morality, women's obedience to husbands and male superiors in the prayer community, and finding the satisfaction of one's "place." These values stand in sharp contrast with those promoted by liberation movements—especially the notion that the individual should consciously choose his or her roles, challenging and overcoming, if necessary, the inequalities produced by traditional role constraints.

These dramatic changes in the private sphere have been accompanied by many rapid changes in the public sphere. A number of events of the 1960s reduced Americans' confidence in their nation and its institutions: the Vietnam War, the failure of the war on poverty, the rapid increase in crime and especially the assassination of several national leaders, disclosures about Watergate and similar corruption in national institutions. By the end of 1973, the Louis Harris poll reported that the Executive Branch of the federal government was trusted by a mere 19 percent of Americans surveyed. Religious institutions were, interestingly, among the institutions least trusted.[24]

American faith in progress and technology became less plausible with threats of economic depression, inflation, and ecocatastrophe. The American dream of unlimited upward mobility appeared fragile in the face of a new kind of depression in the mid-1970s and 1980s, with widespread unemployment and underemployment, rapid inflation in prices and tax burdens, and increasing unavailability of consumer goods such as private home ownership and fuel for cars, boats, and campers, defined as evidence of upward mobility. Such economic reversals are particularly acute for blue-collar, newly middle-class persons—the social classes most represented among Catholics.[25] These problems are not merely a matter of what people cannot have; rather, they present an inability for ordinary people to project matters that count to them into the future (for example, "If I keep saving at this rate, next year I can afford to buy a house," or "If I work hard in college, I'll be able to get a good job.").

These sources of discontent are further compounded by the growing sense of powerlessness in the face of the large bureaucracies directing most areas of the public sphere. Political, economic, legal, educational, and military institutions seem to be inaccessible or unresponsive to the average citizen. They appear to be even out of the control of those in positions of responsibility for them.

Many recruits also fear a world crisis. This problem may be merely because people are more aware of world issues, through mass media, and feel especially powerless to affect problems of such scope. Americans have only recently become aware of the extent of economic interdependence among nations, such that recession in other nations affects this nation's well-being. Similarly, there is a growing awareness (but only vague understanding) of the extent of American resource interdependence with other nations, of the implications of foreign entanglements, and how wars in such distant places as Angola, Vietnam, or the Mideast can influence the American way of life. Even seemingly unrelated disasters come to be seen as indicators of impending doom. For example, members of some prayer groups pointed to such diverse instances as the war in the Mideast, famine in Africa, an earthquake in Central America, and an abnormally severe winter in North America as omens of the imminence of a larger, undefined "crisis"—possibly the end of the world. It is not just the feeling of crisis, but rather the sense of powerlessness and uncontrollable scope of "world crisis," that are significant. The present "coming end" is not like the purposeful apocalypses of the past; it seems to lack any meaningful interpretation.[26] The world view of the dominant American culture cannot adequately absorb, interpret, and thereby control the apocalypse. The crisis, therefore, is not a crisis of events so much as a crisis of meaning.

This discussion has focused on experiences which, in some combination, may have produced a sense of tension or malaise among a number of middle-class Catholics at this time in history, thus creating a pool of potential recruits. This argument does not suggest that these experiences caused individuals to become Catholic pentecostals. It does suggest, however, that without these or similar experiences, the old meaning system would have worked for most Catholics and they would have had no reason or need to change their established ways of doing and believing.

Converting to Catholic pentecostalism is not caused by this tension or malaise, but rather is a response and resolution to problems of order and control. Other responses such as political conversion, alcoholism, psychotherapy, television addiction, and suicide are also possible. Why, then, did these particular persons choose this particular new meaning system? Recruits are often attracted to a particular movement because they share its problem-solving perspective.[27] Thus, for example, Catholics who were socialized into a religion with a strong emphasis on authority might find an authoritarian movement, such as Catholic pentecostalism, relatively agreeable.[28] Similarly, previous experiences may have given the individual a sense of what positive features to seek. For example, many Catholic pentecostals had been active in the Cursillo and Marriage Encounter movements before joining charismatic prayer groups.[29] Their exposure to experiential religiosity in Cursillo and to a sense of community in both movements may have led them to seek these same qualities in a religious movement. Finally, it is important not to overlook purely religious aspirations in recruitment and conversion to pentecostalism.[30] In other words, one of the attractions of the movement may be that it offers a greater opportunity to praise God, to speak to Him, to hear Him, and to serve Him.

Interaction with the Group

In most cases initial contact for Catholic pentecostal recruits was by means of a relative or close friend already in the movement.[31] Recruitment within already existing networks of friendship or kinship enhances the likelihood that commitment will result.[32] Respondents indicated a variety of reasons why they decided to first attend. For many, it was simply curiosity. One high-school student said, "I came to see what was this weird thing my best friend was into." Another common explanation was that the recruit was impressed with a friend's newfound happiness. Implicit in this response is a growing awareness of one's own less-than-perfect happiness. Several others attended their first meeting to get someone "to stop bugging me," hoping to silence the insistence of a pentecostal friend. This was a fairly common reason why men were brought into the group; their spouses were very insistent. These explanations also show that, even in the earliest stages of recruitment, there are differences in levels of commitment.

Not all Catholic pentecostals are aware of their "need" for a meaning system before their contact with the movement. Many recruits felt discontented and some were actively seeking a resolution to their discontent prior to their first contact. Many others, however, "learned" how discontented they were only after exposure to the movement. Conversion to a new meaning system is often made possible through the "mediation of anomie" (sense of loss of normative order) by the new religious group.[33] Thus part of the early interaction with recruits consists of undermining their confidence in their prior world view. The mediation of anomie consists of promoting the potential convert's sense that things are gravely disordered and in need of a new framework. An examination of appeals made in early parts of Life in the Spirit seminars shows this process clearly.

An Explanation Session is the first formal introduction potential recruits are likely to experience.[34] In this first session a deliberately oversimplified explanation of the meaning of salvation is given. The following appeal is typical, "If you don't have God at the center of your life, you can't experience His peace and joy, His power and the direction only He can give. Without His direction, life can seem empty and meaningless; without His power, we are helpless."

If recruits continue in Life in the Spirit seminars (a minor act of commitment in itself), the second session, entitled "Salvation," further mediates their growing sense of anomie. The Team Manual suggests the following outline for the introduction to Session two:

> I. *There is something seriously wrong with the world* (with society as a whole and with individual lives)—something major is needed.
> A. God made the world to be a place of peace and justice and happiness, a place in which he would reign. He still wants the world to be that way (Isa. 2:1–5).
> B. But *everyone agrees* that there is something seriously wrong with the way the world is now (war, poverty, riots, racial conflict, generation gap, exploitation).
> C. There is a growing realization that there is more than just a number of individual problems—society as a whole, the system as a whole, has something wrong with it (*where is it all going?* Social problems are getting worse, *no one on top of the situation*, technology and social change *out of men's control*).
> D. Individuals suffer from the situation and from lack of help, and they experience many problems (*loneliness, isolation, depression, anxieties, insecurities, lack of direction, meaninglessness*, personal relationships characterized by *fear, suspicion, mistrust, exploitation*).[35]

The presentation then explains that "Satan is behind it" and that humans by themselves cannot fight such powerful forces. The solution to world and personal problems is possible through the power of Jesus.[36] Thus not only do recruits grow in their dissatisfaction with their old framework of order, but also they learn to redefine their discontent and other needs in terms of the specific pentecostal ideology.[37]

Through interaction with members, the recruit is gradually resocialized into that group's way of life. Conversion, put somewhat too simply, means "coming to accept the opinions of one's friends,"[38] and is essentially a resocialization, consisting of an individual renegotiation of personal identity and world view consistent with that considered appropriate by the group. The group's social support of newfound fellow believers is especially important. Affective bonds with members of the prayer group affirm the new pentecostal self and meaning system. As the recruit gradually withdraws from competing social relationships, the new group's opinions become increasingly important.[39] New Catholic pentecostals associate themselves more frequently and intensely with other members of the prayer group.[40]

Another important way of supporting the plausibility of the convert's new world view is by converting one's immediate family and friends; if one's spouse, for example, is also a believer, the new member experiences confirmation rather than conflict.[41] Since, however, few Catholic pentecostals live in "total communities" of fellow Catholic pentecostals, most members are likely to experience considerable conflict in facing those who supprt their former world view and who relate to them in terms of their old identities. The more conflict with these persons new members experience, the more important their group of fellow believers becomes. Former attachments compete with new commitments, symbolize a world view that the recruit wishes to reject, and are based upon an identity that the recruit has decided to change.

Symbolizing the Conversion

The part of the conversion process typically identified as "the conversion" is basically some form of symbolizing the transformation that has already been occurring or that the individual has decided should occur. The convert affirms the new identity by some symbolic means considered appropriate in that group. One session of the Life in the Spirit seminars is set aside for a special emotional and spiritual event, baptism in the Spirit. In smaller, less formal prayer groups, a similar conversion experience is encouraged, usually in a separate setting immediately after the regular prayer meeting. The speaking in tongues and witnessing that sometimes accompany conversion are concrete expressions of the inner transformation—symbols which the group and the new convert both understand to mean a change has taken place.

Although conversion is a gradual process, many recruits who have decided to convert adopt some symbols of conversion rather dramatically. Part of the resocialization entailed in conversion involves learning to act, look, and talk like other members of the group. Like recruits to the military forces, the police, or medical profession, new religious recruits often eagerly imitate the behavior of full-fledged members. One particularly noticeable feature of new Catholic pentecostal recruits who had decided to convert was an almost exaggerated blissful smile and starry eyes. Many converts imitated special speech patterns of regular members, so that by the last session of the Life in the Spirit seminars their prayers and witnessing were gross caricatures of the routine style of praying and witnessing of regular members.

Outsiders sometimes mistake such dramatic change of appearance and behavior as indication that the convert has been brainwashed or "zapped." Fellow believers sometimes mistake the transformation as evidence of a dramatic conversion. Actually, acting converted is part of the resocialization process itself, "The way to *be* changed is act changed."[42] By acting the role of the full-fledged member, even to the point of exaggeration, the neophyte learns the details of acting and thinking like a Catholic pentecostal until these patterns are fully internalized and taken for granted.

The data do not support any clear-cut delineation of when Catholic pentecostals become committed converts. Some individuals pointed to an exact moment of their decision. Other respondents said they had attended a long time, gone through Life in the Spirit seminars, received the baptism in the Spirit (with no particular spectacular side effects), and still could not "put their finger on" when they had decided or were sure they were fully committed. As Becker points out, some commitments result from conscious decisions but others develop crescively—the person simply gradually becomes aware that he is, in fact, committed.[43] Although the prayer groups deliberately foster an atmosphere necessitating a moment of decision, analysis of the careers of new members shows clearly that these processes are not all that discrete. Catholic pentecostals themselves refer to the Laying on of Hands for baptism in the Spirit as part of a commitment ceremony, but they acknowledge that it may only symbolize an act of commitment made well before the event itself. Furthermore, some members do not feel strong commitment during the baptism, and their decision may be merely the decision to ask God for further grace to lead them to "real" commitment.

Several researchers have emphasized that glossolalia serves a significant function in the conversion and commitment process. Hine asserts that glossolalia serves as the critical "bridge-burning" act for American pentecostals. According to her analysis, speaking in tongues identifies tongue-speakers with the group in which the act is valued and commits them to changed attitudes consistent with the group's ideals. At the same time, glossolalic speech serves to cut the speaker off from the larger society.[44] Similarly, Harrison observes that baptism in the Holy Spirit, and the glossolalia which accompanies (or follows) it, confirm new members of their faith in the Holy Spirit and the charismatic movement. These same steps serve to alienate them from non-pentecostals and publicly demonstrate their commitment.[45] Harrison disagrees with Hine's isolation of glossolalia as *the* "bridge-burning event," pointing out that (for Catholic pentecostals, at least) tongue-speaking is only part of the commitment process and is only one of several acts that may alienate pentecostals from non-pentecostals. Harrison's distinction is comparable to Lebra's concepts of mechanisms of "involvement" and "abandonment" in religious resocialization. Abandonment refers to renunciation of social ties or possessions associated with one's former social system; involvement means investment of one's self or possessions with the new social system. This dual emphasis upon both aspects of commitment seems useful. Lebra also notes that commitment is made at various stages of entry and post-entry.[46]

Data from this study suggest that, while glossolalia may function as a symbol of abandonment (bridge-burning), the main involvement and public abandonment act for Catholic pentecostals is public or semi-public testimony. Furthermore, testimony (witnessing) serves several other significant functions in resocialization. A description of Catholic pentecostal induction processes illustrates the functions of witnessing as a commitment mechanism, and for the broader process of resocialization of new members.

Commitment

The process of conversion is not ended by officially joining the group and symbolically affirming the conversion; rather the conversion process is continued in the ongoing commitment by which members increasingly identify with the group, its meaning system, and its goals. Persons who are totally committed to a group have fully invested themselves in it and wholly identify with it. Commitment is the link between the individual member and the larger social group—in this case, the prayer community.

Although conversion may resolve problems with former meaning systems and former selves, it alone is not sufficient to resolve new problems, but the group's commitment processes help prevent new doubts and new problems from undermining the conversion. The conversion-commitment process produces new members who will invest themselves in what the group is believing and doing and ensures the commitment of all members, new and old, to the group's values and objectives.

The processes by which the prayer group fosters commitment are similar to the mechanisms of the initial conversion; members are urged to withdraw from competing allegiances and alternate ways of life and to involve themselves more deeply in the life of their prayer group, its values and goals.[47] Some of these commitment mechanisms are developed in more detail in Chapter 8.

Life in the Spirit Seminars

During the earliest years of the Catholic pentecostal movement, induction of new members was relatively informal and abrupt.[48] More recently, however, the movement's leadership has prepared and published a formal, detailed course outline for a series of "Life in the Spirit seminars," designed to prepare newcomers for baptism in the Holy Spirit.[49] Seminars typically consist of nine sessions: one explanatory, one sign-up, four preparatory, one for baptism in the Holy Spirit, and two follow-up. Details of the curriculum and roles to be played by leader-teams are carefully spelled out in the manual. The very idea of attending seminars reveals something about the commitment process. Seminars are a culturally acceptable induction mechanism, clearly appealing to a middle-class audience. They are safe, gradual, and orderly.[50]

In analyzing these Life in the Spirit seminars, it is helpful to view the convert's career as "drift" rather than as a dramatic shift. Neophytes are often already disposed toward the group's views even before attending, become increasingly committed if only by the act of further attendance, and so on. Most new members interviewed could not identify a specific point at which they were converted to the new life. Certainly, attendance at the seminars was no dramatic turning point for many. It was more like one step in a "funneling" process. Of twenty-three seminar participants interviewed, sixteen indicated that they had already decided to ask for baptism in the Spirit before beginning the seminars, two had already previously received the baptism and were seeking "further insight,"[51] and only five could be characterized as relatively uncommitted beforehand (of these, two dropped out). Since attendance at the first session after the sign-up was defined by group leaders as a minor sign of commitment, it is necessary to speak of the neophytes as already well into the process of conversion. The seminars are, therefore, more appropriately considered as a resocializing, identity-forming induction than as a prelude to conversion.

The Significance of Testimony

Testimony (witnessing) has much prominence in the prayer meetings of Catholic pentecostals. It takes two basic forms: (1) "spontaneous" witnessing, by which (at an appropriate time) the member recounts an event or experience which "shows God's power"; and (2) the "teaching," a formal talk given by a group leader in which the individual shares God-given insights and recounts experiences showing God's power and revelation. Both forms of "sharing" (the preferred term) are bound by careful norms and are permitted only for recognized members of the prayer group. Catholic pentecostal use of the term "witnessing" does not usually refer to public evangelizing such as street-corner and door-to-door witnessing. Rather witnessing typically occurs only with an already sympathetic audience, that is, the prayer group itself or friends and relatives.

Observations of Life in the Spirit seminars make apparent the centrality of testimony as a commitment and resocialization mechanism. Testimony is a fundamental—if not *the* fundamental—aspect of the induction process. The following section develops the various social settings, beginning with the recruit's initial exposure and proceeding to recognized, personal public testimony.

Testimony and the New Member's "Career"

Most new members' first-remembered exposure to the Catholic pentecostal movement was the private or semi-private witnessing of a friend or relative. This informal witnessing, in the context of an already-existing friendly relationship, is part of the reason for the movement's relatively successful recruitment. Typically, new members then attended a prayer meeting with their friend or relative, there hearing public witnessing by members and leaders. Several new members interviewed indicated that this activity caught their attention and confirmed the witnessing of their friend. Asked what features of the first prayer meeting attended were more remembered, respondents indicated that glossolalic prayer and witnessing made the most impression on them. These respondents had attended prayer meetings for quite a while before baptism in the Spirit (an average of about fifteen weeks).[52]

Potential members typically attend an introductory talk early in their experience with the prayer meeting. These introductions consist of a highly simplified appeal for commitment (for example, one group leader concluded by framing the choice as between God and Satan). The leader-team's testimonies are especially prominent in the introductory talks (for example, one male leader in his late twenties gave a short, vigorous statement of how Jesus helped him off drugs, and his thirty-five-year-old female counterpart testified to how pentecostalism helped her to adjust to a troubled marriage). Introductory talks did not press for immediate acts of commitment from participants, but referred those interested to a forthcoming sign-up session for Life in the Spirit seminars. The sign-up sessions outlined the expectations of these seminars in such a way that anyone who subsequently signed up considered that act to signify some degree of commitment.

Recruits attend regular prayer meetings concurrent with the seminars, often sitting together at the larger meetings. New members hear testimony on many different themes. The group leader shares a testimony each week, relating these tales to themes prescribed for that session. For example, at a session on the theme of "repentance," one leader gave numerous personal examples of parts of her former life of which she had needed to repent. Themes of witnessing included: the leaders' own experiences of coming into the movement, highlighting the positive emotions experienced (peace, joy, sense of purpose, happiness, enthusiasm), the importance of the prayer community, what aspects of their lives had changed, and specific evidences of God's power (for example, getting jobs, material successes, healings, improved relationships).[53]

A major step in the induction process is when the new members begin to witness in the seminar group. Leaders describe this as discussion or sharing, but the content is essentially witnessing or testimony. This practice of having a discussion consisting of mutual witnessing was part of nearly every session of the seminars observed. New members are encouraged to contribute testimony about any aspect of their lives and are encouraged each week to share something special that the Lord had done for them since the previous meeting. Members are discouraged from discussing ideas or theological questions during these sessions. Although the concept of seminar implies intellectual development, Life in the Spirit seminars are specifically not idea-oriented. Questions seeking clarification of the leader's point are permitted, but the content of the answer is not discussable. In one group, for example, a man had basic theological questions about pentecostalism that were regularly cut off. Eventually the discussion leader referred him to the priest-leader of the prayer group, stating that the seminar was not the right place for such questions. The discussion group was for shared experiences, not shared ideas.

The pattern of verbal interaction between the witnessing new member and the discussion leader was especially significant. In the two seminars in which this interaction was systematically observed, the discussion leader carefully reframed each member's contribution. If the testimony mentioned a relatively trivial event, the leader commented how even small aspects of everyday life reveal God's power. If the testimony did not use appropriate words, the leader translated the testimony into acceptable terms.[54] For example, one seminar member referred to those who had received baptism in the Spirit as "saved," but this usage was regularly corrected by the seminar leader who substituted the phrase "growing in the Spirit." In other instances, the leader changed the significance of testimony altogether, making it mean something different from what the member appeared to intend. One woman recited at length all her physical ailments as examples of "crosses" she was bearing, concluding that God rewards suffering. Without appearing to contradict the witness, the leader gave an altogether different interpretation of the ailments, concluding that it was the Lord's design to overcome suffering. Sometimes the leader would acknowledge witnessing that was completely off the point, but treat it as though it demonstrated the point.

Each testimony was acknowledged and framed by the discussion leader in a restatement. As members gradually began to use the appropriate concepts, the leader often reinforced this usage with a knowing look or smile, sometimes confirming a testimony by sharing a similar insight from personal experience.

New members became increasingly relaxed about sharing in the informal setting of the seminar discussions, such that when the baptism session occurred, everyone was expected to share with other seminar members some testimony about the personal significance of that experience. These testimonies were not, however, different from those that preceded. After baptism in the Holy Spirit, the expectation of witnessing by neophytes increased, and the last two sessions of the seminar were devoted to this activity. In one group, a relatively spectacular baptism took place—a Jewish girl converted to Catholic pentecostalism. She was introduced to the entire prayer group and gave public witness immediately after her baptism in the Spirit. For most members, however, witnessing at the public prayer meeting did not begin so soon. They were encouraged to witness privately and were given much coaching about not "coming on too strong" to their families and friends. After some weeks, they began to witness at prayer meetings, and by three months after the baptism in the Holy Spirit, nearly half had given recognized public testimony. Witnessing in some groups (characterized as "closed" in Chapter 4) is a rather controlled speech act, so the giving of *public* witness at prayer meeting marks group acceptance of the neophyte as a full and trustworthy member.[55] This aspect of approval is important in religious conversion, because conversion is not only an internal process but also social. It is necessary, especially in a small group setting, for new members to be accepted as validly "in." Their witnessing at public prayer meetings serves this purpose.

The induction of new members in smaller, more open prayer groups differs somewhat from that in groups with formal Life in the Spirit seminars. There is more emphasis on private witnessing *to* the newcomer, and the expectation that the new member will not only receive the baptism after relatively few weeks, but will also begin public witnessing earlier. New members in these groups usually began witnessing immediately after baptism in the Spirit and gave testimony regularly thereafter. It should be emphasized, however, that in more open prayer groups, witnessing is more informal, less spectacular, and expected of all committed members. By contrast, in more controlled groups (large and small), only those with approval of the core leadership give public testimony. Even in the more open, less formal groups, however, more advanced, experienced members were distinguished from neophytes in the quality of their testimonies. "Successful" witnessing in both types of prayer group was characterized by its appropriate brevity and timing, its phrasing (choice of both correct and inspiring expressions), its connection with themes of concern to the larger group (healing, attracting new members, resolving recent group crises), its spectacularness (healing cancer versus sore throat), and its modulation and pace (a peppy, upbeat, often jocular mode, a fervent crescendo, and a soft, ethereal mode were the three most successful, depending on the mood of the group).[56]

Witnessing as a Commitment Mechanism

Most sociological attention has focused on glossolalia as a commitment mechanism. Such attention is overdrawn—at least in the case of Catholic pentecostals. This overemphasis may be due to social scientists' fascination with anomalous speech, but observations of actual uses of glossolalia both in and outside the context of the prayer meeting show it to be a relatively minor aspect of the commitment process. As the above career of the newcomer suggests, testimony has greater significance for commitment and conversion. A bridge-burning act requires a certain degree of public exposure to other group members and to outsiders (for example, Caribbean converts from Espiritismo to Protestant pentecostalism are often expected to publically destroy their saint/spirit figurines). Among Catholic pentecostals, glossolalia simply does not have this public function, whereas, testimony to a greater extent, does.[57] Glossolalia is fascinating to the new pentecostal and it has importance as a symbol of "new life." New members usually desire tongue-speaking as a sign of the efficacy of their baptism in the Spirit; members who do not "receive tongues" are often anxious and eagerly pray for that or some other gift, such as prophecy. Nevertheless, unlike most traditional Protestant pentecostals, Catholic pentecostals do not consider glossolalia to be a necessary sign of authentic baptism in the Spirit. Glossolalia is also symbolic of the submission to God required in the baptism, and it functions effectively this way because, as one new member witnessed, it means "allowing God to control my life, even if it makes me look foolish." So tongue-speaking is a symbol of commitment, both to the new member and the group, but it does not really serve the bridge-burning function.

In none of the groups observed did new members speak in tongues publicly. In Life in the Spirit seminars observed, three new members made one or two sounds that were considered the beginning of tongues after their baptism (which took place in private). Two more members witnessed to seminar members in the final session that they, too, had received the gift of tongues. In weeks following the seminar, three more new members privately witnessed that they had received the gift but none of these eight new tongue-speakers were ever heard publicly by the larger prayer group.

In all of the prayer groups studied, most tongue-speaking was reserved for personal prayer. Speaking forth in tongues (public glossolalia) was believed to be a separate gift—a form of prophecy—and was practiced only by a very small number of the core group (see Chapter 4). In other words, glossolalia, while highly desired, is considered to be a prayer gift, for personal devotion. For this reason, members of a prayer group (especially in larger groups) seldom know exactly which members have received the gift of tongues. Roughly six weeks after the Life in the Spirit seminar, new members in one large group were asked which participants of their seminar had "received tongues." Most members named only the five who claimed the gift during the seminars. Not only is glossolalia not public within the prayer meeting, but also it is seldom practiced by Catholic pentecostals before others in their everyday lives. Thus although it might symbolically cut off the new pentecostal Catholic from the rest of society, it need not ever show publicly.

These observations would suggest, therefore, that while glossolalia may serve as a symbol of commitment, it does not involve the new members sufficiently to be considered as a major commitment mechanism. By contrast, witnessing requires more public exposure since by definition it involves talking to others. Testimony calls attention to the new member and is therefore more dramatically perceived as requiring commitment. Furthermore, witnessing includes both involvement (drawing the member into the prayer group) and abandonment (a risk of "turning off" family and friends).

Witnessing as a Resocialization Mechanism

There are several functions of testimony (or witnessing) that promote the resocialization of the new Catholic pentecostal. One seemingly simple function is learning to perceive one's experiences in an appropriate framework. In Life in the Spirit discussion groups and in private witnessing, new members learn to use the appropriate terms for describing their experiences. This translation process is very similar to that reported by Zaretsky in his analysis of Spiritualist churches, except that a specific jargon is not so important to Catholic pentecostals.[58] Nevertheless, the translation process does teach new members how to interpret the everyday experiences which they relate in their witnessing. This process continues less formally, even after the seminars, as group leaders and confirmers of witnesses continually frame public testimonies according to the group's desired interpretation.

A second resocializing function of witnessing involves the learning of group norms and rules governing public pronouncements in prayer meetings (see Chapter 4), carefully controlled in most groups, and subject to important norms in all prayer groups. The new member learns these tacit conventions and an appropriate style by watching and imitating models in prayer meetings and seminars. This use of exemplars is specifically advocated in the seminar manual, in which discussion leaders are advised to always give sample testimony before asking new members to "share."

This way of learning shared rules is similar to how the new member learns to share meanings. Hearing committed witnesses provides models for the newcomer's new identity and commitment. This is especially true of new members' relationships with their particular discussion leader (or in smaller groups, the individual who assumes care for that new member). These individuals personalize their witnessing for newcomers and offer themselves and their own experiences as models. Following their example new members learn through witnessing to articulate the distinctive perspective of Catholic pentecostalism. By talking about the perspective, the neophyte comes to share it. When the new member begins to witness outside the immediate prayer group (for example, to relatives and neighbors), this identification with the group's shared meanings is further strengthened. Trying to express to a skeptical friend how one's newfound faith differs from the friend's ordinary religion further reinforces the testifier's identity as a Catholic pentecostal.[59]

Although this discussion of resocialization has focused on the new member's induction, it is a continuing process. Thus, even when a committed member is witnessing, the act serves the resocialization function. Therefore, for both neophyte and veteran members, testimony confirms the reality of the pentecostal definition of the situation. It serves as conversation in which the new reality is talked through and allotted a recognized place in the "real world."[60]

Testimony converts all events, cognitions and history into significant events, meaningful cognitions, and a history which converges on pentecostals' special religious experience. One way pentecostal witnessing accomplishes this transformation is by devaluing everyday interpretations of events and replacing them with specifically religious interpretations. The following example illustrates this process:

> Man (about fifty): I just want to tell you all about "something that happened to me this week." It seems "kind of little, but it shows how much Jesus wants to do for us." You see, where I work—at the school kitchen—all these kids come in and they're always losing something. Like, I left my lunch money on that tray, or, I can't find my hall pass. [group laughs] So, this past week, one girl comes back and she had left her mouthplate on her tray and it must have gone in the garbage, and she wanted me to look for it, because it cost a lot of money and her folks would be very upset. So, at the thought of going through all that garbage, I wasn't very

happy [laughter], but "I prayed to Jesus that he'd help me and sure enough, it was right on top of the first pail I looked into" [group claps and some respond, "Praise the Lord"].[61]

Most testimonies in all but the most controlled groups are similar to this example; they retell various little events which illustrate God's power in members' lives. In more controlled (closed) groups, in which witnessing is limited to one or two pre-chosen members, testimonies tend to be longer, whole-life experiences, but similarly serve to integrate everyday life with the group's belief system.

This reality-confirming function of testimony is particularly obvious when challenges to the group's belief system are perceived. Real or perceived opposition aids the development of a religious movement.[62] Opposition implies a threat, but in facing that threat, even symbolically, the group can actually come out stronger. For this reason, a large number of witnessing tales include the role of the skeptic, who embodies the opposition's claims and may even embody the members' own doubts. This skeptic role can be clearly seen in the following testimony:

> Woman (about forty-five): Remember my sister that you all prayed for last week on account of her operation? Well, she still hasn't had the operation yet, but I do want to tell you all something that happened since then that just shows you the power of the Lord and how he cares for us. My sister went into the hospital last Monday and they did some tests and said they would have to postpone the operation because her blood pressure was way too high. So she just stayed there, getting more and more anxious, waiting for her blood pressure to go down. So, I was in visiting with her and I witnessed to her about Jesus and his power to heal, and I asked her if she wanted me to pray for her. My husband was real embarrassed by my witnessing, and my sister was none too sure, but said "go ahead." So I prayed over her, and sure enough the next day when they tested her blood pressure, it was down nearly to normal. The nurses were all amazed, but my husband was the most amazed of all.

Friends and relatives are cast in the role of skeptic most frequently in witnessing reports, and this is understandable since their opposition is the most threatening. Also frequent are references to doctors, scientists, and other authorities, whose official definitions of the situation differ threateningly from that of pentecostals.

The most dramatic integrating function of witnessing can be seen when threatening or disconfirming events occur. Catholic pentecostals increase witnessing to their faith when that faith is shaken by certain events as did members of the group Festinger studied.[63] For example, one group had been praying for many weeks for the healing of a member's brother, yet the man had died. At the next prayer meeting his sister testified:

> "We're talking about faith here. And it's strange, because I've gone to all kinds of healing services; I've been to Kathryn Kuhlman six times, and read hundreds of books on healing. And I believe that the Lord heals; I believe that it's his perfect will to heal, and I believe that it is on *our part* that we block it—I mean, if Jesus Christ healed everyone who needed it when he walked the face of the earth, and he's the same today as he was then. It's his command that we go and preach the Gospel (which we do) and we'll be saved. But we think we've got a lot of faith, but we don't. But, even as we are praying in tongues—I mean, many of us have the tongue the Lord has given us (and he wants to bless everyone else with it if they are open to it, I'm sure)—and in the different prayer groups (I don't know which gift each of you has, so I'm not comparing)—some still aren't open to his gifts.
>
> But it's a hesitancy of faith . . . the Lord can't do his work, if *two* are praying *for*, and *two* are are literally praying *against*. I know it's so in the case of my family. There you are with all the doctors and nurses and my brother-in-law and sister-in-law, all having absolutely given my brother up. There you are with all those negative feelings. Some are lifting up and others are pulling down. I'm not judging; I'm just saying that it [his death] did *not* dampen my faith that Jesus Christ is the healer, and I want you all to know it.

This witnessing and the enthusiastic responses which followed served to reintegrate this disappointing experience into the group's belief system and to legitimate the apparent failure of the group's prayers.

Witnessing is telling a special kind of tale. It represents "talking through" an experience. The event described in witnessing was experienced as significant (even if after the fact), but often the actual meanings come out in the very formulation of the story. In other words, many times the act of witnessing involves the formulation of meaning.[64]

What is the relationship between the witnessing tale and the event to which it refers? First, the tale is a recounting and, by its very nature, can never be the event. Something is, therefore, inevitably lost in the telling. Secondly, as a recounting, witnessing refers to a personal experience, not merely an event. This means, for example, that the testimony described earlier was not about school cafeterias, garbage, and lost mouthplates; rather, it was about the believer's experience of what it meant to ask God for help and (apparently) receive it. Goffman asserts that tales "demonstrate a full interdependence of human action and fate—a meaningfulness . . . not necessarily characteristic of life."[65] Testimony, even more than tales in everyday life, are assertions of meaning and order—meaning and order which are not necessarily part of the event to which they refer. As such, they are statements of faith, but they in turn produce faith in the speaker as well as the audience.

Thus witnessing transforms the experience.[66] The telling acts back on the experience and assigns it a place as part of "real reality." Telling the tale confirms the event's reality for the believer. Witnessing is thus an assertion of order, the interpretation of experiences as orderly and meaningful rather than coincidental or chaotic. Group acceptance of the testimony reassures believers that their subjective experience fits the model understood by other group members. This confirming function is part of the reason that witnessing is validated, rather than challenged (see Chapter 5). Thus witnessing has an especially important function for the group in establishing the foundation of an assumed shared social world.

Conclusion

Viewing the conversion and commitment career of Catholic pentecostals as more of a drift than a dramatic shift, it is possible to trace the process by which recruits typically become committed members. The initial encounter is usually the personal witnessing of a friend or relative. This interaction, and later induction procedures, often involve the "mediation of anomie" in which the recruit's sense of need for the movement's solutions is heightened. The neophyte learns to view God, self, and the world from the group's distinctive perspective. Fellow members of the prayer group support the believer's new world view. While the conversion event may be managed by the group, it is usually part of a steady progression toward increasing commitment begun much earlier in the process. In fact, it is difficult to distinguish between the legitimating rhetorics which frame these events and the subjective meanings of the experiences themselves. Commitment processes, akin to the social processes surrounding the initial conversion, continue for all members—new and old alike.

Testimony (witnessing) is especially important in new members' inductions, serving both as a commitment and a resocialization mechanism. Although glossolalia may also serve as a symbol of commitment, testimony is greater because it includes both involvement (in the prayer group) and abandonment (the risk of cutting off family and friends). Witnessing serves several functions for resocialization of new members, and continuing confirmation of the belief system for all members. New members learn to perceive their experiences in the appropriate pentecostal conceptual framework, learn group norms and rules, and imitate their exemplars' models of witnessing and faith. For both neophytes and veteran members, witnessing confirms the reality of the pentecostal world view. This function is especially strong when those beliefs are perceived to be threatened. Thus numerous testimonies embody the role of the skeptic who is effectively disproven by the witness. Also, disconfirming events or experiences are "talked through" in witnessing and integrated into the group's belief system. Finally, the witnessing tale transforms the experience—assigning meaning and order to events of everyday life. Thus testimony is a statement of faith which produces faith.

Four—
The
Prayer
Meeting:
Controlled
Spontaneity

The prayer meeting is the characteristic focus for groups of Catholic pentecostals. The format for this worship service has evolved into a clearly recognizable and relatively uniform feature of every prayer group. One movement spokesman said, "From the very beginning of the charismatic movement, the prayer meeting has been spontaneously adopted as the natural expression of the movement."[1] This "natural expression," more than any other corporate activity, includes a broad range of special pentecostal practices such as prophecy, speaking in tongues, and witnessing. A variety of other social situations also express pentecostal piety; many prayer groups have separate Bible studies, pentecostal Masses, seminars, share groups, prayer rooms, and the like. Some of these other activities are discussed elsewhere in this volume.

In order to understand what happens in a prayer meeting, it is necessary to appreciate the special kinds of interaction and use of language that are appropriate to the gathering. These ways of acting and speaking have particular meaning for participants. While the sociological observer never fully shares the believer's frame of reference, it is possible to perceive more accurately what is going on if one knows what the actions mean to the believers themselves.

Group Structures

Before analyzing the events of a prayer meeting, it is necessary to consider the group structures within which these events take place. Interaction in the prayer meeting is correlated with the pattern of organization of the prayer group. These groups may be visualized as on a continum between open and closed structures. The terms "open" and "closed" refer to the degree to which the general membership and other participants are permitted to influence or speak up in prayer meetings. Highly open groups have relatively fluid prayer meetings. The closed groups, by contrast, have meetings with completely structural content. The more open the group, the more likely it is to encourage and exercise *all* "gifts of the Spirit" during meetings. Highly closed groups, on the other hand, place strict limits on which "gifts" are encouraged and exercised. Open groups tend to have more inclusive membership and participation in prayer meetings; closed groups are more exclusive. Meetings of relatively open groups tend to be more emotional; closed groups are comparatively subdued, and their leaders ensure greater orthodoxy to movement ideology. Open groups are less orthodox or ideologically controlled. Groups with relatively high proportions of priests or nuns in control tend to be toward the closed end of the continuum, whereas lay-controlled groups can be found all along the continuum. Relatively open groups exhibit only simple stratification and an unspecialized participation of members. Closed groups (small as well as large) are highly stratified, and roles performed by members and leaders are highly specialized. Figure 1 shows how the nine groups studied were distributed along this continuum.

Even physical arrangements of seating during prayer meetings serve to reinforce these structural elements. The following is a common pattern. When the group becomes too large for a single circle, chairs are arranged in concentric circles. Leaders, generally men, (with some women, usually in the "music ministry") sit in the central circle. Other core members (frequently including the central leader of the group) sit around the second or third circle or semi-circle, among other regulars (typically active women members). Men who are not in the core group tend to sit on the periphery of the seating arrangement, as do most visitors. Neophytes generally sit on the periphery when they sit with other new recruits, or in the middle seating if they come with active regulars.

The Organization of the Prayer Meeting

General formats for prayer meetings are different for open, as compared with closed groups. These formats reflect the degree of control of "gifts" practiced in prayer meetings. A relatively open prayer meeting usually begins with an opening talk, consisting of a statement of welcome, an invocation of the Holy Spirit, and exorcism of evil spirits. Then follows a period of praise, which includes hymns, scripture readings, praise in English or in "tongues," confirmation of

Medium-sized, non-student groups	Large, non-student groups	Large, student groups	Small student groups	Medium-sized non-student groups	Small, non-student groups	Large, non-student groups

Figure 1
Structure of Prayer Groups Studied

prophecies, and spontaneous prayer. Last comes a "teaching," a longer period of witnessing, and a period for petitions. After the meeting there is usually an opportunity for informal witnessing among participants, a separate prayer room for special petitions and the "laying on of hands" for baptism in the Holy Spirit.

By contrast, prayer meetings of highly closed groups consist only of opening remarks, a period of praise, and the teaching. The contents of the meeting are carefully controlled, and only members of the recognized core group may speak up. Other elements are typically practiced outside the public prayer meeting under carefully controlled circumstances. What follows, below, is an analysis of each major period of the prayer meeting.[2]

The Period of "Praise"

Cues to begin are invariably given by the official leader of the service. His words are chatty and informal, shifting to a matter-of-fact tone as he sets the mood. These initial statements serve the important function of telling the participants what to expect to experience. For example:

> God will speak through the body gathered here. We would ask you to just relax, enjoy being able to sit back and just let the Lord speak in any way He wishes to you . . . You should hear the voice of the Lord in prophecy. If someone speaks in prophecy (which is first-person) it's a time to be very attentive and listen—it's a special message. Sometimes it will happen with tongues, sometimes without. In either case, be very sensitive, very alert and listen hard. The Lord may speak to us in silence, too, and we should be comfortable with silence as well as with Scripture. Or with spontaneous prayer (which is somewhat new)—a particular prayer welling up in your own words. If you do hear speaking in tongues, we ask you to wait and listen. It is the Lord's way of getting our attention. We should be silent until we know what it is he has to say to us.

Opening statements also specify the limitations of speech in closed groups. A typical reminder is,

> "Let our core community, that has been here for months, do
> the hard part of the work, doing the praying and praising
> aloud. This would be true particularly of the music. We'd
> ask you to let the music ministry select the songs so that the
> fabric of our prayer will be a real unity. Also, let the core
> community choose the Scripture selections. . . .

A prayer of invocation and exorcism opens the prayer meeting. This
is marked by a shift to a very serious and sometimes dramatic tone.
The invocation calls the Holy Spirit's presence upon the meeting, and
the phrase often used at this juncture is "a fresh anointing." The exorcism, consisting of a "binding" of all evil spirits, is somewhat low-
key, unobtrusive, and buried in a longer prayer. Exorcism, however, is
clearly part of almost every prayer meeting in both open and closed
groups and is linked with the movement's dualistic sense of Satan's
powers. Examples of exorcisms include, "Lord, we ask that just your
Holy Spirit tonight be upon this meeting, and any other spirit, we
bind in the name of Jesus, and let the Lord take care of it," and,
"Lord Jesus, through your most precious blood, we bind all evil spirits,
all dissensions, all disunity, all evil thoughts." The period of praise
is the main focus of most prayer groups, all parts of which are considered by members to be "prayer" (even hymns and Scripture readings
are "prayed"). Participants immediately assume their prayer postures.
The most common posture is sitting, eyes closed, face relaxed, head
bent slightly upward, hands or arms outstretched slightly, palms up.
In fervent prayer, especially during certain hymns, the arms go high
over the head, palms still up. Another posture of fervent prayer is
standing, arms outstretched, body swaying (usually during hymns or
immediately thereafter). This posture is borrowed directly from traditional pentecostalism, as are some other practices, but Catholic pentecostalism generally discourages highly emotional displays.

Hymns and Scripture readings are used frequently in the period of
praise. In closed groups, the choice and timing of these elements of
the service are carefully controlled by leaders. In more open groups,
members simply read a Scripture selection or start a hymn when they
feel moved to do so. For example, one woman began a hymn, saying,
"I would like to sing 'Amazing Grace.' The Lord is telling me let's
sing it." One special type of singing is called "singing in the Spirit"
or the "Lord's harmony." This singing, which lasts from a few seconds
to four or five minutes, consists of each person singing a "word of
praise" in English or in a "tongue," in a combination of several notes
or on a single note. Members believe that the Lord gives them the
harmony which results. Only four of the groups studied sang this
"harmony"; two others tried occasionally but were unsuccessful. This

singing resembles something of a combination of chanting and a sixty-four–fold choral "Amen." The group leaders are typically quite prominent in the singing in tongues; they stop song as soon as the harmony is well established.

Throughout the period of praise, individuals murmur "words of praise." These are short ejaculations of praise, usually repeated many times in a sing-song pattern. Some of the most frequent are: "Praise you, Lord," "Thank you, Jesus," "Glory, Halleluiah," "Praise thee, Lord Jesus," "Glory and honor to thee," "Bless you, Jesus." Simultaneous with these praises, other individuals in the group use their "gift of tongues" to praise. This prayer in tongues is done in the same tone of voice and volume as the praise in the vernacular. One woman explained the value of praising in tongues:

> Tongues is a prayer-gift given by the Holy Spirit—you know, praying in a language other than our own. And, in doing this, I experienced a new *feeling of prayer*—a new freedom—which I couldn't have sticking to English. When God gave me the gift of tongues, I could express what was in my heart, because I wasn't restricted by the English words. We don't understand the languages we are given, although I do have a sense that I am praising God. All I know is that I am given this gift and I experience a new freedom.

Some Catholic pentecostal literature plays down the importance of speaking in tongues.[3] This idealization of group practice, however, does not reflect the actual meaning of tongues to individual members. Tongue-speaking is very important as a recognizable sign of baptism of the Holy Spirit. Thus while praying in tongues is a minor aspect of the public meeting, it is very important to individual members who treat glossolalic prayer as "really real"—far more significant and holy than prayer in English. The potency of tongue-speaking as a sign of acceptance was exemplified several times during witnessing and petitions. For example, two couples prayed that if one member of the couple received the gift, the other would too, so as not to divide them and cause jealousy. Unlike many Protestant pentecostals, Catholic pentecostals do not, in theory, consider tongue-speaking to be a necessary sign of baptism in the Spirit. But, in practice, those who do not have the gift suffer considerable anxiety, unless they have some other dramatic gift, such as prophecy.

Also, during this period of praise, several of the more open groups frequently have spontaneous prayers of praise and something rather like litanies of praise. Litanies of praise frequently arise out of a spontaneous prayer, and are not necessarily led by a formal leader of the prayer meeting. They are characteristic only of the more open type prayer groups, because they engender precisely that heightening of

(P-prayer; R-typical response)

P	Lord	Jesus,/	we ask	you to	come	upon us/	and be	with us/	tonight.
R						Yes,	Lord/	come	upon us.
P	Send	down	your	Holy	Spirit/	in a	fresh	anointing/.	
R	Be with	us, Lord					and your	Holy	Spirit,/
P	Take	our	hearts/	as we	lift	them up/	to you/.		They are
R	Lord.						Yes,	Lord.	
P	yours/	Lord.	And	show us/	how to	love	you	better.	
R	They	are	yours/	Lord.					
P	Cleanse	us/ of	all that	would	keep us	/from	knowing	you/ and	serving
R				Yes/	Lord/	make us	clean,	Lord.	
P	you.	Free us	from all	sin and	sadness/	Jesus.	Take all	anxiety	away/
R					Free us	Lord.	Yes/	Jesus/	all
P	and show	us your	peace.						
R	that	black	sin.				Yes/	Lord/	yes.

Figure 2
Praise-response pattern

emotion which more controlled groups try to limit. These litanies are very dramatic, resulting in a crescendo of emotion. It is difficult to describe, in print, the characteristic praise-response pattern because the words of the responses overlap the words of the next part of the prayer (Figure 2). This praise-response pattern appears to be borrowed from classical Protestant pentecostalism, although it is unclear how the practice has been introduced into the groups observed.

The two spoken gifts that attract the greatest attention during the prayer meeting are "prophecy" and "speaking (forth) in tongues." Both gifts are spoken publicly, louder than other elements of praise. The rest of the prayer group falls silent as soon as prophecy begins. Prophetic utterances are believed to be directly from God; that is, God Himself is believed to be speaking through the person. These pronouncements are always in the form of a first-person statement. To Catholic pentecostals, prophecy means "forth-telling" rather than "fore-telling." One member described this gift, "Prophecy is the forth-telling of the mind of God to His people. God had things He wanted to say to us as a community, like tonight when He used me to speak His message. There was a certain phrase that kept coming through my mind, and I knew I needed to start speaking that."

The content of prophecies observed was never strongly negative and almost never recommended or predicted specific action. Rather, prophecies were usually vague, soothing or merely mildly urging, and spoken in relatively loud voices, with men typically speaking them very strongly and firmly, and women usually speaking only the first few words strongly with the remainder in a sighing or crying tone of voice.[5] Most prophecies are brief—only a few relatively short sentences. The general form of the prophetic statement consists of a greeting (for example, "My children"), several somewhat repetitive statements on one or two themes, closed by a single final statement. The following example is typical of most prophecies observed:

> My children,
> I want to be part of your world.
> Surrender your home to me.
> Surrender your heart to me.
> Surrender yourselves to me.
> Let me work in you.
> Let me pray through you.
> I will need to take over your lives.

Glossolalic pronouncements are also considered prophecies, except that they are spoken in tongues. They may be called "speaking (forth) in tongues" to distinguish from "praying in tongues," in which the gift of tongues is used in individual prayer. Like prophecy in the vernacular, glossolalic prophecy is spoken loudly (whereas glossolalia in personal prayer is quiet). Typically, however, speakers use less inflection, although this difference may be due to variations in skill of tongue-speakers. Prophecies can also be sung in tongues and in English, although this is rare.

Glossolalic prophecy requires that someone else in the group receive the "gift of interpretation." In the Bible verse upon which pentecostals base this practice, St. Paul said, "If any speak in a tongue, let there be only two or at most three, and each in turn; and let one interpret. But *if there is no one to interpret, let each of them keep silence* in church and speak to himself and to God" (I Cor. 14:27, RSV, emphasis added). Therefore, immediately after a glossolalic prophecy, the group observes an intense silence, awaiting an interpretation. When the interpretation comes, it is usually in the same form, except that it is often briefer than vernacular prophecy. In both open and closed groups, prophecies and interpretations nearly always come from members of the recognized core group.[6] Indeed, non-recognized members are often openly forbidden from speaking prophecy or interpretation. Specific mechanisms for control of prophecy are analyzed in detail at the end of this chapter.

Frequently there are several different interpretations of the same glossolalic pronouncement; for example, (1) "I am here among you, my people. (pause) Rejoice in my presence." (2) "The Lord has given me similar words—Abide in me, for I am your Lord always." (3) "Even though I walk through the valley of evil, I shall not fear, for Thou art with me." The second interpretation above is stated in the form of a "confirmation," a common, but important, pentecostal affirmation consisting of a statement that the participant had received a message similar to one spoken by another member. Almost every kind of public statement was confirmed at one time or another during prayer meetings observed. In open groups, hymn and Scripture selections are frequently confirmed, for example: "I want to confirm that reading and the prayer. I opened to Jeremiah, at the end of Jeremiah." Confirmations of prophecies and interpretations of tongues are received with much enthusiasm, as an important sign that the prophecy given was truly from God.

The supportive role of confirmer is frequently assumed by regulars who seldom speak up in any other capacity, and is a relatively safe gift, requiring little initiative. Members see so many confirmations that words and acts outside prayer meetings frequently are seen as confirming a large variety of inspirations. As shown in Chapter 3, confirmation is a major factor in witnessing; it serves to affirm that a personal reality is a shared reality. Confirmations are rather rare in highly structured and controlled groups, and there they are made only by members of the core group. When leaders have a separate "meeting of discernment" to evaluate the input of the previous meeting, there are far fewer public confirmations given than usual. Absence of public confirmations makes it possible for the leaders to filter public pronouncements; whereas if speech were publicly confirmed, it would be harder to contain.

Another charism which occurs occasionally is the "word of knowledge" or the "gift of wisdom." This act is not related to the "message" or formal teaching and is usually spoken by recognized members other than the official leaders of that meeting. In open groups, a word of knowledge might come at any time. For example, at the very end of one meeting, a woman had the "gift of knowledge that the Lord wants us to pray for the healing of the eyes of all present," after which all who had bad eyesight gathered in the center circle and, for about ten minutes, blessed each others' eyesight. This "word of knowledge" has a different meaning to members of closed prayer groups. To them it means a "personal vision," a "personal conviction," or "being struck by" the presence of God. It has no specific message content, but refers only to this awareness. This individualized interpretation of the gift further exemplifies how closed groups preclude unpredictable disruptions.

Silence is very significant to Catholic pentecostal prayer groups, especially the more closed groups. Leaders use a variety of techniques to create silent periods. One leader stopped an interval of spoken praise, saying, "Let's close our eyes, lean back in the arms of the Lord. Be still to let the Spirit get a word in edgewise." In another group, a woman had requested a hymn, and the central leader of the group (who was not formally a leader of that service) said, "No, the Spirit wants us to be silent and listen to *His* word now!" An intense silence followed, and a prophecy occurred after about four minutes of silence.

In closed groups many glossolalic and vernacular prophecies follow periods of extended silence (three to ten minutes). In relatively open groups these pronouncements are much more likely to come after other activities. It is more common for glossolalic prophecy to emerge from quiet glossolalic prayer or during the babble of "words of praise" in open groups. Closed groups are far more comfortable with longer periods of silence and during the process of socialization into this type of pentecostal piety, new members are taught to expect and welcome the silence. Another reason why longer periods of silence do not cause so much restlessness as in more open groups is that members know that the whole order of worship is "under control," and that if the leadership permits or encourages silence, that must be a good thing. In the more open groups, silences of longer than about three minutes usually evoke a hymn request, Bible reading, or some other innocuous filler.

In both types of group, there are times when silence is especially tense or meaning-laden. For example, one relatively open group felt threatened by an outsider—a nun from that parish who attended the meeting and attacked their beliefs and activities. They felt helpless to argue openly with her, and they could not easily eject her, as they would a less important lay person who caused trouble. To end her tirade and avoid further conflict, the leaders called for silent prayer for guidance. The silent prayer which followed was very tense and fervent. Frequently silence creates or expresses a sense of expectancy.[7] In another group, a long term member asked to "be prayed over" since he had never received the gift of tongues. The silence that accompanied and followed this group prayer was extremely intense. The group was highly sympathetic with this man and genuinely expected the silence to end in his reception of the gift of tongues (which did not occur). Another occasion of expectancy which occurs frequently is the silence between a glossolalic prophecy and its interpretation. A similar intensity is felt when the leadership holds the group to silence to listen for a prophecy or an answer to a specific prayer.

Closure of silence is more difficult than opening it. In open groups any member can end the silence, often by some minor activity. On the other hand, in closed groups for whom silence is more meaning-laden, bringing it to a close is more complicated. If the silence is not ended by a prophecy or some other dramatic event, then usually a succession of eye-contact cues between the central leader and the service or music leader occurs. As long as the central leader's eyes remain closed, the silence continues. When he changes posture and opens his eyes, the service leaders (who are already watching him) proceed with the service.

Several observable norms govern language use in the period for praise. These norms differ according to the degree of control exercised by the group's central leadership. In both open and closed groups the length of segments of praise aloud is limited (two or three minutes maximum in closed, five or six minutes in open groups). Both types require that the "words of praise" and "praying in tongues" not be spoken too loudly, although the open groups tolerate greater loudness in moments of group fervor. Both types prefer that items for praise aloud should be general rather than specific, referring to group or abstract causes for praise (rather than purely personal reasons). Both types of group also discourage use of negatives or sad thoughts, or references to serious evil during the period for praise, although the tolerance for negatives varies greatly from one meeting to another.

In open groups, the leader of that meeting is the only one who may start and stop the period of praise, but other core members may initiate litanies, hymns, Scripture readings and other elements of praise. By contrast, in closed groups, only formal leaders of the meeting may do so. Often further control is exercised by a single central leader (not one of the official leaders of the service) who cues most important changes. In open groups, anyone is permitted to speak—even one not baptized in the Spirit. In closed groups only core members are allowed to speak out. In fact, in some cases visitors are not allowed to speak at all. Furthermore, in closed groups, regular members are permitted to praise in a louder voice than are visitors or neophytes. These groups have additional norms discouraging (or forbidding) emotionalism and encouraging (or imposing) many periods of silence. These operative norms illustrate the degree of ordering and control governing even a seemingly spontaneous prayer meeting.

These norms, together with their legitimations, have become sufficiently crystallized to be officially promulgated in the movement's publications. One manual on how to participate in prayer meetings states that order is essential. One order-promoting aspect is for the prayer group to agree to submit to a leader. Another is to follow a set pattern (with the first part of the meeting reserved for prayer and praise and the latter part set aside for testimony and teaching). The unity of the prayer meeting is thus enhanced, because everyone expects to pray in a certain way at a certain time. The manual also urges clear norms for the reception of prophecy and glossolalic prophecy, so they can have their proper impact.[8]

To speak of "norms" is to imply sanctions for failure to comply, but the full range is not observable since many of these take place in private. Two overt forms of sanction are noticeable, especially in the more open type of group. One is that the leader simply terminates the offender's speech. A more subtle method is to let the person talk but to ignore it and continue praying quietly.

In the more closed groups, sanctions tended to be much less subtle and more formal. In smaller closed groups, they are handled directly by the key leader (or leaders) outside the public meetings. Participants either comply with admonitions or are excluded from the group. Leaders of the small groups studied carefully screen visitors and prospective members before their first meeting and give them strict instructions about what is permitted.

In some larger controlled groups, the core leadership has separate meetings to discuss the previous prayer meeting. One function of these meetings is to discern which speech acts of the previous meeting would be accepted as validly "from the Lord." If a member's speech were considered problematic, he (or she) would be counselled and asked to refrain from speaking out. In one group studied, the central leader was believed to have the "gift of discernment" from the Holy Spirit. One core member described this discernment, "_____ has the gift. He is very sensitive about who is real or false and who is within the community. If he feels at the meeting there is a kook or someone speaking out in a way that is disruptive, he will take one of us [other leaders] aside and tell us to get to that person and tell him to be quiet. If that person will not conform, then he is asked to leave and not return."

The "Message"

The second major portion of the prayer meeting, markedly separate, is set aside for the "message" or a "teaching." Sometimes the period begins with the "laying on of hands" for the person who is about to speak, asking the Spirit to give a special anointing to the speaker, and there is often a major change in physical setting. For example, one group changed the lighting from dim to normal during the message. Another group turned their seats away from the center of the concentric circles to face the back of the room where a separate podium was used for the message. The "teaching" is also given in a different tone of voice—matter-of-fact and authoritative. The message is one of the least important parts of prayer meetings observed.

If dull or badly done, the negative effects on the group were not nearly so great as when the praise or witnessing periods were disappointing.

The "message" is a further manifestation of control. Even though it is called a "teaching," its main purpose is not to discuss ideas or to present theological points, even in popular style. Rather, it is more of a meditation or a sharing on a single theme, often amplified by many Scriptural references. In both types of group, the leadership decides in advance who is to give the message. In closed groups, however, further control is exercised by the central leadership over the exact content of the teaching. In some groups the speaker must submit the talk (or outline) in advance for the leader's approval; in others, the leader (or leaders) simply inform the speaker what the content of the message will be. Such control is consistent with the closed groups' emphasis on ideological orthodoxy. This orthodoxy is strongly related to the movement's beliefs about the sources of legitimate authority. While maintaining loyalty to the Catholic church, they see the immediate authority of the Holy Spirit manifest in their own leadership, and more concretely in the authority of their own prayer group.

The Period for "Witnessing"

Catholic pentecostals' use of "witnessing" or "testimony" is an adaptation of the traditional pentecostal idea of testimony and consists in the public recounting of an event or idea that the believer considers a manifestation of God's power. As Chapter Three shows, it has broad significance beyond the confines of the prayer meeting itself. The place of witnessing in the prayer meeting varies considerably between open and closed groups. In highly controlled groups, there is relatively little public witnessing, and when testimony is given, the segment tends to be short—seldom more than one or two minutes. By contrast, most open groups devote an entire major portion of the prayer meeting to public witnessing, ranging from twenty to seventy minutes altogether.

In relatively closed prayer meetings, the leader occasionally asks one or two members to tell something specific that has recently happened to them, and in introducing them, carefully frames what they are to include. A summary or commentary on their testimony follows, with an explanation of the context in which the audience should find it meaningful. Witnessing members almost always belong to the core group or are recognized regulars. Operative norms for these testimonies include that they should be very brief, enthusiastic (humor and humorous exaggeration are acceptable), that they describe simple events, and that they be spoken only by those permitted and introduced by the leadership. Four themes are prevalent in closed groups. In order of frequency, they are: (1) the Lord's solution to some emotional problem or personal difficulty, (2) improvement of interpersonal relations either as the answer to a prayer or merely due to receiving baptism in the Spirit, (3) physical healing, and (4) a report of the Lord's work in some other prayer group or in some special event (like a prayer weekend).

In the more open groups, witnessing assumes a greater significance and a greater portion of prayer meeting time. Witnessing usually evokes exclamatory responses, such as "Praise the Lord!" from the rest of the prayer group. There appears to be a measure of judging the witnessing. Testimonies that are very dramatic, such as cures, or persons for whom the group has much sympathy (for example, a woman whose son was on drugs) evoke especially enthusiastic responses. Themes considered by these groups to be relevant topics for witnessing are much broader than in closed groups. About forty percent of the testimonies are brief descriptions of specific favors done by the Lord (finding lost objects, getting car started, help on first day of a new job). Descriptions of a recent healing account for about twenty to twenty-five percent of the testimonies. Like more closed prayer groups, these also delight in witnessing about other pentecostal events and how well the movement is doing (15 to 20 percent of the testimonies). These include a number of instances, however, that closed groups would not discuss (for example, a nearby Protestant faith-healer's successes, a favorite fundamentalist radio program, a mission to convert the Jews).

Another major category (accounting for about 20 percent of the witnessing in open groups) is especially interesting. These themes include a variety of interpretations of personal or public crises. Public issues which received particular attention during observations included, for example, the energy crisis, war in the Mideast, and problems in the government. Witnesses interpreted these events variously as signs of God's will, evidence of the truth of certain Biblical prophecies, and omens of the coming of the Millennium. Other issues receiving attention were the appearance of the Kohoutek comet, UFOs, and various interpretations of the End of the World. Witnesses' interpretations of personal crises included an explanation of a dear one's death, a woman's beliefs about her husband's indifference to the pentecostal movement, and another woman's interpretation of her sister's unpleasantness. Such testimonies tend to be much lengthier and more complicated than witnessing about simple events.

It would be a mistake to view these testimonies primarily as descriptions of fact. Although they are supposed to represent factual occurrences, their primary function is expressive. Members, therefore, accept even seemingly weird testimonies without questioning their factual content, because they accept the expressive intent of the witness. Nevertheless, there are some norms for witnessing, even in the most open prayer groups. One norm is the rather nebulous distinction between a "witness" and a "teaching." For example, one night an older man witnessing was interrupted by a group leader who said, "What we should be doing is telling each other these things before the meeting. Our witnesses should be about what Jesus Christ has done in our lives, and when a witness is given that way, it uplifts us. A *teaching* is given at a certain time; a *witness* is given at another time." The implication is that witnessing should be about a specific event, but in practice the main difference between a teaching and a testimony is primarily one of length. The offender's mistake had been not only talking too long but also in usurping the giving of a teaching, the leader's prerogative. In practice, norms regarding the length of witnessing are quite flexible. Most open groups prefer testimonies of no more than five minutes, but some last for fifteen minutes or longer. If the events described in these long testimonies are of considerable interest to members, they are tolerated.

As shown in Chapter 3, witnessing is a significant aspect of the conversion and commitment process. The prayer group also evaluates witnessing as to how uplifting, enthusiastic, or heartfelt it is. The giving of testimony is, like other pronouncements in the prayer meeting, a special kind of performance—affirming the group's belief system, attesting to the witnessing member's commitment and identification with the group, and giving ordinary members a chance to participate and shine.[9]

The Period for "Petitions"

In closed groups, petitions are not a significant part of the main prayer meeting. Rather, there is usually a separate period for petitions after the meeting (often starting as late as 11:00 P.M.), in a different room and presided over by several core members. One group asked members to write their petitions on cards beforehand. Although the petitions were not presented aloud, the group prayed over the basket full of petition cards during the prayer meeting, and members took home the petition cards of others to include them in prayer during the subsequent week. This partition of prayer activities serves several functions. It serves to maintain the positive atmosphere of the prayer meeting in which little evil or suffering is mentioned. It filters out frivolous petitions and discourages anyone who does not have a specific request. It enhances the counselling function of the core members who supervise the prayer room, and it removes the possible spectacle of a claimed healing to a safe environment.

In the open type of prayer meeting, by contrast, the period for petitions is an integral part of most meetings. Often nearly everyone present requests one or more petitions. All persons (including visitors and non-members) are encouraged to participate. The atmosphere is less urgent than in the prayer room; the attitude is more one of "sit and think about what else you want the group to pray for."

Different degrees of fervor arise in responses from the rest of the group. After a petition is spoken, other members often echo it in their own words. These responses are quite intense in certain situations. One such situation is when the group thinks the problem is "really a shame" (for example, a grandmother praying for her grandson who was "into Transcendental Meditation"). Another occasion is when the group knows the person being prayed for or really sympathizes with the petitioner (for example, a prayer for one leader's wife who was dying of cancer). Also, the response becomes intense if a crescendo of prayer (similar to the overlapping pattern for praise on Figure 2) is developed. In these crescendo-prayers it is common to extol the virtues or recount the sufferings of the person, for example, "Blessed Jesus, we ask that you heal our sister ———, who is suffering from MS. You know how she has loved you and served you these many years. You know, Lord, how those three little children of hers depend on her, and how much her family needs her, Jesus. And how hard it is for them to manage without her, Lord. Heal her, Lord. Heal her." Usually the response to petitions is only verbal. Sometimes in an especially fervent petition, members lift their hands high, as during the praise, except that at this juncture the posture has the added connotation of supplication. If the individual being prayed for requests it, members use the laying on of hands, but this is relatively infrequent.

Themes of prayers of petition differ markedly between the open and closed type of prayer groups. In groups where petitions are presented in a separate setting, most petitions are for private intentions—usually for oneself or close friend or relative. The topics are mainly emotional (for example, anxiety, lack of self-confidence, or difficulty in a marriage). Also, there are frequent petitions for health problems. In open prayer groups, on the other hand, the very format of petitions encourages a much larger range of themes, about 25 percent dealing with broader problems. One main theme is matters that would divide or hurt the prayer community (dissension in the group itself, disapproval of spouses who are not members, or conflict with persons in positions of authority in the parish or diocese). A second important theme is the evils of the world (pornography, the occult, the energy crisis, the faithlessness of people in this nation). Unlike closed prayer groups, these groups do not hesitate to pray frequently and fervently against the "Devil in the world," "the powers of Satan," and "the Evil One's influence in our group and in our families."

The petition period, except for occasional outbursts of fervor and tension, is a denouement from the rest of the meeting. The prayer meeting ends rather quietly when the leader offers a very general prayer, gathers the petitions, and asks the Lord's blessing on the entire group, then closes with a final hymn. Members frequently linger afterwards, over coffee and cookies, talking in small clusters, often witnessing further or simply arranging practical details such as asking rides home or offering to visit a sick member. Some peruse the literature table, buying books, magazines, or tape-cassettes.

Analysis of Language Use in the Prayer Meeting

This analysis of Catholic pentecostal prayer groups shows the development of distinctive patterns of worship and interaction. These patterns borrow much from traditional pentecostalism, but maintain clear boundaries from many older practices which leaders of the Catholic pentecostal movement disparage as "cultural baggage." The patterns of speaking and norms described here are sufficiently crystallized to be idealized in detail in several manuals for group leaders, as well as in popular literature for members.

The most interesting feature of the prayer meetings is the element of control. There are strong conflicting strains running through the ideals of the movement: egalitarianism versus appeals to authority, spontaneity versus order, freedom versus control.[10] Only some of this conflict would be observable in the public prayer meeting, but the distinct stratification of roles and the strong control of language use in prayer meetings provide two such examples. The ranks of real authority, power, and prestige are clearly defined by the answers to such questions as: Who controls the volume and pace of the meeting? Who is permitted to speak publicly and who does in fact speak publicly? Who speaks the more powerful and prestigious kinds of speech? And who has the power to limit the speech of others?

The existence of such firm lines of stratification among members is problematic because of a strong egalitarian ideal in the movement, and is especially awkward in smaller groups where there is no structural need for specialization of tasks and group roles. On the other hand, the stratification system appeals to many members who desire strong and clear sources of authority. Its unpleasant impact is, however, modified by the group's belief about the source of differentiation in the group: It is believed to be from God. If the group pattern of dominance and control is God-given, then it is less oppressive. In one group, for example, the teaching was about how to know what is the will of God. Members were instructed to pray fervently to God for His guidance, and then to seek the advice of one of the superiors (or Shepherds) in the group, who would give authoritative guidance as to what God's will for that person really meant. This interpretation is similar to their belief in the authority of the persons given special charisms, especially the gift of "discernment." If the person's actions which control or direct the group are believed to be the result of a special gift of authority from God, then the dominance is more acceptable. Theoretically, in his role as believer, the leader is an equal; in his role as representative of God, he is a powerful superior.[11]

Another strong reason for Catholic pentecostal emphasis on control in prayer meetings is a felt need for less fallible sources of authority, the assertion of which is one of the basic appeals of the movement. This need for authority derives, in part, from the sense of void resulting from the undermining of traditional religious authority and norms after Vatican II. Another source is the challenge to societal norms and authority arising from rapid social change and unrest. For Catholic pentecostals, authoritative order is communicated by God to the individual or group in such a highly subjective way that it is not so vulnerable to disconfirmation or debunking. A new framework of order is sought to replace the old, undermined source; indeed, a desire for strong bases of order was a central theme in the responses of many members interviewed. For example, one respondent stated:

> The church is failing us all on this. People need to know exactly what's right and what's wrong, what's okay to do and not. They used to be clear on this. I mean, for example, it used to be clear that divorce and homosexuality, and all that, was completely wrong. But now, they're this way and that about things. Not that I want to go back to the fish on Friday bit, but the church can't keep changing their minds about what's right and wrong. They can't have it halfway either. It gets so you can't believe them when they do take a stand.

In addition to these external forces for order and authority, there are some elements inherent in pentecostalism (classical as well as neo-pentecostalism) which require responsible leaders to seek strong order and control. In classical pentecostalism, this control was accomplished by a different pattern of leadership—the preacher who regulated all charismatic behavior in the prayer meeting.[12] The Catholic charismatic movement has a pattern focusing on strong multiple leadership by the core group—usually with several leadership roles and a greater repertoire of control mechanisms. This spread of leadership roles creates a semblance of egalitarianism, but the subsequent control is often more effective than that of the single preacher. Thus the prayer meeting is, as Lane characterizes it, a set of highly routinized rituals with opportunities for individual virtuoso performances.[13] These routines prevent disruption and maintain control, but apparent spontaneity and creativity is allowed in individual performances of testimony, glossolalia, prophecy, and so on.

The very nature of the pentecostal belief system makes control both difficult and necessary. Beliefs that the Holy Spirit directs and is the source of much input into the prayer meeting mean that the entire group must be open to a wide variety of ideas, acts, and emotions as being possibly divinely inspired or even the direct action of God. "The Spirit blows where it wills" is a popular phrase among pentecostals. Thus the Spirit itself is a potential source of disruption (not necessarily, in the pejorative sense). In the belief system there is, simultaneously, another theory of disruption—the influence of Satan. This means that input into prayer meetings might be inspired by the Holy Spirit or it might be inspired by the Devil. Some groups believe that some input comes from a more neutral source—human influence, which is not evil but merely banal. With this belief system, the abilities of the central leadership to maintain control are highlighted. If unpredictable input does occur, in spite of control, then the leadership is required to discern the input's source—is it from God or the Devil? While most members are fascinated with this dual possibility, they also fear it and gladly defer to the leadership's judgment.

Another element inherent in such highly personalized group-religiosity is emotionalism. Unlike their Protestant counterparts, Catholic pentecostals discourage displays of extreme emotionalism, especially in public. Nevertheless, the order and interaction of prayer meetings are geared to the subtle manipulation of emotional fervor. This fervor is, in fact, one of the central appeals of public prayer meetings. For instance, members frequently evaluated the success of that night's meeting according to how "exciting" it was or how good they "felt" during the meeting. The primary difference between these and classical pentecostals is that Catholic pentecostals do not encourage or appear to enjoy the greater extremes of emotional fervor.

Furthermore, the emotion-laden possibilities of the prayer meeting encourage another source of disruption—the individual who uses the meeting to bare serious psychological difficulties or to promote an "ego-trip." Catholic pentecostals try to preclude these disruptions by not allowing contributions freely from "just anyone," but to a newcomer the apparent openness of the meeting often encourages intrusion. Most relatively closed groups formalize their exclusion of outsiders by announcing at the beginning that only members of their core group may speak up at meetings. During the years of this study, all of the groups observed moved toward increasingly formal and strong controls against non-members' open participation.[14] Groups that were newly pentecostal encouraged less controllable types of behavior, but as routine patterns of ritual developed, they increasingly controlled or discouraged spontaneity. Highly routinized forms of pentecostalism discourage unpredictable behavior (such as authoritative prophecy) altogether.[15]

Finally, Catholic pentecostals have an additional need for strong control and assertion of authority within the prayer group. Many of these Catholics are seriously concerned about maintaining their ties with the Catholic church and the hierarchy. They are interested in convincing church authorities that there is nothing irregular about their charismatic practices, so they need to make sure that elements of their prayer meetings would not give the hierarchy cause for forbidding or limiting their movement. More importantly, however, Catholic pentecostals are concerned to legitimate their practices to fellow Catholics. They try very hard to show their direct connection with Catholic tradition, and they are aware of the appearance of various practices to potential members. Thus there is considerable attention paid in their literature to the orthodoxy of their movement and to possible unorthodox practices which should be avoided.[16]

The emerging patterns of interaction in Catholic pentecostal prayer meetings may be viewed as resolutions of conflicting strains in the movement itself. These patterns have developed in the direction of stronger authority, order, and control. This direction is understandable, not only as an example of "routinization of charisma" (literally, as well as in the Weberian sense of the word), but also as a result of several themes in the appeal of the movement itself.

The Social Context of Prophecy

A detailed analysis of the social arrangements surrounding prophecy in the prayer meeting shows clearly how ambiguous and potentially disruptive events are managed, routinized, and are ultimately used for the validation of the leaders' authority in the group.

Prayer group leadership tries to control the situational ambiguity of special forms of communication in prayer meetings. The very nature of communication such as "interpretation" and "prophecy" means that, every time these are spoken, the group must act anew to construct or maintain a collective "definition of the situation."[17] The group needs to arrive at a collective meaning for events—with the diversity of perspectives and motives of the many group members surmounted. Situational ambiguity is resolved by creating a common interpretation of the experience which satisifes individual members and enhances group unity. This resolution process is, significantly, a *group* process, although some members are clearly more influential than others. Thus the production of resolution itself contributes the unity of the group.[18]

This process can be analyzed best by examining the division of labor in the reception of prophecy. Such a division is not unlike that discussed by Shibutani in his analysis of the reception of rumor.[19] Like the audiences described by Shibutani, prayer groups are engaged in the process of seeking a satisfactory common definition of the situation in the face of the ambiguity inherent in the very nature of prophecy. In fact, as Samarin points out, the history of movements such as the new pentecostalism is "a study in the sociolinguistic aspects of the institutionalization of religious roles."[20]

As previously noted, prophecy is believed to be God speaking directly to the prayer group through one of its members, and refers to "moments" of prophetic utterance, rather than to a generalized lifetime prophetic role. Nevertheless, pronouncement of these prophetic utterances often becomes a distinct role within the prayer group. For example, one movement authority explained, "Yet in this instance we are referring to prophetic utterance, to a word-gift given for a moment to an individual. The individual is not necessarily a prophet therefore, but he sometimes exercises a decided gift for prophecy, a gift for speaking out in the Lord's name as he is prompted."[21] Catholic pentecostals believe prophecy to be a "forth-telling" of the mind of God.[22] These beliefs, together with the mystery and awe which surround the pronouncement, account for the centrality of such a relatively brief event in the prayer meeting.

The success of the event depends entirely upon the satisfactory management of the social context of prophecy such that it "comes across" as being truly "from God." The ambiguity lies in the fact that the words spoken are, in fact, spoken by humans. Thus prophecy has meaning— or lacks meaning—as human communication. Also, the persons assuming key roles (for example, speaking prophecy, interpreting glossolalic prophecy, discerning valid prophecy, etc.) are known to fellow members as ordinary people rather than "prophets" or religious celebrities. Furthermore, there is continually the built-in possibility that the communication may not be from God, but from the Devil, or the speaker's own imagination. All of these problems must be overcome in the management of successful prophesying.

The leadership's control over prophesying is more important than any other element because prophecy has the inherent potential to undermine their authority in the prayer group. Leaders take care that only "responsible" members are allowed to prophesy. Nevertheless, such domination runs counter to the ideals of spontaneity and egalitarianism. Thus the management of the social context of prophecy must create the semblance of freedom and equality. How, then, is the social context of prophecy arranged to promote the desired common definition of the situation—that the "mind of God" be spoken to the prayer group?

The Reception of Prophecy

The sense of spontaneity and equality are promoted by a division of labor in the reception of prophecy. The process involves several different social roles, each with its own norms and prerogatives. Although some of these social roles are clearly more important than others, the spread of gifts among several members distracts from the stratification that exists within the prayer group. The fact that prophecy is given and interpreted by several persons rather than only a central leader also enhances the conviction that it is valid, from God.

The role of "speaker of prophecy" is a very important one in the prayer meeting. The whole group desires to receive prophecy, so it is very desirable to be the one through whom this important communication comes. The primacy is also due, in large measure, to the borrowed authority which the speaker gains in prophesying. One's words have great importance, but not as one's *own* words. The issue of authority is why leaders control the element of prophecy; the speaking of prophecy serves as a validation of their authority in the prayer group. This use of prophecy is directly connected with the egalitarian-authoritarian conflict in the movement's ideals. As Willems points out, "The closer a sect comes to the egalitarian model, the more its leaders feel the need to validate their authority by seeking supernatural sanctions for their decisions."[23]

One pattern of prophecy seems to contradict these generalizations about authority. This exception is that, while women are virtually unrepresented among the key leadership of prayer groups, they are frequently speakers of prophecy. Does this use of prophecy represent a usurpation of the male leadership's power? Probaby not. Indeed, the women's frequent exercising of prophetic roles may actually function as a safety-valve by making them feel as though they indirectly share prestige and power in the prayer meeting. In reality, however, prophecies given by women are more likely than those of men to be vague, unspecific, and expressive rather than directive. As such, they constitute no challenge to the male leadership's control. The overall frequency of purely expressive prophecy has increased steadily in the groups studied. The developing patterns retain the element of prophecy—because it fulfills other important functions—but the element is divested of its authority-challenging potential. This increase may be related to the consolidation of leadership authority. Simultaneously, in social groups with strong core group leadership, leaders' prophesying has become increasingly specific and directive.[24] While these differences may reflect partly the greater expertise of experienced speakers of prophecy, they also reflect the effective consolidation of authority in these prayer groups.

To speak of high levels of control is not, however, to deny that the role of speaker of prophecy is a very creative one. Bracketing the question of whether the *content* of the prophecy is created by the speaker, it is still certainly possible to show that the *performance* of prophecy is very much the speaker's creation. The speaker has the choice (with God's guidance) of timing the pronouncement as effectively as possible. The dramatic elements of presentation of the pronouncement are also under the speaker's control. And—very significantly—the individual can choose not to speak a certain prophecy. Prayer group members respond favorably to prophecies that are performed well, and a prayer meeting is frequently evaluated by members as more exciting if prophecies and other important elements are carried off well.

Prophecies spoken in tongues pose a problem, since they must be interpreted. Some groups have an individual member who is singled out with the specialized role of "interpreter of glossolalic prophecy"; usually such a person is a member of the leadership team. Another common pattern is for several different persons to provide interpretations from meeting to meeting. Yet, in all groups (closed, as well as open) prophecies and interpretations come primarily from members of the core group. These gifts are seldom exercised regularly by more than a few (that is, two or three members in a medium-sized group).

In one group (medium-sized, with few leaders), a sense of crisis developed one night when the chief leader spoke in tongues and no one gave an interpretation. The group waited a very uncomfortable thirteen minutes (very serious for a group with no other observed periods of silence of more than four minutes) after which the same leader "received" an interpretation to his own pronouncement. Such failure to provide an interpretation can sometimes be wielded as a tool to invalidate the authority of the tongue-speaker.[25] Thus the role of the interpreter is a powerful one.

The interpretation of tongues is considered to be a separate "charism" from prophesying in tongues. The interpretation is not a translation, nor does the interpreter purport to understand the literal meaning of the tongues. Rather, "He receives a distinct inspiration about the meaning or sense of what was said, without having understood the words themselves."[26] Two very different patterns of group attention to interpretations were observed. One common pattern was to treat interpretations as equal to prophecies. In this arrangement, the role of interpreter is very powerful and authoritative as is that of speakers of prophecy. The prestige of the interpreter is somewhat diminished in this model, however, by the fact that the prophecy is actually pronounced by the tongue-speaker. The person who "speaks (forth) in tongues" attracts considerable group attention, and that role promotes a sense of awe and mystery that enhances this special type of prophecy. Theoretically, a tongue-speaker of stature could deny the validity of an interpretation,[27] but this was never observed in the nine Catholic pentecostal groups studied. Authority emerges through the interpretation. The role of speaker of glossolalic prophecy poses little threat to group leaders; the interpretation is the more powerful authoritative element.

Another pattern, increasingly common among the groups studied, results in the diminished importance of interpretation. In this mode, the content of interpretation is less important than the fact that one be given.[28] Accordingly, the speaking of glossolalic prophecy is highlighted and the interpretation is a denouement–something to be gotten out of the way in order to proceed. This pattern results in interpretations which are purely expressive or affective. As such, neither the glossolalic prophecy nor the interpretation pose much challenge to the leaders' authority, except that they still constitute prestigious types of speech. Nevertheless, in groups where prophecy, glossolalic prophecy, and interpretation of tongues became totally expressive acts (rather than directive or authoritative), more members claimed the gift of prophecy and many prophecies were given at each meeting. The leaders' control was already consolidated and purely expressive prophecies did not threaten it.

Another role in the reception of prophecy is the "confirmer" of a prophecy or interpretation (that is, one who states that God had communicated a similar message as had just been spoken in prophecy). Confirmations of prophecies and interpretations of tongues are received with much enthusiasm, as a sure sign that the prophecy is a true one, from God. Members believe that confirmations of various events and pronouncements can come at any time, even long after the events occur. The public pronouncement of a confirmation is potent, since it validates a prior assertion of authority.

The supportive role of the confirmer is simple but important. It is frequently assumed by one of the regulars who seldom speaks up in any more assertive capacity. Confirmations are common in open groups (that is, prophecies are confirmed nearly half of the time, and interpretations of glossolalic prophecies are almost always confirmed). By contrast, confirmations in closed groups are rather rare. When given, they are pronounced only by core group members. This restriction makes it less likely that a prophecy which challenges their teaching-authority will be confirmed. Even fewer confirmations occur in prayer groups where the leaders practice discernment after the prayer meeting. Thus group leaders are able to evaluate and filter the public pronouncements, whereas if prophecies were publicly confirmed, it would be harder to contain or repudiate them.

A further social role in the reception of prophecy is that of the "hearers," the rest of the membership of the prayer group. Rather than view hearers as a passive audience, it is important to see their role as bound up with the task at hand of constructing an acceptable definition of the situation. Usually the hearers of prophecy and interpretation at prayer meetings are believers—that is, they too define the content as directly from God. By their tacit consent, then, the speaking of prophecy is supported and encouraged. This supportive role of the audience is especially evident when a member of the audience challenges the definition of the situation which the group members are co-producing.[29] A dramatic instance of this kind of challenge occurred during one meeting observed. The group responded spontaneously by forgoing all spoken gifts, and praying intensely in silence for the entire remainder of the meeting. Thus the role of hearer of special pentecostal speaking has considerable complicity with the roles of speakers (as Chapter 5 develops further).

A far more powerful role in handling interpretations and prophecies is that of the "controller" of the meeting. For instance, leaders of the meeting frequently use the "floor" to react to prophecies and other input. The effect of these commentaries is to reinforce or restate favorable input and to soften or redirect what leaders feel is misguided or wrong. Further control is exerted by the leadership, especially in closed groups, in the function of "discernment" (the evaluation of which pronouncements of the previous meeting were validly "from the Lord"). In some groups this is done by prayers asking the Lord to confirm the major events of the previous prayer meeting to the leaders. This private discernment meeting also includes discussion of various members' contributions, relative to their spiritual progress, their emotional stability, and their closeness to "main themes of group interest."[30] If members' pronouncements are considered problematic, they are counselled and asked to refrain from speaking out. In other groups, a single individual (typically the central leader) is believed to have the gift of discernment, and his sense of the matter is accepted because of his God-given authority.

The role of discerner is the single most powerful role in the reception of prophecy. Exercising this role is the ultimate validation of authority and is therefore typically invested in the central leader.[31] Even in groups where discernment is practiced by a group of leaders, the role clearly carries the power to invalidate the authority of speakers of prophecy, glossolalic prophecy, interpretation, or confirmation. Discernment is directly tied to the exercise of controls and sanctions over the interactions of the prayer meeting. If speakers are discerned to be false and do not accept the leaders' counselling to keep quiet, they are usually asked to leave the group and not return.

In dramatic cases, these sanctions are applied during the prayer meeting itself. For example, in one large group (roughly in the middle of the continuum between open to closed), a woman about forty pronounced a very ominous, specific prophecy. Her prophecy was threatening to the leaders, not only because the content was not in keeping with their own teachings, but especially because it was given skillfully and effectively with obvious impact on the audience. While the prayer meeting leaders were trying to undo the immediate effect, one of the central leaders moved to the woman's side, spoke a few words, and walked out with her to "counsel" her. She never returned to that prayer group. More typically, however, discerners are not likely to exercise this gift immediately during the prayer meeting, but the knowledge that they will do so alters the quality of the prayer group's input. In groups with actively practiced discernment, members are more cautious about pronouncements they make and less likely to contribute when they are not completely sure of themselves. This reaction further ensures that virtually only the core leadership will speak the more important input. Because they are confident that the discerner will evaluate pronouncements, members of these prayer groups are less likely to attempt evaluations themselves. Thus the active practice of the specialized role of discerner successfully consolidates authority and control.

There are additional means for controlling prophecy and related pronouncements—mostly by way of guidance, advice, and encouragement for the inexperienced. This teaching of supposedly spontaneous speech is not inconsistent with Catholic pentecostal understanding of the nature of these word-gifts. Members believe that the Spirit offers the prayer group many such gifts and that, due to inexperience, misinformation, or fear, these gifts are not used or are used improperly. The purpose of "how-to" instructions on prophecy and other word-gifts is to encourage and clarify their proper use. Such guides communicate group norms regarding what should be considered prophecy, when it should be spoken, and how it should be spoken. One guidebook explained that an important sign that a person should prophesy, give a message in tongues, or give an interpretation, was the "anointing of the Spirit," which is described as a sense of urgency or expectancy. Even with this anointing, the member is counselled to seek direction from the Lord whether to prophesy, and when is the appropriate time. The guidebook suggested that if one is supposed to prophesy, one will feel a "sense of peace from the Lord" indicating that one should speak. A leader told the group, "We ask you to refrain from speaking, hold your prophecy and pray for a confirmation either in scripture or in another prophecy that would prove your prophecy is truly sent by God. Then, if you feel strongly enough that your ability to speak valid prophecy has been proven, you will feel confident you speak God's will." Members are cautioned to wait their turn, not to interrupt, and to wait for the appropriate atmosphere for their prophesying. The guidebook gives this advice about pronouncing a prophecy, "Administering the word of prophecy or interpretation is very important to its effectiveness. The prophet should speak loudly enough for all to hear, but not so loud as to frighten everyone. He should speak the word *in a way that is appropriate to God*. Also, a prophetic word should be in ordinary English" (emphasis added).[32] The social roles of pronouncing prophecy, speaking (forth) in tongues, interpretation of tongues, hearing, controlling, and discerning together contribute to a successful "event." They make it possible for the group to achieve the desired definition of the situation: God Himself is immediately present and directly communicating with the group. One further element is needed—orchestration of the event. These various roles must be integrated and managed to ensure the event's success. A poignant example of a group's failure to "bring off" its weekly prayer meeting is provided by Westley.[33] The group she studied, while large enough to become successful, failed to organize or control its meetings, resulting in banal input.

In classical pentecostalism, orchestration is less difficult because the preacher or minister himself or herself performs most crucial roles. In the Catholic pentecostal movement, however, the ideals of spontaneity and egalitarianism have encouraged a spread of roles among several different members of the prayer group. Thus the orchestration of roles becomes a greater problem for the group and leaders. Nevertheless, as the above descriptions show, most prayer meetings (especially in the more closed groups) are neither totally spontaneous nor egalitarian. In effect, in Catholic pentecostal prayer meetings the division of labor among a larger number of persons makes the meeting appear spontaneous and egalitarian; in practice, however, the actual assignment of roles is carefully controlled and managed by the core leadership.

Themes of Prophecies

Participants view prophecies as directed to the building up of the entire prayer community, in addition to prophecy's value for personal inspiration or instruction. In closed groups this focus is further intensified, and the content of prophecies is believed to have meaning only for that prayer group and can be understood properly only by members fully immersed in its life. This belief is one reason they firmly restrict the act of prophesying to group members. Nevertheless, prophecies recorded in all groups studied follow a pattern remarkably similar in form and content.

Themes of prophecies are usually very general. For example, one common theme is the presence of God:

> My people,
> Know that I am Lord, that I am God.
> I will move in power and majesty among you this night.
> Be ready both in listening to my voice.
> Hear me as I call to you.
> Hear me as I speak to you.
> I am in your midst.

And again:

> You are my children.
> Believe in me.
> Believe in my presence within you.
> Stretch forth your hand, and I will lead you.
> You are mine.

A second recurring theme is surrender:

> My children,
> I want to be part of your world.
> Surrender your home to me.
> Surrender your heart to me.
> Surrender yourselves to me.
> Let me work in you.
> Let me pray through you.
> I will need to take over your lives.

Another example:

> My people,
> There is only one thing I ask of you—
> That you surrender yourselves to me completely, without
> regret.

The idea of surrender is significant to Catholic pentecostals and is often used to refer to the necessary condition for baptism in the Holy

Spirit. Sometimes the theme of surrender in the prophecies takes on the specific interpretation of submission to prayer group authorities. The following concluding fragment from a very long prophecy illustrates this theme:

> Surrender to me.
> Surrender to my will.
> Be obedient to those I have set over you.
> Do not be rebellious against the due authorities I have set over you.
> Respect and be thankful for their leadership and authority.
> Their authority is my authority over you.
> Submit to them for I have ordained them to speak my word to you.
> I appreciate the efforts of those leaders and servants.
> Come to me.
> Sup with me.
> I am your Lord.
> Forget your cares and troubles and just surrender yourself to me.

Also linked with the theme of surrender are themes about the power of God. These two ideas are usually combined in prophecies, embodying pentecostals' belief in their own total powerlessness and God's gift of power to them if they surrender their own wills. For example:

> My people,
> I want to move powerfully in your midst this night.
> I am here.
> I am your Lord.
> Surrender to me.
> I am in power among you.
> You can limit my power by not expecting enough.
> Believe in me.
> Believe in my power.
> Expect great things and you will receive great things.
> I am here.
> I am with you.
> I am in power among you.
> Surrender to me.

Combined with the theme of surrender is the theme of security and trust:

> My child,
> I would speak a word to you.
> Do not be afraid of my presence.
> Do not look away, but to me . . . (pause)
> For I wish to pour out my speech (?) upon your heart.

You can trust in that.
You can trust in me.
For I love you.
For I am your God.
And I want you to experience that God.
Open your arms wide, my child,
And let me come in.

These themes—immediacy and power of God, self-surrender, security, and trust—are directly related to the movement's basic appeals. The content of prophecies in these groups is almost never strongly negative and seldom urges or predicts specific action. Instead, it is usually vague, soothing, or only mildly urging. This vagueness is functional, because prophecy in such groups is often used affectively, thus diminishing its potential as a challenge to the authority of group leaders.[34] Such vagueness and ambiguity in the content of prophecies also allows greater flexibility in the group's creation of its interpretation and response. This explanation is expecially plausible for the closed groups, in which the authority issue is more critical. Such affective use of prophecy is particularly significant for Catholic pentecostals, because such prophecy is not likely to challenge the authority of the Church hierarchy.

Most prophecies tend to be directed toward personal interior spirituality; occasionally they refer to interactions within the prayer group itself. Seldom, if ever, does the theme relate to involvement in the larger society except as evidence of the impending Millennium. These themes are consistent with the movement's focus on interior concerns and personal religiosity and its devaluation of social activism.

Social Functions of Prophecy

Sociological analysis of the element of prophecy must, of course, bracket the crucial question: Is it communication from God? Whatever its religious validity, however, prophecy can be shown to fulfill several important social functions in the life of the prayer group, having significance, not only for the cohesion and interaction of the larger prayer group, but also for the individual.

Prophecy promotes three interrelated elements in the prayer meeting: expectancy, sense of mystery, and immediacy of God. Thus it contributes to the desired definition of the situation within the prayer meeting and to the success of the event. At the same time, prophecy serves to heighten these same elements on a personal level for each participant. The atmosphere of expectancy is directly related to the group's belief that communication from God will be forthcoming. Silence and glossolalia are especially important in fostering such an atmosphere.[35] The idea of the anointing of the Spirit expresses theologically the feeling or mood which can also manifest itself in sociologically observable behavior at such junctures in the prayer meeting.

Prophecy, with its characteristic use of the first person, impresses the hearer with a sense of the immediate presence of God and with a feeling of one-to-one, highly personal, communication. Furthermore, the specific content of most prophecies enhances this sense of immediacy, since a substantial majority contain some statement to the effect that God is present.

The atmosphere of expectancy and the sense of immediacy of God both promote the other element, mystery. The quality of mystery is created, primarily, by the interpretation of pronouncements as "from God" rather than the result of purely human action. This approach sensitizes participants to endow all behavior during the prayer meeting with possible special meaning, communicated by the mysteries of the Holy Spirit. Thus the choice of hymn or Scripture reading, for example, could become endowed with supernatural meaning. Glossolalic pronouncements are especially forceful in promoting this sense of mystery. Speaking in tongues is mysterious simply by its unintelligibility to the hearer and speaker alike. For Catholics, changing the language of the Liturgy to the vernacular de-mystified much of the Mass; the pentecostal emphasis upon glossolalia constitutes a re-mystification of worship.[36] Finally, all word-gifts (especially prophecy, glossolalic tongues, and interpretation) are felt to originate outside the speaker. This attitude toward speech is a major departure from everyday conceptions of human speech, and it accounts for the awe, mystery, and different manner of "listening" in the prayer meeting. This mode of speaking and hearing is developed further in the next chapter.

The element of prophecy fulfills additional social functions for the prayer group. It enhances unity, the feeling of being "chosen," and it promotes stratification and reinforces lines of authority. When preceded by an intense silence, the moment of interpretation of prophecy is characterized by an almost tangible sense of group unity. The only other event of the prayer meeting which approximates this unifying force is the occasional swell of a special hymn or, in open groups, a healing or a relatively emotional prayer-litany.

Prophecy also enhances the feeling of the group's chosenness because speakers and hearers feel especially selected by God for His revelation. This attitude is particularly important for Catholic pentecostals as a legitimation of their new style of religiosity. For Catholics in particular, pentecostalism represents discovery of the democratization of the power to be the vessel for the divine. Prophecy demonstrates that the hierarchy and the Saints are not God's only human mediators.

Stratification of the prayer groups is, nevertheless, very evident in their patterns of language. The ranks of real authority, power, and prestige are clearly defined by norms for speakers, hearers, and controllers of special forms of pentecostal speech. Because of the centrality of prophecy and because of the unpredictability of non-core-members' use of it, the prayer group's leaders especially control the use of this gift, limiting who is allowed to prophecy, to discern whose prophecies are valid, and to interpret, redirect, or soften misguided prophecies.

Finally, prophecy should be seen as contributing to believers' assurance of the authoritative teaching of the prayer group. If it is God who is speaking directly, His word is hardly subject to the change or disconfirmation which befalls human teachings. This function of authority is especially important for Catholic pentecostals. The debunking of religious authority and norms resulting from Vatican II and its aftermath, together with the ambiguity of societal norms and authority resulting from rapid social change and unrest, have contributed to a desire for an authority (in the case of this movement, the Holy Spirit) which is outside the influence of all change. For pentecostals, this authoritative order is communicated by God to the individual or group in such a highly personal and subjective way that it is relatively safe from debunking and disconfirmation. The element of prophecy is the paramount source of this kind of authority and order.

Summary

The Catholic pentecostal movement in America has developed its own distinctive pattern of language, as seen in this analysis of interaction during prayer meetings. While borrowing much from classical and neo-pentecostal Protestant counterparts, this movement has maintained behavioral boundaries from the other variants of pentecostalism, partly because of the necessity for legitimating their practices as orthodox within Catholicism.

Specific elements of stratification and social control can be analyzed in these prayer-meeting practices. The very nature of charismatic communication, with the ever-present possibility of any behavior or speech being directly from God, poses a threat to the authority and control of group leaders. Thus the manipulation and limitation of pronouncements during prayer meetings constitutes a necessary control. While conflicting with other ideological values in the movement, the stratification of roles in the prayer group and social control serve specific functions of providing authority, order and control—all features valued by members.

The diverse roles in the reception of gifts, such as prophecy, help develop and maintain a common definition of the situation—that God is immediately present to the group and communicating directly with members. Prophecy and related gifts foster an atmosphere of expectancy, a sense of the immediacy of God and a feeling of mystery. They promote the unity of the prayer group and enhance members' feeling that their group is "chosen" for God's revelations of Himself. The use of prophecy and related gifts embodies group stratification and promotes leaders' control. The spread of social roles in the reception of prophecy creates a sense of spontaneity and egalitarianism, but ultimately charisma is firmly controlled.

Five—
Religious
Speaking
and
Religious
Hearing

As the foregoing analysis of prophecy and other pentecostal interaction has shown, the beliefs and practices of Catholic pentecostals represent a dramatic departure from certain everyday assumptions about behavior. One of the most interesting departures is that the prayer meeting operates under very different rules of speaking and hearing than do other human gatherings. Although glossolalia is the most obvious difference, there is a broader context within which this, and other special forms of religious speaking, are meaningful. This chapter examines the larger setting of "religious speaking" and "religious hearing" in pentecostal prayer meetings.

While based on considerable field evidence (much of which is presented in descriptions elsewhere in this volume), this chapter takes a heuristic and somewhat speculative approach to the matter of religious speaking and hearing because many other interpretations of pentecostal speaking are enmeshed in very limited theoretical perspectives. For example, alternative interpretations fail to realize the extent to which glossolalia is merely an instance of a much broader phenomenon which has far more interesting theoretical implications. Enough research on religious speaking has been done to enable one to move toward this broader perspective.

Alternate Realities

The prayer meeting, as an example of a religious setting for speaking and hearing, differs fundamentally from everyday reality in two ways: it operates on an alternate definition of reality and it exists as an alternate sphere of reality. An appreciation of the radical differentness of these two aspects of the prayer meeting puts the prayer meeting interaction into perspective. First, the prayer meeting may be viewed as operating on an alternate definition of reality—the pentecostal world view (developed in Chapter 2) which not only differs dramatically from that of other Catholics and from that of secularized world views, but implies alternate views of speaking and hearing. For example, the Catholic pentecostal world view holds that God can and does communicate regularly and directly with humans through the gift of prophecy. Thus, this alternate world view creates the possibility of alternate modes of speaking and hearing which are consistent with the belief system of the group and are highly meaningful.

Second, the prayer meeting itself functions as an alternate sphere of reality. The exact nature of this different reality is somewhat complex, and existing theories are not adequate to explain all of the factors involved. Much of the literature starts from the assumption of a dichotomous relationship. Individuals are seen as either "in" or "out" of everyday reality (that is, "dissociated"). Much of the psychological literature on these "states" focuses primarily on the phenomenon of dissociation, assuming a clear dichotomy.[1] Some anthropological approaches to such phenomena as trance and possession also share this assumption of dichotomy, although anthropologists less frequently infer pathology from the "states."[2] Sociologists, on the other hand, have typically focused exclusively on the sphere of everyday life, seldom even broaching the question of alternate spheres of reality; these spheres do not fit neatly into their "over-socialized" conceptions of human behavior.[3]

One sociological attempt to explain alternate realities is Schutz's theory of "finite provinces of meaning," which posits that various finite provinces of meaning will have different "cognitive styles." Each different province will have a "specific tension of consciousness and, consequently, a specific epoche [suspension of doubt]; a prevalent form of spontaneity, and specific form of self experience; a specific form of sociality, and a specific time perspective."[4] All these qualities are internally consistent within that province of meaning but are likely to be inconsistent with qualities in other provinces of meaning. Furthermore, according to Schutz, the commonsense world of everyday life assumes the character of paramount reality, since it is within that sphere that communication of intersubjectivity takes place. Schutz treats these finite provinces as totally discrete realms, moving to and from which the individual experiences a "shock" in attention.

More recently, Goffman has approached the same phenomenon, explaining it with a complex analysis of "frames" according to which individuals organize their experience.[5] Goffman's analysis is more singularly sociological, examining rules and relationships in the various frames, and allowing for an interpretation of those "frames" in which an individual can be fully absorbed yet not define them as "real" (for example, the theater). Goffman's approach is useful, especially since it recognizes a whole array of intermediate circumstances which are neither "everyday reality" nor "dissociated," but his emphasis on the purely sociological concomitants of these frames leaves psychological and physiological aspects unexplored.[6]

How, then, should the different sphere of reality of the prayer meeting be envisioned? Rather than the dichotomous version, a continuum may be a better model.[7] One extreme of the continuum is "everyday reality," the taken-for-granted sphere of social life, built on the strong assumption of intersubjectivity. At this level such assumptions are based primarily on the pragmatic mode (that is, members do not ask questions about "what do we really mean," because communication is aimed at "getting things done"). Much of daily life is conducted in this sphere of reality. It is the sphere of buying groceries, getting cars started, arranging for babysitters, asking directions, striving for promotions, planning vacations, and being on time for meetings.

At the opposite end of the continuum, "alternate reality" refers to spheres of reality that are totally subjective experiences, and therefore fundamentally unshared and unsharable. In fact, the very attempt to communicate them is, by definition, social and thus a transformation of the experiences themselves. Examples of spheres of reality toward this extreme of the continuum include dreams, hallucinations, drug "trips" and mystical experiences. Even these examples, however, are relative; for example, some mystical experiences are more unrelated to everyday life than are others. Transitions from this extreme end of the continuum to everyday reality produce a much greater sense of shock. In other words, the individual feels a strong sense of partition between spheres (as, for example, on awakening from a dream).[8]

While the two extremes of the continuum are relatively easy to characterize, the immense middle range of "modified reality" is more complex, depending upon the interplay of two factors: (1) the extent to which the sphere of reality is shared or private, and (2) the extent to which the individual (or group) absorbed in that sphere is removed from attention to the sphere of everyday reality. Examples of modified realities show clearly the diverse range in the middle of the continuum: drama, a chess game, a rock concert, discussion of mathematical theories, daydreams, private prayer, a sense of exhilaration at the beauties of nature, poetic imageries, being slightly "high" on alcohol or drugs, erotic euphoria, being absorbed in a good book, and so on.

The reality of the prayer meeting is one of these modified spheres. It is shared, and thus is not a fully alternate reality. For example, members are usually alert to each other and often exchange smiles. In fact, because the prayer meeting is a group activity, it is seldom the occasion for individuals to slip into a fully alternate sphere. Those members who desire to have mystical experiences do not seek them during prayer meeting, but in private.

One dissociated sphere of reality valued by some Catholic pentecostals is called "resting in the Spirit," comparable to fairly deep meditation. Although this practice was mentioned in movement literature and observed at some large healing services in the region, it was not practiced in any of the prayer groups studied and none of the respondents interviewed at that phase of the study had ever experienced it. Nevertheless, the reality of the prayer meeting does effectively absorb members' attention from the realm of everyday life. Somewhat comparable to involvement in an exciting game or moving drama, the ongoing reality of the prayer meeting itself absorbs the members into a sphere of its own. Unlike the game or the theater, however, this sphere is defined as "really real"—perhaps even more real than everyday life. Similar to the game (and to a lesser extent, the theater) the prayer meeting is not partitioned by a noticeable "shock" of attention upon entering and exiting, because the beginnings and endings are built into the social interaction itself. For example, participants are led by the order of the prayer meeting back to the sphere of everyday reality (for example, concerns such as: Where did I leave my coat? Will I have gotten a parking ticket? It's getting late, I wonder if my children went to bed on time, and so on).

The above theoretical distinction shows that the speaking and hearing in prayer meetings can operate under dramatically different rules, because the members are in a different sphere of reality from that of everyday life. Furthermore, as this analysis suggests, it is not necessary to make the dichotomous assumption of "dissociation" to explain the different forms of speaking in prayer meetings.

Inspired and Ecstatic Speaking

Although this analysis applies to some extent to all shared religious meaning, it takes on specific significance when applied to pentecostals for whom a key premise of the alternate definition of reality is that human speech can be "given" by God. In other words, certain occasions of human speaking derive, in content and/or inspiration, directly from God. Prophecy, prophecy in tongues, and interpretation—are all believed to be direct interventions of God into human speaking. Other speech is also believed to be possibly from God, but less dramatically so. For example, some teachings and testimonies during a prayer meeting are thought to be of immediate divine inspiration. Catholic pentecostals also believe that God can, and regularly does, influence the choice of Scripture readings and hymns. The firmness of this conviction can be seen in the regularity of "confirmations" of even minor aspects of the prayer meeting: "Let's sing 'For You Are My God.' The Lord wants us to sing it," and, "I want to confirm that Scripture reading. I've been thinking about a problem I've got, and I asked the Lord for a text, and he gave me (verse number) and then he gave me (verse number), and now you've read (verse number), so now I know for sure he's telling me how to handle my problem and my anxiousness over it."

These examples show that a wide range of speaking in prayer meetings is considered to be "special," set apart, and particularly valued, because it is believed to be derived wholly or partially from a source greater than the speaker himself. The dramatic first-person pronouncements, as well as much other speaking (testimony, teaching, Scripture reading, and hymns) are believed to be "from God." The distinctions are clearly social definitions; that is, the group imputes the special quality to the speech. Although the speaker might claim (for example) to be speaking for God, it is the group which must validate the claim. It is possible to distinguish degrees of this imputed divine authorship: ordinary speaking, inspired speaking, and ecstatic speaking. Much speaking in prayer meetings is treated as "ordinary" in its authorship; speakers are believed to be speaking their own words, their own ideas, and on their own authority. Most witnessing lies toward this end of the continuum. However, a large proportion is considered to be "inspired"; that is, speakers are believed to be using their own words, but the content and mode of presentation are to some degree directly inspired by God. Many teachings by group leaders are believed to be inspired in this sense, and speakers seek a special anointing comparable to that which precedes a prophecy.

Especially dramatic are pronouncements which are here considered "ecstatic" speaking; that is, the speaker is believed to be speaking the words and ideas of a source other than himself. The term "ecstatic" is here used in the literal sense—"standing outside" oneself. The use of this term should not imply, however, that ecstatic speaking is necessarily trance-related or done in the context of a religious peak-experience. It means merely that the group believes that the speaker is speaking the words of, and on the authority of, another being.

This belief alters fundamental assumptions about the relations of the speaker to the speech. The speaker is seen as the medium—not the author. As medium, the speaker acts as a non-participant in the communicative act, somewhat like a third-party go-between. As such, the medium is freed from some of the rules of participation. This relationship has obvious parallels with possession shamanism, in which the shaman is believed to act and speak while possessed by a spirit. By contrast, ecstatic speaking in a Catholic pentecostal prayer group is rarely, if ever, trance-related, nor are the roles of the speakers themselves usually spectacular or specialized roles like those of shamans. Catholic pentecostals themselves assert that trance-related speaking is not involved.[9] Medium roles in other religious groups involve written rather than spoken messages (for example, "automatic" writing) and communication with lesser authorities (saints, "ascended masters," extra-terrestrial beings, and so on).

Glossolalia

Glossolalia is one type of religious speaking which attracts the attention of social scientists and the curious public, so an interpretation of Catholic pentecostalism requires an explicit statement about this phenomenon. In a linguistic analysis, Samarin defines glossolalia as "A meaningless but phonologically structured human utterance believed by the speaker to be a real language but bearing no systematic resemblance to any natural language, living or dead."[10] Glossolalia, *per se*, is not religious behavior and occurs in numerous non-religious settings.[11] In the social context of a religious ritual or belonging to a religious group for which it has value, a religious meaning is attached to the act. Samarin's study concludes that glossolalia is basically a learned ability, made possible by a relaxed self-consciousness and a social setting in which such speech is valued.[12] He gives the following transcribed example of a glossolalic prayer in a neo-pentecostal prayer group:

> kolama siándo, laboka tohoríămasí, lamo siándo, laboka tahandoria, lamo siando kolămasí, labo siándo, lakatándori, lamo siambăbă kătándo, lamá fia, lama fiandoriăkó, labokan doriasandó, lamo siándoriako, labo siá, lamo siandó, labăkán doria, lama fiá, lama fiandolokolămăbăsí, lăbo siandó, lama fiatándoria, lamokáyămasi, labo siandó.[13]

Although the utterance may be meaningless, pronouncing it is a highly meaningful act for Catholic pentecostals. Two different theories were expressed by respondents. One common explanation is that the tongues are real languages but not known by the speaker, and that if someone from that foreign country were present, the exact translation would be possible. Other informants explained that the tongues are not human languages but divine languages (since their purpose is communication with God) and therefore it does not matter that they cannot be translated. The former theory finds much prominence in early

Catholic pentecostal literature; whereas, later literature tends to be more circumspect. For example, in 1971 O'Connor clearly identified the glossas as foreign languages, but he went on to say, "It is not the foreign tongues in itself which is important. This is only an external sign . . . that the Holy Spirit is the principal author of the given prayer, even more than the person who utters it."[14] This interpretation links glossolalia with the broader context of "religious speaking" which this chapter will develop further.

Thus the exact meaning of the "words" they utter is relatively unimportant to Catholic pentecostals, although they believe that what they are saying is meaningful.[15] Furthermore, the act of speaking in tongues is highly valued and meaningful within the prayer group. It is valued foremost for religious reasons—namely, that tongue-speaking is central to the pentecostal definition of what it means to be a Christian. Social scientists are often too quick to write off believers' own reasons for doing something as merely a symptom of some latent purpose.

The following summary of Samarin's analysis illustrates the variety of functions which glossolalia can serve.[16] First, it can be symbolic of change. This function is especially important, because speaking in tongues is unusual for middle-class Catholics, and its use can, thus, function as a bridge-burning event in the commitment process.[17] Second, for many individuals glossolalia is a proof of the validity of their baptism experience. Although the leaders of the movement downplay this function, individual members continually look for such proof. This search for validation of their experiences is strongly correlated with their desire to know their personal standing before God (that is, "Am I saved?"). Third, glossolalia functions as a symbol of submission. The term most often used is "yielding"—to tongues, to other charisms, to God's will. The obvious parallel would be submission in possession-cults, but possession–cults typically have different beliefs about the degree of control exercised by the possessed person.[18] Catholic pentecostals believe that, especially with the gift of tongues, the individual retains total control over the use of the gift. One can stop and start at will and does not require a special inspiration each time the gift is used.[19] This control is related to the fact that glossolalia, both in the prayer meeting and outside it, occurs as part of the "modified reality" relatively close to the sphere of everyday life. For example, respondents reported playing with tongues and using them casually as they went about their everyday activities.[20] Fourth, according to Samarin, glossolalia is a symbol of self-assertion. This use by Catholic pentecostals is clearly illustrated in Chapter 4, where public use of glossolalia is related to the authority structure of the prayer group.[21]

Samarin points out that glossolalia can also be simply pleasurable.

Speakers enjoy a sense of mastery over something which they once considered impossible. They enjoy the fantasy and reverie and also the ecstasy which is associated with glossolalic speech. "Ecstasy" here refers to any "pleasurable state of intense emotion—whether natural or linked with an altered state of consciousness."[22] Samarin emphasizes that glossolalia is not necessarily related at all to dissociation or altered states of consciousness, and this assertion is supported by observations in this study, as well as by the opinion of Catholic pentecostals themselves. As O'Connor states, "The subject is fully conscious, both of himself and of all that is going on around him, . . . The person who prays in tongues is likewise in calm control of himself before, after, and even while he is doing so."[23]

The control which Catholic pentecostals and other middle-class pentecostals exhibit is important counterevidence to the culture-bound theories (held in popular notions as well as by social scientists) that glossolalia is the product of a trance-state. There is simply no evidence in the years of this study that *any* of the special forms of religious speaking considered in this chapter are necessarily trance-related.[24]

Most researchers assume that altered states of consciousness (trance or dissociation) are psychobiological phenomena, with observable and measurable physical correlates.[25] If glossolalia were necessarily identified with these states, it could be considered part of an altered reality, rather than merely a modified one. Recent research on neo-pentecostals, however, has not found any significant physiological correlates.[26] Theories which presume trance-production are probably based on evidence from cultures or subcultures in which trance is *also* valued and, therefore, likely to occur *alongside* glossolalia.

Similarly, theories which presume that this phenomenon is based on some psychopathology may also be culture-bound.[27] Recent studies of Catholic pentecostals and Protestant neo-pentecostals do not bear out the thesis that glossolalia, *per se*, is related to psychopathology; indeed, the whole experience (especially the group ties) may be therapeutic.[28] It is probable that any unusual religious group will attract a disproportionate number of persons with problems, including psychological problems. The particular belief system of any group or movement will be likely also to attract certain kinds of people who share its problem-solving perspective (see Chapter 3). This self-selection process is likely to include certain psychological correlates, and in the case of pentecostalism such self-selection probably accounts for reported characteristics, such as submissiveness, suggestibility, and dependency on authority figures.[29]

To focus on glossolalia, however, merely because it is anomalous, is to miss the broader theoretical perspective. Glossolalia is merely one member of a larger class of religious speaking: all speech which is believed by a group to come from the deity rather than the speaker. This belief alters fundamental assumptions about the relationship of speakers to their speech. It is worthwhile, therefore, to examine these assumptions and the social context in which they become possible.

Authorship of Speech

People make very explicit assumptions about the human authorship of speech in the sphere of everyday life. For example, if individuals are found to have told a lie, they are considered culpable for their speech. Or if they pay a compliment, they are believed to be responsible for thinking of the compliment. Or, if their words hurt someone's feelings—even unintentionally—they consider it appropriate to apologize. The possibility of the divine authorship of some human speech, however, alters this relationship. Speakers experience a different sense of responsibility for their speech, a concomitant freedom from everyday constraints in speaking, increased potential for the expressiveness of speech, and a borrowed authority for their words. As any given speech is considered to be on the continuum from "ordinary" to "inspired" to "ecstatic" speaking, the degree to which the person experiences these other alterations increases.

It is not only from divinely given speech, however, that individuals can gain this sense of freedom from responsibility. There are several specifically social circumstances in which the group feels that individuals are not speaking "for themselves." Other, relatively mild, forms of reduced responsibility include jesting, use of sarcasm, irony, innuendo, folk sayings, and adages.[30] For example, when speakers invoke folk sayings in a culture in which folk wisdom is considered to be a source of authority, they are using words "other than their own" and speaking on the authority of the larger group. Other social circumstances, less mild instances, also result in reduced responsibility. When individuals act and speak as official representatives of a social role, they assume part of the authority of the whole institutional apparatus of which that role is a part. Thus a judge, in pronouncing the judgment "of the bench" is believed to be speaking, not personally, but on the authority of the entire legal institution.[31]

By extension, then, individuals frequently try to claim exculpation for acts, including speech acts, in the performance of a role—the extreme case being war crimes. An excellent example of the parallels this kind of freedom from responsibility can produce was in the My Lai massacre trial, in which one of the psychiatrists testifying said, "I do not believe that we should hold any one person responsible for My Lai. . . . I do not believe that we should hold any one person or the nation responsible. If you want to hold someone responsible, I think the only one you could point to would be God."[32]

The point of these comparisons is that religious ecstatic speaking is not altogether unlike these everyday forms of ecstatic speaking; in both instances, individuals believe themselves not fully responsible for their own speech. The important qualitative difference about religious speech is that the ultimate referent is God. Unlike human referents, God does not publicly disavow (except through other human mediums) those who mis-state His messages; thus His mouthpieces are less subject to disconfirmation. Furthermore, because the ultimate referent is so much more powerful, religious ecstatic speaking is potentially more powerful and awesome. It is simply impossible to evaluate the crucial element; there is no way of objectively validating or invalidating the claims that it is "from God." Thus religious "ecstatic" speaking is qualitatively different from other socially understandable forms of ecstatic speech. The following analysis examines the resulting altered relationships.

Within the context of pentecostalism, religious speaking implies a different sense of responsibility. If the speech is "from God," the speaker is not responsible for its content or effects. There is, however, the responsibility of being attentive to the "right" source of inspiration. That is, the speaker must earnestly desire to express God's message and not that of the Devil or that borne of one's own human weakness. The responsibility for the speech is not direct; rather religious speaking, in this context, means being responsive to the "right" source of speech, that is, God.

One of the main effects of this altered relationship to one's speech is the generation of a sense of freedom. In the sphere of everyday life, one is bound by rules and responsibilities that seem no longer to hold when one is speaking in the pentecostal context. For example, one is free to literally speak non-sense (glossolalia).[33] As such, religious speaking permits self-revelation without risk.

This function suggests one of the basic fallacies in the theories of those researchers who attempt to show that glossolalia and related religious speech are pathological. It is not the form of speech that should be the object of interpretation, but rather the relationship of speakers to their speech—a relationship which permits and encourages anomalous speech.[34] The view of glossolalia as psychopathological focuses only upon speaking in tongues (anomalous speech) and not on the whole realm of special forms of religious speaking, such as prophecy and interpretation of tongues. The differences between a member who prophesies in tongues and one who prophesies in the vernacular are not explained by psychological factors. The differences are primarily sociological factors, such as learned skills, relative power in the prayer group, and the extent to which the whole prayer group values and encourages the particular form of speech.

Furthermore, this production of a sense of freedom is not purely individualistic. The prayer meeting is not a gathering in which each member goes off into a private world of religious experience. Rather, the production of a sense of freedom is a group experience in which individual speakers contribute to an overall feeling of spontaneity. Thus religious speaking is primarily a social phenomenon.

This attitude of freedom from responsibility in religious speaking is tied to specific values of the pentecostal belief system—"trust" and "faith." Members believe that God's gifts are good, that God would not give bad or misguided tongues or prophecies, and that to trust God means to "trust His gifts." This trust leads to the idea of "surrender,"[35] one of the primary themes of pentecostal piety; the ultimate goal is complete surrender to God's will. Specific acts of surrender are focused on yielding: to the gift of tongues, to God's inspiration in one's life, to baptism in the Spirit, to guidance by the "Shepherds" of the prayer community, and so on. Thus glossolalia and other religious speaking become not only symbols of commitment but also symbols of surrender to the source of authority outside oneself.

Another effect of this attention to God as the source of authority is a freedom from the pragmatic motive that governs the sphere of everyday life. Certain boundaries are lifted—boundaries of space and time, boundaries of everyday definitions of the possible, boundaries of actuality. If God can tell the believer what to do and give the power to do it, then the believer can experience a sense of freedom from everyday concerns with "how to" and "in order to." Even religious statements about "what to do" take on an expressive function, in addition to the purely communicative one implied in the pragmatic mode. For example, when a woman stated during prayer meeting, "Let's sing 'For You Are My God.' The Lord wants us to sing it," she was not merely directing members to sing a song. Rather, the request was an expression of both the speaker's feelings and her belief that God moved her to sing that hymn. Boundaries of what is possible are changed, for even the basic premise of religious speaking among pentecostals implies such a dramatic change: it is possible for an ordinary Christian to be chosen as a vehicle for speaking "God's mind."

Concomitant with this expressive function, there is a decreased emphasis on the purely communicative functions of speaking. Those forms of religious speaking which make the strongest claims of divine authorship (prophecy and interpretation) are often especially vague, non-directive, or ambiguous.[36] This expressive function may account, in part, for the great deal of poetic, metaphorical, or allusory speech used.

This discussion of freedom is not to imply that pentecostal speakers operate without norms or responsibilities. Rather, the pentecostal community's rules of responsibility are transformed in the specific setting of the modified reality of the group. There exists a social context within which this changed relationship between speaker and speech is permitted and encouraged. The prayer group values God's speaking through its members. Given the alternate world view of the group, deviance is defined differently from the way it is defined in everyday life. Within the prayer group, deviance is defined as expressions of doubt—specifically doubt in God's authority and His expression of His will in and through the prayer group. The expression of doubt on the part of the individual member is indicated by a refusal to yield to special word-gifts—especially glossolalia. The larger group may also be considered culpable in its unwillingness to yield to or encourage word-gifts important to the community, especially prophecy.

Furthermore, there are specific pentecostal norms for religious speaking. For example, given the negative connotation of doubt, expressions of negative thoughts or failure are firmly discouraged in prayer meetings. There are also clear operative norms as to who may prophesy and how. Finally, there are definite ways of dealing with violation of those norms; the most significant form of sanction is the use of discernment. The role of discerner is to distinguish pronouncements of divine authorship from those deriving from other sources. The discerner confirms God's authorship of certain speech and institutes sanctions against those who claim divine authorship for speech from other sources.

Implicit in this practice of discernment is a theory as to what the other sources of pronouncements might be. All of the groups studied firmly believe that Satan is very powerful and is particularly concerned with confounding pentecostals and other highly committed Christians. Specifically, he is believed to be the source of much non-divine speaking. This dualism is understandable in light of the groups' strong emphasis on trust in God and the goodness of His gifts. In other words, if persons are speaking by an authority other than their own, but their pronouncements are discerned not to be good for the group, then the source of their speech must be "the Evil one."

Some prayer groups hold an additional theory of human weakness to account for invalid pronouncements. In those groups members are counselled to be attentive lest their speaking be from themselves rather than from God. Movement pamphlets explain that the Spirit gives a special "anointing" (experienced as a feeling of expectancy or anticipation) when the speaker should give God's message. Even with the anointing, however, members are cautioned to follow certain norms, such as waiting for an appropriate moment, taking turns, speaking in a proper tone of voice, and so on.[37] In other words, even valid divine speech is constrained by the social norms of the prayer meeting.

A third and highly significant function of such speech is borrowed authority which could not be gained from mere personal speech. Thus religious speaking is an indirect assertion of power. For example, glossolalic prayer serves to confirm the average believer's baptism in the Spirit, and glossolalic prophecy and prophecy in the vernacular serve to confirm the authority of the leaders. The gift of discernment confers authority on the sanctioning of deviant behavior and confirmation of valid speech is done on the authority of God. Religious speaking serves both to validate authority and to express authoritative statements. A prophetic statement is simultaneously an assertion of authority and an expression of an authoritative pronouncement.

The possibility of divine authorship of speech also alters the "hearing" or reception of spoken messages in the prayer group. Hearers are, for the most part, believers. Thus they desire to contribute to the group definition of the situation that God is present and communicating with the group. This role of hearer is not a passive one, but means that one is actively involved in promoting such valued speaking. This attitude toward hearing implies a number of differences from "ordinary" hearing.

One result is that the hearers (individually or collectively) attempt to impose an interpretation on spoken words, even the most difficult to understand statements. For example, a testimony about some seemingly irrelevant theme, or a Scripture choice of some esoteric passage, would become the object of meditation, a seeking for deeper meaning to the statement. In this connection, the hearers often actively imposed metaphorical, allusory, and poetic expectations on the content of religious speech. For example, one woman claimed that God had given her the "gift of knowledge" that He wanted the group to have a special prayer for the healing of eyesight. While the group did subsequently have a blessing of eyes (laying on hands) and prayer for healing, the immediate reaction to this "gift of knowledge" was several testimonies about the metaphorical significance of healing of sight. Samarin suggests that this kind of expanded expectation accounts for the sense of connection between a tongues-message and its interpretation, because the audience actively works to contribute meaning to the message.[38]

This imposition of allusory or poetic expectations on religious speech is partly a learned process. In Life in the Spirit seminars new members learn to reformulate experiences and ideas according to the meaning system of the group. Neophytes are encouraged to share descriptions of any events of God's power in their lives and then the seminar leader explains what that event "really means." If a member witnessed to some trivial aspect of life, for example, the leader would re-frame the testimony as an "example of how God touches every portion of our lives." Reading deeper meanings into human speech is not uncommon in non-pentecostal religious hearing. Most Christians, for example, take the words of the Bible as symbols of some deeper reality. This quality of belief in the Bible is quite similar to the pentecostals' belief in certain forms of religious speaking—both are considered to be of divine authorship. Thus pentecostals believe that if the overt meaning does not make sense or is not especially significant, then God must have intended a deeper meaning. The hearers, then, must exert themselves to discover this deeper significance. As such, religious hearing becomes an active role.

Another result of the altered source of religious speaking is that hearers tend to focus on the expressive intent, rather than the details of logic and content. Thus religious hearing, as well as speaking, is highly expressive. For example, confirmations of prophecies often focused on the apparent expressive intent of the prophetic message rather than the detailed content. Witnessing was respected for the feelings expressed rather than for the details, and so responses to witnessing tales freely reinterpreted the content.

This emphasis is not inevitable, since (theoretically) any first-person expressions of "the mind of God" ought to be significant in content as well as intent. The strenuous de-emphasis of content persists among Catholic pentecostals (as well as other diverse religious groups, such as the Jesus people, Divine Light Mission, Spiritualists, and Jehovah's Witnesses), partly because of the strong belief that the human mind gets in the way of the real truth. One respondent stated firmly that unless a person had received a special charism such as the "gift of wisdom" or "knowledge," a prophecy would be seriously distorted by concentrating on its content. The appropriate reception of prophecy, as well as other forms of religious speaking, is to meditate on the broader meaning of the words, incuding the expressive elements.

Part of this expressiveness in religious hearing is due to the fact that this hearing is selective—members of the audience tune in to those parts of the statement that strike a responsive chord. This is similar to the reception of speaking at a political rally. Such audiences are actively seeking—not primarily to be informed—but to be inspired. The inspiration process is, understandably, more fragmentary and disconnected than the information process. In other words, hearers selectively hear not merely those ideas or thoughts they want to hear, but, indeed, are often satisfied to hear single words or phrases rather than whole ideas. As Zaretsky points out, in his analysis of listening during Spiritualist services, many members seem to regard certain referents "only as a stimulation to cathect with their own thoughts, visions, and spiritual concerns."[39]

Religious hearing involves listening to speakers, not with an intent to disprove their statements, but with the intent to confirm and build upon their speech. Thus hearers do not notice mistakes or "communication out of character."[40] For example, no attention was paid when one leader slipped from first to third person in pronouncing a prophecy. Hearers ignore fallacies in witnessing and reinterpret seemingly meaningless pronouncements. This mode of hearing is directly related to the problem of validating religious speaking. "Validation" here refers to the necessity for any group to decide which acts fit into any given large group of special (valued or disvalued) acts, so they can respond accordingly. It means audience-classification of an act and, on the basis of this classification, acceptance of the actor and the actor's claims. This need for validation is particularly acute for several forms of religious speaking. For example, the prayer group must decide which are valid instances of glossolalia in baptism in the Spirit, which are valid prophecies and interpretations of tongues, which testimonies and teachings are valid instances of inspired speech, and so on.[41]

For the most part, members of Catholic pentecostal prayer groups are quite ready to validate the claims of any member (even new members) if the claims fit into the already established pattern of speaking and acting in that group. Almost any kind of verbal activity is accepted as glossolalia, so long as members use their tongues for personal praise rather than prophecy. Samarin suggests that this acceptance results because members "approve it on nonlinguistic grounds; the person's total behavior is accepted in the immediate religious context."[42] It is likely that this kind of acceptance is actually a conscious effort to reassure members that their Spirit-baptism was genuine. Since personal use of tongues in prayer is purely private, aiding individuals in their spiritual growth and ability to pray, the prayer group can afford to be generous in its validation of this form of speaking. Other forms are public, so the group needs to be more cautious.

Even with these public pronouncements, however, hearers are seldom willing to judge a contribution as meaningless, irrelevant, or wrong. The more toward the ecstatic end of the continuum the speaking appears to be, the less likely regular members of the prayer group are to judge it, even privately. Since such speech might possibly be from God or, at least, inspired by Him, the prayer group listens carefully—reinterpreting, or imposing meaning, if necessary. For this reason the leadership often imposes firm controls over who is allowed to speak the more dramatic forms of ecstatic speech. Nevertheless, unless specifically discerned to be invalid (which rarely occurs publically), many irregular statements go unchallenged in prayer meetings, and individual hearers allow that these statements are probably true and inspired by God.

In the sphere of everyday life, speaking is regularly judged, partly because of the pragmatic motive of everyday communication. Advice given is judged by the hearers as good or bad; facts related are judged as accurate or inaccurate; tales told are judged as fanciful, probable, or lies, and so forth. In the prayer groups, however, much speech (such as witnessing, confirmation, and the like) is irrelevant, fanciful, of doubtful accuracy, offbeat, or just strange by everyday rules of judgment. For example, one woman testified to having laid hands upon a leaking faucet to cure it; another member's confirmation of a Scripture reading involved an inaccurate hearing of a key word in the text; another testimony involved a detailed mathematical calculation of the number who would be saved on the Last Day; and many speakers' witnessing involved interpretations differing from official Catholic pentecostal teachings. Respondents indicated privately that they did not believe the factual content of all such statements, but still valued them as meaningful.

Especially in relatively open groups, there appears to be a strong norm against challenging the validity of a member's testimony.[43] A simple element is ordinary tact, but tactfulness does not begin to account for the strength of this norm. One interpretation of this latitude is that the testimony is heard as an expression of commitment to the group and its belief system (see Chapter 3). An expansion of this idea would be to interpret the validation of these testimonies as an expression of communion between participants.[44]

Another factor may be at work, however, in the ready validation of testimonies. It may be that to challenge members' witnessing would be to strike at the heart of what holds the community together, and thus be a threat to its very existence. Schutz states that "Reciprocal understanding and communication already presuppose a community of knowledge, even a common surrounding world (and social relationships) and not the reverse," and "Only upon such a transcendental *We* can a community be founded."[45] A religious group bases its sense of community on the presupposition of a shared religious experience. Every instance of witnessing in the prayer group, therefore, is a reference back to that underlying shared experience; thus, witnessing is a very potent source of group unity. On the other hand, there is an underlying concern that perhaps the referent experience is *not* the same. In other words, how do individual members know that their crucial experience of God (which is, by definition, largely subjective) is really like that which other members individually have had? The only way one member can know what another has experienced is through the communication of that experience in formal or informal witnessing. But to raise the question about whether the experiences of all members have the same central referent is too threatening to the unity of the community, and so strong norms develop against any comment on the validity of these testimonies. Thus members benignly accept—and even confirm—each others' witnessing, turning their attention away from problem aspects and focusing upon the expressive intent of the speaker.

All of the above aspects of hearing religiously show clearly that the receivers of religious speaking are far from being a passive audience. Rather, in the pentecostal setting, hearing means being actively involved in receiving religious speech in accordance with the group's alternate definition of reality.

Conclusion

Among Catholic pentecostals certain forms of speaking and certain attitudes of hearing are dramatically different from speaking and hearing in the sphere of everyday life. Glossolalia is merely one, relatively minor, instance of these modes. Pentecostal belief in the possible divine authorship of much religious speaking radically alters the relationship between speakers and their speech, resulting in a different sense of responsibility for what they say, a concomitant freedom from everyday constraints in speaking, increased potential for the expressive functions of speech, and a borrowed authority for their words. Not only does the pentecostal context alter religious speaking, but hearing also is conducted with different attitudes. Religious hearing serves to contribute to the definition of the situation that God is present and communicating with the group. Thus hearing religiously involves a readiness to validate speakers' claims, not looking for slips, and not disproving the speaker. Rather, hearers focus on the expressive intent of the speech, and actively impose metaphorical, allusory, and poetic expectations on the content.

This analysis has described some of the ways everyday, taken-for-granted, modes of speaking and hearing can be altered fundamentally in a given religious setting. Within this setting, and given these altered relationships, certain kinds of anomalous behavior (prophecy and glossolalia) become understandable. Attempts to analyze religious speaking and hearing need to appreciate the radical differentness of the under-

lying assumptions of the religious sphere of reality. One such belief—
that God gives them their speech—makes the speaking and hearing of
Catholic pentecostals appear to be anomalous, but the ultimate evaluation of that belief is not sociologically available.

Six—
Wholeness,
Holiness,
and
Healing

The development of religious healing practices within the Catholic pentecostal movement is an understandable product of its belief system, and analysis of these beliefs and practices is critical for a sociological interpretation. It is a predictable development, not only because of the historical precedents from classical pentecostalism and the numerous Scriptural references to healing,[1] but especially because healing is intimately linked with two key elements of the belief system: order and power. Any sociological interpretation of religious healing in pentecostalism must take into account the full sociological implications of these two themes. The theme of order is very important for an understanding of healing practices, because suffering and death are probably the most order-threatening experiences of human existence.[2] Questions about "how could God permit? . . ." are age-old, but they take on even greater significance for any group whose members believe that God touches their daily lives in miraculous ways. One of the main experiences characteristic of the pentecostal movement is a sense of being in touch with God's power—whether through ordinary personal prayer, or more strongly, through the various "gifts of the Spirit" such as prophecy. It is a logical extension of this relationship to God's power to include the area of healing. Indeed (as argued in Chapter Seven) power is one of the key concepts for a sociological interpretation of any system of healing—not just religious healing.

The beliefs and practices described in this chapter can be termed "faith healing";[3] this is consistent with Catholic pentecostal usage. Some Catholic pentecostals, however, do not agree with theological implications that faith itself produces the healing nor with the stereotypical image of the faith healer.[4] In order to achieve a radically sociological perspective in this phenomenon, it is necessary to discard some common misconceptions. One is that faith healing is merely an alternative healing practice, something to which people resort when all else fails. For most Catholic pentecostals in a group with a healing ministry, faith healing implies a totally different definition of medical reality, an alternative etiology of illness, and a specific theory of health, deviance, and healing power. Thus in order to fully understand the process it is necessary to delve into members' root conceptions of health and illness and to ask questions which explore all functions of healing practices and beliefs.

We must also set aside the assumption that the medical reality as promulgated by the dominant health specialists in this culture is necessarily the true reality. From a sociological perspective, the medical definition must be seen as one among many competing conceptions of illness, its causes, and treatment. It is interesting that sociologists have adopted a relativistic stance in their studies of religion, family, and political systems, but few sociologists of health and illness have bracketed the assumptions of the Western medical establishment.[5] Such oversight is probably due largely to the success of the medical profession in establishing itself as an arbiter of definitions of reality in this society.[6] Its success in getting its viewpoint taken for granted has been so great that even professional students of "definitions-of-reality" fail to see that medical reality, too, is socially constructed. Explaining one belief system in terms of another may be a useful legitimating device, but does not really explain. For example, to say faith healing worked in A's case because it included X, Y, and Z from psychotherapy, may be an accurate parallel but does not *explain* either belief system.

Faith Healing "Works"

One of the first questions people ask about faith healing is "Does it work?" The assumptions underlying this question are problematic, because this type of healing is not merely a technique, and there are several different senses of the word "work." The key functions of all medical systems include, not only healing practices *per se*, but also: construction of the illness experience, cognitive management of the illness experience (through categorization and explanation), and management of death.[7] Faith healing is clearly successful in all of these meaning-providing senses of the word. Indeed, part of the appeal of this kind of medical system is that, unlike modern "scientific" medicine, faith healing creates no sharp dichotomy between meaning-providing elements and healing practices.

Traditional ("non-scientific") medical systems succeed because they are effective in providing meaning and they provide empirical proofs in support of their explanations. The nature of such proofs is that the sickness episode is consistent with the expectations of the participants.[8] If the quality of the evidence supporting the success of faith healing is broad enough to incorporate those proofs which are meaningful to the participants, they can accurately affirm that faith healing works.

Most analyses of faith healing have viewed it only as a technique rather than an entire system of medical knowledge.[9] Most have assumed the criteria of the Western medical paradigm; that is, they have accepted Western medicine's definition of health, illness, and healing as a baseline against which faith healing is evaluated.[10] Few studies take seriously the claims of faith healing to have influence over biophysical illness, but many are willing to allow its possibilities in the realm of psychological problems. This perspective gives rise to a number of studies which treat faith healing and other non-scientific medical systems as "primitive psychotherapy."[11]

Even fewer authors have analyzed the relationship between faith healing and socio-cultural bases of illness. Some anthropologists have pointed out the significance of this relationship in other cultures[12] and in subcultures of Western societies.[13] Studies which utilize a socio-cultural perspective point to a number of interpretations of faith healing which the more narrow biophysical or psycho-therapeutic interpretations miss.[14] A comprehensive analysis of the ways in which faith healing is successful must go beyond usual assumptions about what it means to say a medical system succeeds. It needs to take into account biophysical, psychological, and socio-cultural aspects of illness and healing.

The literature on faith healing and other marginal medical systems generally implies that these systems of belief and practice are characteristic mainly of the lower classes and less educated, that they are basically vestiges of earlier folk medicine, and are likely to wane as education and socio-economic levels increase.[15] Marginal medicine is sometimes viewed as the poor person's alternative to expensive medical care.[16] Some authors state that certain systems of therapy might be adequate for simple (folk) societies, but are not suitable for modern Western society.[17] Nevertheless, the acceptance of what might be broadly categorized as "alternative medical systems" or "marginal medicine" by many middle-class persons raised the generally unresearched issue: Does the root conception of health and illness held by middle-class persons really resemble the officially promulgated one? It is entirely probable that the congruity is less than social scientists have supposed.

For this reason, it is difficult to say for certain whether belief in alternative medical systems represents a deviation from the belief system into which persons were initially socialized. It is entirely possible that many middle-class, relatively well-educated persons were socialized into a set of medical conceptions that are neither officially acceptable nor internally consistent: a curious mixture of elements of folk beliefs, religious explanations, partially-understood "scientific" explanations, superstition, recipe-knowledge for everyday situations, mass media caricatures, and cocktail-party versions of "pop" therapeutic concepts. In light of these empirical issues, the study of Catholic pentecostal faith healing is especially interesting; these groups are middle-class, moderately well-educated, and generally not the "type" social scientists would expect to be attracted to an alternative medical system.

Development of Catholic Pentecostal Healing Practices

In the early stages of the movement's development, healing was acknowledged as one of the gifts of the Spirit, and prayers of petition for healing were common in regular prayer meetings and private prayers.[18] Nevertheless, most prayer groups hesitated to pray for healings and were ambivalent about faith healing in classical Protestant pentecostalism. A major change began in 1974, dramatically highlighted by the prominence of faith healing at the movement's annual International Conference, attended by some 25,000 persons.[19] Father Francis MacNutt, one of the leaders of that mass healing service, became the movement's chief spokesperson on healing ministries.[20]

The resulting flood of Catholic pentecostal literature [21] proclaimed that healing is central to the Christian message and, therefore, the "healing ministry"[22] should be a regular part of every prayer community. Two of the nine groups studied in this research were chosen specifically because they had highly developed healing ministries. Of the other seven groups studied, three developed extensive healing ministries; three others continued to include petitions for healing in regular prayer meetings but did not extend either the scope or settings for such prayer; and the remaining group was generally uncomfortable with faith healing. Highly developed healing ministries were found mainly in larger groups where core members gave healing activities high priority (as compared with, for example, teaching or writing). The focus of the following chapters will be on those groups with relatively well-developed healing ministries, but many of the qualities of these beliefs and practices apply to other groups as well. Prayers for healing are very common in the groups studied and many members claim to have experienced multiple healings. This frequency is in sharp contrast with Pattison's findings in a classical pentecostal group in which faith healing appears to have become highly routinized and uncommon.[23]

Catholic pentecostals practice faith healing in many contexts: prayer meetings, mass rallies, special "healing Masses," smaller home-centered "share" groups, informal interpersonal settings, special visitations of the sick (especially by Eucharistic ministers within a parish), and private prayer. The groups with developed prayer ministries had a special prayer room for individual needs. This prayer room, together with visitations of the sick, accounted for the main activities of the prayer-ministry team of core members (also called "healing ministers").

The prayer room is for all types of prayer requests; in groups which emphasize various kinds of healing, however, requests for healing are predominant. Leaders of these prayer ministries cautioned against assuming that the healing required is solely physical or emotional. They said that many times the individual initially presents only the surface of a much deeper problem. Using only the problems presented, however, the following is the range of frequency of prayer requests in the prayer room in several groups: physical healing, 30–50 percent; mental/emotional healing, 30–40 percent; healing of relationships, 10–30 percent; God's favor in job-, education-, social-, or financial-related matters, 5–15 percent; guidance in decision-making, 0–5 percent; general or vague requests, 5–10 percent. Furthermore, many persons come to request prayer for someone else. One prayer minister said:

> I see it as a sign of growth that more and more people are coming in to request prayer for themselves. We have no hesitance to ask the Lord to help our loved ones, but we are either too proud to ask for ourselves or we think there's some virtue in not praying for our own benefits. Our prayer room used to get nine of every ten requests for others. Now, I'm not knocking praying for others, but I think it's a good thing that we are now getting as many as a third requesting prayer for themselves.

A composite sketch of what occurs in the prayer room is helpful in showing the place of healing in a prayer group. The regular prayer meeting is over and most members stay to chat over coffee. During the prayer meeting one of the leaders had announced that the prayer room would be open in the library down the hall, and the three prayer ministers go there to wait. They are women, ranging in age from mid-thirties to mid-fifties, and all have been active core members for several years. They sit on library chairs in a small circle with a vacant chair almost inviting someone to complete the circle. After several minutes a woman comes in and closes the door behind her. Joining the prayer ministers, she explains that she had had recurrent splitting headaches that have disrupted her everyday life. The team invites her to join them in a period of praising the Lord. They continue the prayer, even after she ceases; they ask the Lord for guidance and enlightenment in praying with them. One minister begins to pray in tongues briefly and then the prayer ends. They ask the woman if she has anything further to share about her request and she cannot think of anything to add. One prayer minister "receives" a Biblical text about trusting the Lord. Another suggests that she should regularly "hand over" every worry and concern to the Lord in her daily prayer, adding that sometimes people are not even aware of the matters that bring on physical problems like headaches, but that it is a good idea to "turn these over" to the Lord anyhow. The prayer ministers then pray over her. The two sitting next to her lean over and put their hands on her arm and hand; the third member rises and stands behind her with both hands on her shoulders. They pray briefly, one minister praying in tongues. When the prayer ends, they remain touching for a few seconds and then move away. The woman thanks them and leaves.

Three others enter, one by one, during the next twenty minutes. One woman requests prayer for improving her relationship with her thirteen-year-old daughter; she receives similar counselling, spiced with much warm sympathy and humorous anecdotes of one minister's similar experiences. The atmosphere is friendly and casual, as perhaps a session around a neighbor's kitchen table might be. Another woman comes to request prayer for her sister in another state who is about to undergo an operation. There is no discussion with this request— only the prayers and assurances of continued concern. The last person who comes in requests prayer to overcome her fear of being alone in the house. Her husband's new job has required him to be away more often and she cannot bear to be left alone. In their initial prayer, the prayer ministry "has a clear sense" that her problems are deeper than the fear itself, but feels the Lord has not "given them exact guidance" about her needs. They pray fervently for her request, but the prayer is very broad and includes statements that the "Lord cast out the spirit of fear" (a mild form of exorcism). They urge her to come again to be prayed with, suggesting that when the Lord gives them clear guidance about her needs, the prayer will be more effective.

This capsule description is typical of most prayer room ministries, except that in some groups individual members of the prayer ministry are believed to have received special "gifts of the Spirit" which enhance their healing ministry. One of the most important of these is the "gift of discernment." In the healing ministry the gift of discernment enables a prayer minister to tell which problems are from which sources, since clear discernment of the "real" problem enables the group to focus its power. Sometimes discernment also refers to the Spirit-given ability to discern the presence or activity of evil spirits, but this is a more specialized kind of prayer ministry than most groups studied employed. Two other special gifts were considered to be closely related: the "gift of faith" and the "gift of knowledge." The gift of faith was distinguished from ordinary faith which presumably all Christians are given; it refers to a special ministry-gift enabling one to pray with complete confidence in the successful outcome. This gift is often inspired by the gift of knowledge, through which God reveals His will to heal in a specific situation. The more general gift of healing may incorporate all of the special gifts described above; it refers to the particular gift given to some enabling them to heal directly as God's vehicle.[24] The parallel with the gift of prophecy is useful. Prophecy is to ordinary inspired speaking as the gift of healing is to ordinary prayers for healing. Both the gifts of prophecy and healing are believed to be God acting directly through human vessels. Ordinary inspired speaking and ordinary prayers for healing are still valued but are considered to be less powerful because they are not directly from God. Some persons with this specialized gift of healing have received it only for certain areas of healing. For example, one healing minister claimed a special gift for inner healings but felt she had no special gift for purely physical healings.

The Healing Process

As the above instances show, Catholic pentecostals seek many different types of healing. Each type of healing is keyed to a different root cause, which is why discernment of causes is sought before the healing prayer is begun. Thus in the description of the prayer ministry above, a distinction between diagnostic and therapeutic actions may be made, even though the overt action in both is the same: prayer. In the diagnostic procedure (especially discernment), prayer is directed toward being enlightened by the Lord as to the real nature of the problem. In other words, the prayer ministers seek categories into which the problem fits and according to which they can focus their further action. Unless a member were believed to have the gift of discernment, this discernment is done through "the body" (that is, the whole ministry team rather than one member). The diagnosis alone is a significant way in which faith healing works. It provides a way of explaining events and experiences; it gives meaning to unstructured and problematic episodes; it locates the problem firmly within the belief system of the group. Because in all medical systems— including Western scientific medicine—disease definitions are socially constructed and socially sanctioned, these definitions entail commitments about how to deal with the illnesses.[25] Therefore, the process of diagnosis is critical in establishing which set of socially established approaches shall be invoked in any given instance.

Diagnostic Methods

It is important to see the transformative nature of all medical diagnoses. "Signs" (behavioral or biophysical expressions) are transformed into "symptoms" (socially understandable indicators of a specific category of illnesses).[26] In this transformation process, some signs are discarded or recede in importance; others are expanded or elicited. The symptoms are not, therefore, merely products of the illness itself, but are rather socially constructed, fitting into pre-existing socially available categories of meaning. Diagnostic action typically involves a social interaction (even if mediated by technological devices) between the healer, or healers, and the person presenting a problem; the healer guides or controls the interaction toward constructing the diagnosis.[27] In the case of faith healing, and other healing with a strong supernatural base, the diagnostic stages may sometimes seem to be passed over through direct divine action (especially likely in mass healing meetings). Nevertheless, the diagnostic processes are very important functions; in some cases discernment of the causes of illness may even be more important for the individual or group than the actual therapeutic actions which follow.[28]

The influence of the Lord's actions is not limited to guiding the discernment process but is believed to figure importantly in the preparation of the ministers for discerning and healing. One member said:

> We believe that praying according to His will is what brings the most provident results, and we may be requesting one thing and He may see the need in another way . . . I find that the Lord would prepare us. Like, during the day, if you'd pray, there'd be Scripture, or maybe there'd be someone you'd be talking to and . . . you wouldn't see anything special in it and then, later when someone came in [to the prayer room], you'd realize that—hey!—you know, our minds had already been prepared for them in a sense . . . It isn't as though you realize that you're going to need that later on, but . . . He sends us very, very little that we haven't been prepared for.

Members also believe the Lord is acting directly, showing people areas that need help and inspiring them as to the sources of healing they should seek out. Members cited instances of being guided by the Lord to certain Scriptural passages that aided in a healing, being led to certain experiences or relationships that promoted a healing, being directed to seek certain doctors, or to change doctors, and so on.

Catholic pentecostals distinguish four basic types of illness, each with a different root cause. There is a corresponding appropriate healing prayer for each type. MacNutt gives a highly refined explanation of these categories. Ordinary members studied used similar categories but they attached different meanings to each type. MacNutt explains the following types of illness: (1) physical illness in our bodies, caused by disease or accidents, (2) emotional illness and problems (for example, anxiety) caused by the emotional hurts of our past [other authors also include relationships that are disrupted or hurt], (3) sickness of our spirit, caused by our own personal sin, (4) demonic oppression, which may result in physical, emotional, or spiritual illnesses. Prayer methods appropriate for each of these are: (1) prayer for physical healing, (2) prayer for inner healing ["healing of memories" is one special form of this], (3) prayer for repentance, (4) prayer for deliverance (exorcism). MacNutt adds that Sacraments and sacramentals of the Church (especially penance, anointing of sick, and exorcism) are appropriate therapeutic approaches in conjunction with these methods.[29]

Many prayer group members emphasized that it is impossible to separate the emotional, physical, and spiritual areas of a person's well-being, and they criticized the medical profession for trying to do this. A holistic approach did not, however, prevent the Catholic pentecostals from distinguishing among the different types of healing. Most persons interviewed felt that physical healings were the least important type. Many members stated that there were very few purely physical illnesses. One respondent said, "Your physical healings are really a result of other things that are being healed. I think one goes with the other."

Emotional healings and "healings of memories" figure prominently in the Catholic pentecostal scheme, and Fichter[30] correctly relates this particular form to the entire conversion process. Emotional healing is believed to release one from the "bondage" of numerous hurtful past experiences in order to enter into a fuller Christian life, and so this form of healing, together with repentance, is important in enhancing members' commitment[31] (see Chapter 8). MacNutt includes the healing of emotions and memories, but other Catholic pentecostals include the healing of relationships (for example, a family feud). The broadness of this category of illness allows for treating every imaginable feeling: fear, anxiety, anger, doubt, sense of worthlessness, depression, shyness, pride, jealousy, and so on. Some members interviewed included one's opinions and thoughts as needing healing in this area. For example, one woman said, "You have to heal not only for health, but healing of thoughts and minds and that's why I feel it [healing] is so important. You know, your opinions, that you really get the right opinions. You have to pray to the Lord and ask Him to guide you and direct you and lead and heal your opinions and your feelings towards people and things like that."

Members described spiritual healings usually in conjunction with some other type of healing. For example, one member stated, "I asked for a healing of my stomach problems, and He showed me that I needed to repent of all my pent-up anger and unforgiveness." Another said, "Before I could be healed in my relationship with my son, I had to repent of the pride that kept me from getting close to him." Prayer ministers generally consider spiritual healings to be more important than did ordinary members. One prayer ministry team included prayer for repentance as part of every healing prayer, because they felt it was so often a fundamental cause of illness.

Exorcism, or what is termed more broadly the "deliverance ministry," is far less common and considered to be a special ministry. Ordinary exorcism is distinguished from the official exorcism of the Church, for which specially appointed priests are required.[32] Ordinary exorcism occurs routinely in Catholic pentecostal prayer meetings as a precaution against the influence of evil spirits. It is often used by individuals to protect themselves in ambiguous situations (for example, some respondents in this research prayed prayers of exorcism before being interviewed).

In the context of a healing ministry, ordinary exorcism is considered important when the person seeking help is possibly being harassed by evil spirits (that is, oppression rather than possession by evil spirits). One prayer team "head" explained:

> I haven't had experience with [the deliverance ministry], but it is very much a part of healing. Sometimes you realize that there is an area under the control of evil spirits. We [Our prayer group] don't have a deliverance ministry, but we do pray a simple prayer of deliverance which anyone is capable of. Sometimes you do get a sense—like one time a person had such unnatural fear—that possibly it was a harassment by evil spirits—not a possession. They [evil spirits] get into a natural weakness and use it against us. I explained this to the person and took authority over the evil spirits, because they do have a way of stifling, harassing. It is simple to just take authority because Jesus has given us this authority, but deliverance is a special ministry. . . . If the person needed deliverance—if the body [prayer team] discerned this—we could, on the spot, take authority over any and all evil spirits and then we would take this up with the pastoral team and we would speak the truth with the person and put

them in touch with someone who could help them—such as Father ———. He has a real deliverance ministry.

Although healing ministries that deal with evil spirits have not developed as extensively as other kinds of healing, they provide a potent ritual expression of the dualistic belief system and fulfill important functions for the whole group.[33]

Therapeutic Methods

Healing techniques may be distinguished from the larger concept of healing method. Techniques are important in the Catholic pentecostal movement and some have become institutionalized healing practices. Different prayer methods refer to a more general focus of prayer according to root cause, as described above. Persons involved in the prayer ministries studied cautioned against considering various prayer techniques to be necessary. One woman asserted, "The way we pray with people is important, but we mustn't box God in. He can choose to heal however and whatever He wishes. The Lord usually follows certain patterns, which is why we pray according to certain patterns, but we can't say for sure that any one way is necessary."

In general, persons active in prayer ministries tended to emphasize the faith of the healing ministers or an atmosphere of faith as very important for success.[34] This is well expressed by one experienced prayer minister:

> What's important is the faith-filled atmosphere. A person of very weak faith can come in where there are three or four people who are confident in their faith, and that in itself is faith-building, can provide the necessary atmosphere. But if you've got a bunch of people questioning, throwing cold water on everything, then you're not as likely to have a healing. But then I'm not going to limit the Spirit, who blows where He wills! At the same time, if I have faith, I should share it with you and let the Lord use that so more healing will occur in a faith-filled atmosphere.

Another prayer minister added that she believed that the Lord honors the faith of the group, even if they are misguided about how to pray.

By contrast, regular members were more likely to emphasize the faith of the person being prayed for.[35] This attitude was often correlated with a tendency to view prayer for healing as an individual activity, while prayer team members were more likely to see it as typically situated in a group context. Regular members were more inclined to consider faith as necessary for healing, whereas prayer ministers were concerned lest the individual feel guilty over lack of faith.

A number of respondents felt that it was often necessary to "claim one's healing" in order to experience healing. This practice, borrowed from classical pentecostal faith healing, refers to a stance of strong confidence on the part of the person prayed for that the healing has, in fact, already occurred. One member, for example, described how she had sought healing for her recurring ear infections, but had come down with another one and returned to the prayer room for further healing. Although the prayer ministers did pray again with her, one of them "had a word of knowledge" that she had been already healed the first time and needed only to claim that healing. So every time she gets any symptoms of earaches she re-claims that healing. In this conceptualization of the process of healing, the actual healing and the experience of healing are clearly separated. A similar sense of efficacy of individual faith is evident in the frequent use of Oral Roberts's concept of "seed faith." For example, one respondent said, "With seed faith, I had to pray for other people. But I made that pact, that blessed pact with the Lord: I pray for these people, knowing that You will give it back to me. In three weeks time, the healing started to come . . . the Lord said: if you want the healing, you've got to do something for it. Not only praying, you've got to do something." Other factors that members believed to contribute to the efficacy of healing include various techniques and settings: the laying on of hands, visualization and other imagery, use of special objects, Scripture, glossolalic prayer, and Sacraments. Members exhibited three characteristic orientations to these factors: human, spiritual, or magical. Instances of all three orientations were found in members' attitudes toward every technique or setting—including the Sacraments.

The human approach is exemplified by one member's evaluation of laying on of hands for healing:

> It's not important in healing, but I think it's a good thing because I think we tend to be enclosed in ourselves. And I think that when somebody touches you, that there's communication in touch. I think it's a very basic instinctive kind of thing. And I think it's good because it does communicate love. A lot of people don't like to be touched and that's a psychological thing of their own rejection of themselves and you know there's a lot of acceptance in having somebody touch you.

The spiritual orientation is illustrated by another woman's evaluation, "It's [laying on hands] definitely important. I think . . . it's almost like cobalt; it's like the power of the Lord working through the person who's laying on hands and then it's through the hands directed into the person who's being prayed for and it's just like the Spirit, the power of the Lord going through that person right into the other person." Sometimes the borderline between the spiritual and the magical orientation was unclear, but a magical orientation is well exemplified by one woman who witnessed in prayer meeting that the power in laying on of hands was so great that Christians should use it for everything that is "not right." She had used this technique on her cat, her checkbook, and her broken doorbell.

Almost all members interviewed felt that laying on of hands was very important for the success of the healing, but only a few considered it to be essential. These latter persons were more likely than the others to believe that the power to heal was given only to specific persons and that laying on of hands could not be done effectively by just anyone. By contrast, the large majority of persons interviewed emphasized the democratization of the power to heal. Although they felt that some persons were blessed with special gifts of healing (healers often mentioned were Kathryn Kuhlman, Oral Roberts, and Francis MacNutt), they emphasized the power (albeit lesser power) of the prayer of ordinary Christians. They contrasted this "discovery" with their prior notion that healing was something totally extraordinary, done only by the Saints. For example, one woman stated:

> In fact, people now are keeping olive oil in their house that's blessed and anointing their children when there's sickness or anything. I see that down the road as really a ministry of the laity, rather than the hierarchy of the church. That could be complete heresy [laughter]. That's what I would like to see, though. I think after a period of time, it will just become so natural. I think it will just become a natural thing.

Some of those who felt laying on of hands was very important had additional notions about how it should be practiced. Several cautioned that one should always seek "the Lord's discernment" about where to focus their prayer, so that the prayer's effectiveness would not be dissipated. This discernment meant not only guidance as to whether the root cause was physical, emotional, spiritual, or from evil spirits; it also meant seeking concrete direction as to which portions of the body were afflicted and what was the appropriate prayer mode. Words, thoughts, and touch should then be directed to those discerned parts. For example, one of the groups was praying with a person with extensive cancer. They felt they had clear direction to pray in the area of the chest, even though the cancer was apparently more widespread throughout the body. The group then focused prayer accordingly, and were pleased that the person experienced much relief from congestion and pain in that area. Such elaborations were typically described by members of healing ministries. Another elaboration was that for certain ailments (such as headaches) you should not touch the afflicted body part because that would make it worse. Also, if you are praying in a group and you cannot all touch the person to be healed (as in cramped quarters), it is just as satisfactory to form a chain of touching such that all persons praying are conducting the laying on of hands through each other to the sick person. A further suggestion was that, in praying for children or anyone, for that matter, who would not understand and cooperate with usual healing prayer, one could lay on hands while they sleep.

Another large group of techniques supplemented prayer. These are generally techniques of visualization and imaging, by which the praying individual focuses the prayer through a recommended set of experiences. One prayer minister said: "I've learned a very good way of doing this kind of prayer. I visualize them [the persons needing healing], and in my prayer I see them healed in praying for them. By visualizing this concrete healing, the prayer takes form. It's much more effective." Another explained, "Most of the time I would pray for a specific result. Sometimes I don't know what I should specifically pray for, then I would pray in tongues—that is called a soaking prayer. I soak the person in Jesus' love—just to see that person being soaked in His love. This way I figure I'm covering all grounds [laughter]."[36]

Prayer ministers recommended similar visualization and imaging in the "healing of memories"—a process of "getting in touch with" memories of past hurts, forgiving the hurt, and handing over the experience to the Lord. This healing of memories is considered important for anyone whose root problem is believed to be emotional or spiritual. It is also recommended as a technique for maintaining health, and some authors suggest using it daily; some recommend it in preparation for Confession.[37] Although prayer for healing of memories can be done by the individual alone, more typically the healing minister guides it. Two particular visualization/imaging processes are practiced by Catholic pentecostals: "calling forth" and "walking back." "Calling forth" refers to a prayer-process in which a painful memory is called forth into present consciousness and re-experienced, prayed for, and handed over to the Lord. "Walking back" is a process in which a prayer minister guides a person's recounting of memories from the present back to the time of conception. Whenever the person indicates sadness or anxiety, the minister guides the person to a fuller explication of the situation (remembering one's age and physical location, as well as relationships, etc.); each painful memory is prayed for separately to be healed.[38]

Such specific guidance in healing of memories was not practiced in the groups studied, but many members had participated in such guided visualization at charismatic conferences or at mass healing services. The following visualization was guided at one such large service:

> Members of the large audience had been told to relax and close their eyes; then they were to picture someone who had died with whom they had not been reconciled—someone who needed their forgiveness. Then the healing minister led the visualization in a quiet, almost hypnotic tone of voice: "Visualize Jesus . . . He tells you to walk with Him . . . and you get to a bridge . . . but you are afraid to cross that bridge . . . Jesus is holding you very securely . . . Now look at that person the Lord has revealed to you . . . that person needs you . . . that person may even have a chain around their body . . . it is heavy . . . Jesus is holding you securely . . . now Jesus puts his hand on your shoulder. . . . Suddenly something within you melts . . . and you say . . . I forgive you . . . and the person glows, rushes to you and embraces you. . . . Then Jesus steps into the center and embraces you both . . . You have freed another, so you have been freed . . . You stand tall and can smile."
>
> "Lord, only You can hear. Many of us are bruised by problems in life and in our past. We ask You, Jesus, to walk through the dark areas of us and shine your light. Replace the cobwebs with your love."[39]

In the groups studied, the healing of memories frequently focused on only one or two problematic areas which were suggested through the gift of knowledge (direction of the Spirit). Examples of memories healed included: being ignored by one's father, having hurt one's mother in childbirth, having been terrified by priests in the confessional, having hated a younger sister who died before being reconciled, having overheard one's mother say she wished she did not have six children (this person was the last born).

Rituals in Faith Healing

Healing rituals, whether in the context of a faith healing service or in a medical doctor's office, consist of two elements: things said and things done,[40] because healing ritual is aimed not only at effecting a cure but also at providing meaning. Modern medicine, partly because of its lack of interest in the meaning aspect, has highly truncated the "things said"; the "things done" are typically done *by* medical specialists *to* the person treated.[41] The major exception is the treatment of mental illness, in which "things said" are considered very important, because the problem of meaning is a central consideration.

Nevertheless, even highly technical medical procedures often have a ritual quality that increases their potency for performers and audience alike.[42]

"Things done" and "things said" are very important in healing rituals of Catholic pentecostals, although no single element is considered necessary. "Things done" include manipulation of objects, for example: the laying on of hands, "leg-lengthening" (ritually lengthening one, presumably shorter, leg to re-align the body), anointing with blessed oil, touching blessed water, holding a Bible, giving a blessing, making the sign of the cross, and keeping blessed objects (such as special cards) close to oneself.[43] In this context, then, it is possible to understand such objects as the blessed oil or the Communion host as medicine in the broadest sense of the word.[44] The application/ingestion of blessed substances—especially oil, salt, and water—has greatly increased among Catholic pentecostals, specifically because of healing practices. For example, in one group at the end of the monthly healing Mass, the priest announced he would bless whatever the people had brought. With a great rustling of brown paper bags, all the members produced large containers of mineral water, salad oil, and table salt, carefully opening all lids to make sure the blessing got in.

"Things said" include not only the words of formal prayer but also Scripture (especially inspired readings), words of advice or instruction (especially inspired "words of knowledge"), glossolalic prayer and song, hymns, prophecies, confirmations, and so on.[45] Unlike the practice of most medical doctors, pentecostal healing ministers would consider "things said" to be of great importance—not merely for encouraging the patient or inspiring hope, but in effecting the cure itself. According to their belief, there is power in the words said.

A related set of beliefs tells how to know when healing is accomplished. It is critical to realize that Catholic pentecostals treat *healing* as distinct from the *experience of healing*. Sometimes they believe a healing has already occurred but the person cannot experience it, because the healing has not been "claimed." Similarly, people often attest to having had an experience of healing even when the healing is not complete. For example, one woman shared at prayer meeting that she had received a healing of her hearing; it was much improved over what it had been a year earlier and she was continuing to pray for full restoration. Even though a condition continues, in Catholic pentecostal usage a healing has occurred if the person experiences partial improvement, relief from some of the discomfort of the condition, or even stabilization. This broad use of the term "healing" suggests that a wide variety of experiences may indicate that a healing had occurred. Furthermore, members believe that the Lord often gives some sign of accomplishment such as a "word of knowledge" that the person has been or is being healed or a "confirmation." Knowing when healing is accomplished requires linking events surrounding healing prayer with a much wider set of social and psychological experiences (for example, being "sent" tears as a sign of inner healing). These connections result in a complex narrative that is very important for understanding faith healing's capacity to bestow meaning.

Attitudes Toward the Dominant Medical System

Another set of related beliefs and practices pertain to Catholic pentecostals' attitudes toward and interactions with orthodox medical practices (doctors, hospitals, medication, surgery, and so on). The Catholic pentecostals studied lacked neither access to (geographically or financially) nor knowledge of standard medical practices—both usually assumed to be the main reasons why people turn to faith healing. Thus it was hypothesized that their beliefs and attitudes toward the medical establishment discourage their use of such services. While this hypothesis was partially confirmed, a mixed picture emerged from the data.

On the level of idealization, members generally believed that doctors were instruments of God in the ordinary healing process; therefore, the medical profession was respected, not on its own merit but rather as a vehicle for God's healing action. For example, one woman explained, "Oh, you consult the doctor for all illnesses. After all, the Lord is going to take care of every illness, but also, if you have cancer, for instance, you can't say the Lord is going to just heal me. You're going to need Jesus to go help that doctor take care of you. That's how I see it." Similarly, most members believed that a person who is seriously ill should get medical help and not shun medicine or other measures prescribed by the doctor. Also at the level of idealization, several members described what they would consider the perfect medical arrangement: a clinic/hospital staffed by Spirit-filled doctors and nurses, who interwove faith healing and Christian counselling with the technologically advanced methods of modern medicine (many cited the proposed medical school at Oral Roberts University as an example).

Assessing their practical experiences with medical professionals, however, members were far less positive. Attitudes toward the medical profession in general ranged from disappointment to outrage. Members who acknowledged that they would pray first and postpone consulting the doctor until absolutely necessary were also those with strongly negative opinions of the medical profession. Typical dissatisfactions include: too many doctors are in that profession only "for the money," treatment is too depersonalized, doctors do not really listen to patients, treatment is too specialized and fails to treat the whole person, doctors treat the symptoms and not the real causes of the problem, doctors are too likely to prescribe medications or surgery, too often doctors treat patients like children and do not explain things or include them in decisions. Respondents liberally illustrated these criticisms with anecdotes of unpleasant experiences.[46] Some respondents singled out mental health professionals, especially psychiatrists, as even worse; they saw psychotherapeutic interactions as being often altogether counter-productive—making the patient worse.[47] A physician whose actions are not guided by the Spirit would be merely less effective; an unguided psychiatrist would be very harmful.

A superficial look at these criticisms of the medical profession indicates that they do not differ in some ways from the opinions of most middle-class persons. There are unique aspects, however, to these pentecostals' criticisms. They comment that doctors often fail to treat the whole person, emphasizing that emotional and spiritual, as well as physical aspects, should be treated. Similarly, often they complain that "the doctor didn't know what was wrong with me." This description would imply an experiential base for their lack of confidence in doctors. While such statements must be accepted as descriptions of their true subjective experiences, they do not necessarily reflect other interpretations of the episode (for example, the doctor's). As one woman commented, "The doctor was this way and that way about the cause. He didn't know. He did explain it to me medically speaking, but I could see that it wasn't just that."

Many members interviewed were attracted to numerous non-religious marginal medical practices, such as chiropractic, natural foods, and mega-vitamin therapy. A relatively large percentage (roughly a fifth) had continued contact with one of several therapeutic groups (for example, Alcoholics Anonymous, various suburban-style psychotherapeutic groups, and smoke-stopping and weight-watching therapeutic groups). Another kind of group—not strictly therapeutic in nature—had particular influence on members of several groups: Marriage Encounter, an intensive, marathon-style group experience to enhance married couples' relationships. It is difficult to evaluate the significance of Catholic pentecostals' participation in these alternative therapeutic practices, because there is so little accurate data on the practices of comparable groupings of persons not in this movement. It is highly probable that belief and involvement in marginal and alternative medical systems are relatively widespread among suburban middle-class persons. Before the beliefs and practices of these Catholic pentecostals are assumed to be deviant, it is necessary to study the root conceptions of health and illness of the population upon which the norm is presumbaly based.

Definitions of Illness and Healing

One of the most serious problems with many studies of faith healing is the assumption that the concept of healing as used by pentecostals means the same thing as it does to the medical professional or to the "person on the street." Because of this misunderstanding, these studies miss the breadth of meaning in the practice of faith healing. The usual notion is that a person with a physical problem turns to faith healing either out of desperation or as a sign of total commitment to the pentecostal belief system. Actually, neither of these patterns characterize the members of the Catholic pentecostal groups studied.

Levels of Involvement in the Group

The meaning of healing changed as members became more deeply involved in the prayer group and its beliefs and practices. Furthermore, as members asserted, it is faith-building—an experience of healing produces faith in the process. The minority of pentecostal members who did not believe in faith healing at all were those who had no experience of healing. Members who did believe cited personal experiences of multiple healings (an average of four instances per interview, but this figure is low because the interviewer had to cut off some lengthy testimonies in order to continue the interview). Although most members stated that physical healings are the least important kind of healing, having experienced physical healing was strongly correlated with belief in faith healing.

What are the characteristics of these different levels of involvement? Initially, the member is already involved in the larger prayer group and is already persuaded of the pentecostals' approach to prayer and the existence of Spirit-given gifts of power. It is an understandable step to expand these beliefs to the power of healing. Members' first experience with faith healing was typically with a physical problem, for which they thought, "It's worth a try," or "Why not, I might as well request prayer for healing it." At this level, faith healing is perceived as another way of trying to solve a problem—an alternative technique. Many persons are not even particularly committed to the pentecostal belief system upon their first exposure to faith healing. For example, one woman felt drawn to join the prayer group because of the loving concern shown by the prayer ministers when they visited her husband in the hospital. She believed she was now able to understand what happened then, even though she was unaware of faith healing at the time. Similarly, a number of fringe members (especially those discussed as "cultic adherents" in Chapter 8) viewed faith healing as merely an alternative technique: that is, those who "knew" were able to use the technique when the need arose. One woman explained:

> I'm not into all that most folks here are, but I do believe in faith healing. I probably wouldn't go to their prayer ministry unless I had a desperate need, though, because they're into a whole big thing on healing. I'd prefer to go to a big healing service—like I went to Kathryn Kuhlman once a few years ago—because like, if it works, fine, and if not, you haven't got them thinking about you.

Nevertheless, most members defined healing broadly. The greater the member's involvement in movement ideology, the greater the expectation of healing in a wide variety of situations. This expectation led to more awareness of problems that might have previously been overlooked or lived with, such as tiredness and aches. One woman recounted:

> I've been prayed for for minor little things like toothaches and backaches and all sorts of minor things and I don't ever recall any miraculous cure . . . but you know, like what happens is you put it out of your mind, you forget about it and the next thing you know, it's gone. And I think there's just something very relaxing in putting your faith in God and your faith in your brothers and sisters. You've been prayed over, you've been ministered to by others. I don't know. It's just something that relaxes you so that even if the problem doesn't immediately go away, it doesn't bother you anymore.

Without prompting, respondents often mentioned books and articles they had read on the topic which had spurred them to consider the broader possibilities of healing. Most frequently mentioned were Oral Roberts and Kathryn Kuhlman (both classical Protestant faith healers); by contrast, specifically Catholic pentecostal sources (for instance, MacNutt and Scanlan) were cited only by prayer ministry leaders. Beliefs about healing held by ordinary members of the prayer groups varied widely from the official ones promulgated by the movement leadership.

At the most extensive level of involvement, faith healing is defined as a normal, regular process of Christian growth. The healing process includes discerning other areas needing healing. Thus "healing" means overcoming various problems of growth in emotional and spiritual, as well as physical, areas of life. One prayer minister said:

> I got the clear sense within myself that the Lord was promising to make me whole. This has been going on for the last three years, but it has accelerated in the last year. Right now, I am experiencing healing on all three levels: emotional, physical and spiritual. I gave my life over to the Lord, but when I have a problem, it means that I haven't given it over as fully as I should have. The Lord brings into your life the things you need for healing, all of us need healing. We all have emotional wounds and scars from our childhood. If it's the desire of your heart to give your life over to the Lord and you still keep having difficulties, then you need healing. In my own case, I had no idea how much healing I needed at first.

The underlying definitions of "healing" implicit in these various levels of involvement differ so greatly that one cannot speak of faith healing among Catholic pentecostals as though it were a unified set of beliefs and practices. Furthermore, the breadth of these conceptions shows clearly that faith healing does not refer to healing in the same sense as understood by non-believer doctors or lay persons. Some examples of diverse episodes may further elucidate the dramatic distinctiveness of what healing means to Catholic pentecostals.

Episodes Defined as Healings

What kinds of events are described as healings? What kinds of situations are described as needing healing? Members interviewed described experiences of past healings, healings currently being prayed for, and healings they felt they needed. One category of events described as healings includes a wide variety of experiences in which there was no prior sense of discomfort or negative condition; in other words, it is not necessary to feel bad—physically, emotionally, or spiritually, in order to have a healing. One man, for example, described going to a group leader with a theological problem (he could not relate to Jesus as the son of God but rather thought of him as a father); he was referred to the prayer ministry which prayed for a healing of memories regarding the man's relationship with his own father, after which he realized how much he must have been "hurting" without ever knowing it. This testimony can tell us nothing about whether the man actually had a psychological problem; it does illustrate, however, that a problem need not be the immediate object of the healing. Other events of healing in this category include: being healed of inability to appreciate the Mass, needing healing for a merely average degree of faith in Jesus, getting a promotion (confirmed faith), and finding money when financially desperate (confirmed faith). Most examples in this category tend to refer to vaguely spiritual types of healing.

Another broad category of episodes described as healings would be considered primarily "inner healing." Examples include: relief from anxiety or depression, healing of painful memories of relationships with parents, overcoming fears, losing self-centeredness, increased peace in life, becoming able to control anger, mending a relationship with someone, and improved self-image. It is important to appreciate the entire episode as it is recounted by a respondent, because these descriptions demonstrate the member's sense of all related factors, helpful influences, what the skeptics said, doubts overcome, signs experienced, and so on. For example, a narrative describing how a woman was healed of her fear of being alone in the house might include: descriptions of how often her husband had to be away, details of various ways she tried to avoid being alone, having mentioned it to her doctor and being told it was nothing, events perceived as leading up to deciding to ask for a healing, descriptions of relationships with certain members of the prayer group, relationships with others who derided her claim of being healed, experiences which tested her healing, and an event considered to be a sign of her healing. All of these elements are considered to be significant parts of the healing episode.

We must also consider healings categorized as "physical" in the context of whole episodes. Healings in this category ranged from mild maladies (colds, headaches, tiredness), to moderately serious problems (a deeply slit finger, frostbite, hepatitis, vision problems), to very serious or potentially very serious (cancer, peritonitis, loss of hearing). Catholic pentecostals would include as healing events which non-believers would attribute to merely natural or human agency. It is not inconsistent with their beliefs to see a healing where, for example, a person under medical care recovered sooner than expected. In theory, at least, it does not bother them that a doctor labels an unexplained cure as spontaneous remission, because "God can work that way, too —through the body's own power to heal itself." In practice, however, they are understandably more impressed by supernatural explanations of healing. Even in seemingly ordinary kinds of healing processes, however, they would see instances of divine intervention. The following examples are not uncommon in descriptions of healing episodes: the Lord led me to go to the doctor, the Lord urged me not to go to my regular doctor but rather to a chiropractor, the Lord guided me about which medicine to buy for my family, the Lord worked through the physician to help me better than was possible without the Lord, the Lord led the doctor to discover what was really wrong.

Another kind of episode is one which describes the need for a heal-ing, measures taken (such as medication, doctor's examination, or prayer), the apparent failure of the healing to occur, and the discovery that an unexpected healing had occurred in another area or to another person. One woman stated, "I think healings are always successful, but it might be your own healing when you're praying for healing for someone else." Learning to live positively with an irremediable handicap would also be considered a healing. Many episodes described fit the following model: "I felt bad and was sure I had X [something serious], so I prayed to the Lord, and I didn't feel bad anymore." One person said, "I tripped coming up the stairs and I was sure I broke my toe. I couldn't even put my foot down. And I cried, and then said, 'why am I crying, all I have to do is pray.' And He did [heal me] and I put my shoe on and I was fine. But I thought I had a broken toe—my big toe was as black as it could be. And I didn't even go to the doctor; I just put ice on it."

A related type of healing episode follows the following pattern, "I felt much pain, and I was so afraid it might be X [something very serious], so I prayed to the Lord, and then went to the doctor and. . . ." The endings of these episodes vary, for example: "And it was diagnosed as Y [something minor]"; "And he found nothing wrong [therefore I was healed before he saw me]." Examples of healings of this type include: severe headaches (feared it was a brain tumor), chest pains (thought it was a heart attack), abdominal pains (feared cancer), blurred vision (thought it was incipient blindness), loss of breath (thought she was dying), irregular heartbeat (thought it was a heart attack), a very bad case of flu (thought she was dying). These examples do not denigrate the experiences of these believers; the fear of serious illness is very real and probably more common than recognized. Rather, these examples point out that healing can refer to episodes in which one's worst fears are not confirmed; having a medically diagnosable condi-tion is not necessary to experience a healing. In the light of these beliefs, the self-confirming potential of faith healing can be appreciated. For example, many members prayed regularly for a healing before going to the doctor for diagnosis, tests, X-rays, or exploratory surgery. Negative test results and favorable diagnoses were then perceived as confirmations that those prayers were successful.

Many respondents mentioned, without prompting, areas of their lives which they felt needed healing. In contrast to those previously experienced, none of these were basically physical, although if new illnesses or accidents were to occur, the individual would presumably pray about them. The two most common areas cited can be broadly described as relationships and personal/emotional traits (for example, self-centeredness, fear, resentment, nervousness, anxiety, family problems, shyness, and holding grudges). Also frequently cited were habits, viewed as symptomatic of some more serious emotional or spiritual problem. The woman who felt she needed to be healed of her reliance on a cup of coffee before starting each day was not describing a physical addiction to caffeine but was rather evaluating the lack of total faith demonstrated by her dependence on anything except Jesus. Other areas cited as needing healing were attitudes (for example, not being satisfied with being a housewife) and thoughts (for example, holding the wrong opinions).

The above descriptions of Catholic pentecostals' definitions of healing demonstrate that their entire system of explanation is different from that of both the medical profession and most non-pentecostal persons. Although the pentecostal system of explanation borrows terms from medical usage, this application does not denote that these terms mean the same to them.[48] If a member witnesses in prayer meeting that he was healed of impaired hearing, for example, the term does not necessarily refer to a formally diagnosed medical category. What is relevant to the witness and to the hearers is the experience of God's love and power in perceiving oneself to be healed. Therefore, there is no deception involved in testifying to something, while using terms in a different sense from their biomedical meaning. Nevertheless, the members want to believe that the healing is also medically factual, so there is much appeal to using scientific-sounding terms.

Etiologies of Illness

Narratives about healing episodes are also useful indicators of Catholic pentecostals' etiologies of illness. The idea of "etiology" is broader and more sociologically relevant than the notion of "cause." Anthropological studies of healing show that part of the healing process in all cultures is the sick person's and healer's co-construction of an illness etiology. This etiology incorporates an organization of both physical and social events (for example, violation of a moral norm) prior to the occurrence of the illness. These etiologies are typically in the form of narratives with conventional formats. They are analytical, focusing on certain facts and discarding others as irrelevant; they result in a culturally meaningful explanation of the illness that specifies causal relations among selected facts and connects them with the larger, socially prescribed, or "ideal" relations of that group.[49]

Thus the co-constructed etiology of each person's illness fits a set of culturally understandable explanations; it serves to link the ill person with the larger meaning system of the entire social group. It is almost impossible for the researcher to be present during the entire process of construction of an individual illness etiology, since this is often very private and takes place over a period of time in a number of settings. Numerous narratives of past healings, however, yielded indications of the social nature of this meaning-constructing process.[50] For example, a common statement began, "But then I talked to——— [typically a prayer minister] and she helped me realize that my problem was because of. . . ." Nevertheless, these interviews were conducted after the construction of the etiology and therefore embodied the retrospective reconstruction of events consistent with the etiology; facts remembered were those that were interpreted as causally related or significant for appreciating the value of the healing.

Nevertheless, it is possible to note the available repertoire of possible etiological factors which are meaningful to pentecostal Catholics. MacNutt's categorization of types of healings (discussed above) implies one such set; illness may be caused by personal sin, influence of evil spirits, emotional hurts, disease, or accidents.[51] Underlying all of these specific explanations is a more fundamental explanation, which connects the etiological statement with the necessary treatment: "The basic source of a sickness is the primordial evil which weighs upon man and can only be lifted by a power beyond our human intelligence and activity."[52]

Respondents indicated etiological categories both in their narratives of specific sickness episodes and in their discussions of the general problem of illness. The most frequently cited etiological category was "sin"; however, the respondents' use of this category appears to be somewhat broader than MacNutt's. The Scriptural sources are exemplified by this passage from the Epistle of James: "Therefore confess your sins to one another, and pray for one another, that you may be healed" (5:16, RSV).

One usage is the idea of sin as a general quality; this etiological category was used by approximately one-third of those interviewed. Two or three respondents said (half-jokingly) that it was all Adam's and Eve's fault that there is so much sickness in the world; this general category is like "original sin." In this sense of the word, sin refers to all things that are out of right order. Relationships with other people and with God that are out of order are sinful; social and political situations that are considered out of order are sinful; attitudes, habits, opinions, or personal traits that are out of order are sinful, and so on. For some respondents, the definitions of "illness" and "causes of illness" overlap or are identical. In other words, that of which they need to be healed is perceived as a cause of illness.

Similarly, the other use of sin as an etiological category also overlaps the definition of illness, when sin refers to personal sin. This category was applied by more than two-thirds of all interviewed, sometimes in combination with the general notion of sin. Most respondents were adamant that it was sin itself that brought on the illness and that God did not send the illness as punishment for sin. One person said:

> I really believe it [sickness] is the result of sin. I really do. I really do. I mean we pollute our bodies with additives or whatever, you know. You can't see the direct link. But for example like when I had my first job, I had severe stomach problems after I was first married and you know, really bad. I was in and out of the hospital and stuff . . . and that was just worry and anxiety and that sort of thing . . . all from not turning it over to Jesus and trusting the Lord.

While these respondents believe sin to be the root cause of illness, they frequently attribute illness to other, more immediate causes as well. A person might begin by saying he needed to be cured of a bad case of eczema, but that he had come to realize that the condition was really caused by his nervousness and anxiety, and although that needed healing the root cause was really his personal sinfulness in not being willing to turn over his whole life to the Lord.

The second most frequently used etiological category includes evil spirits and Satan. Virtually all respondents believed Satan or evil spirits are significant forces in causing illness; approximately one-fourth of the respondents believed them to be the chief causes. The following statement exemplifies this category:

> I think Satan does his best. I think it's time we recognized that the power of evil lives in the world and that we as individuals have to cope with the evil that's in the world today. And again that's another thing, another advantage of having a prayer community. It's because we gather together for strength and you sort of get to be invincible in a group. If you try to hit it out on your own, I mean obviously, you just can't with those devils. You just don't stand a ghost of a chance. You know, I know a lot of people don't believe the devil exists, but I really don't think things would be as bad as they were, the evil in us, the evil in man. The evil that's in man is the evil that's an extension of possession of the devil. The devil is using that person just like God can use us . . . I do believe that a lot of evil, a lot of sadness and sickness in this world is brought on by Satan. I think it's in his scheme of things to turn us against God.

There are two orientations toward this etiological category. Just as for the category of "sin," in which general sin implied only moderate responsibility, whereas personal sin implied high responsibility on the part of the sick person, there are also two levels of responsibility with the category of "evil spirits." In one usage, evil spirits are considered to be highly potent external forces whose negative influence is independent of the individual's will or disposition. Within this framework, the individual has very low responsibility for illness. A moderate level of responsibility is implied by the notion that evil spirits are very potent and the individual cannot combat them alone, but they gain entry to the mind and body through a fault in the person's spiritual or emotional life. The following etiological explanation illustrates this approach. It is quoted in full length to demonstrate the way these narratives weave events and beliefs into meaningful explanations. The member responded to a question about ways in which Christians can prevent illness or protect themselves from disease:

> I put on my armor. I just read this book, *Trial by Fire*, and I really felt that this whole year, I've been bombarded by the devil. I really do. With this thing about TM [she had previously taken courses on Transcendental Meditation], I've left myself open to be used and manipulated by him [the devil]— by letting my mind get over into this other level, this other plane. And I guess he really just didn't want to let it [the mind] go, and he kept making it very hard for me to follow the Lord. I kept having the physical pain and the nervousness—and with TM I didn't have that. I had that positive energy and everything was running smooth. [Satan said] "Remember how your life was back then. Go back to it." So I had a conflict within myself and I said, "No, I'm going to follow the Lord, there's no turning back." The cross before me; the world behind me, you know. But I just read *Trial by Fire* and about how if you have left yourself open to the devil to use you by yoga, by mind control, by TM, even believing in horoscopes, anything like that, you've left yourself open to be used by the devil and you have to repent of that, because it is sin.

> That's number one; now the next thing to do is to put on your armor (that's in Ephesians 6), which said start the day off by putting on your helmet of salvation, your breastplate of righteousness, your belt of truth, the shoes to announce the good news, and my left hand is my shield of faith, and my right hand is the sword of the Holy Spirit. And then you're armed! You've got your suit of armor. The thing is most of us don't realize that the devil and all of his forces are one step above man and then there's God who's over him and it's because of His redemption that we have the power to fight back. So, put on your armor and know that the power of Jesus is in you, too, and say [to Satan], "Go to hell where you belong."

The third most frequent etiological category, cited by about one-third of the respondents, might be called "environment," including evaluations of the impact of the social, physical, and emotional environment of the individual. Men were more likely to use this category, whereas women were more likely to use the supernatural category (for example, evil spirits). Most of these explanations implied only moderate responsibility of the sick person. Examples cited of environmental causes of illness were air and water pollution, harmful emotional experiences in childhood, unhealthy social situations such as slums and warfare, influence of the media, pressures of the job situation, and so on. This category was, however, closely linked with the categories of "sin" and "evil spirits" in many respondents' explanations, such that it is difficult to distinguish among them. The following explanation illustrates this multiple interpretation:

> It [all this sickness] is because of the constant bombardment with the junk in the movies, on television and on the newsstands. And the Church having its difficulties with abortion, and war and the breakdown in society. All these things can be a terrible detriment . . . because, you know, maybe twenty-five to thirty years ago, everybody didn't have television, so people were content doing what they did. I know or I knew when I was a young person growing up, a lot less about life than these kids know. But I think it comes on them much too fast. So you have sexual permissiveness, the taking of life through abortion, the racial problem, the problems that people who are maybe poor never knew about what other people had so they didn't complain. Now with television, they see all these things and it's "I want, I want, I want." The work ethic has gone down by the boards—the economic difficulties that the country is faced with. All of these things apply eventually incredible pressure on individuals. And I think it's just that without the Lord, there's more depression, probably more suicide, and pill-popping to escape reality. The only way that we can keep on an even keel and continue to deal with all these evils is to turn to the Lord.

The final category, mentioned by about one-eighth of the respondents, and then usually after applying one of the more important categories, implies a very low level of personal responsibility for illness; it could be described as "accident." Included in this type would be birth defects, physical accidents, and diseases not accountable by the above categories. In application, this classification accounts for very few physical conditions or diseases, because most of them are attributed to greater personal responsibility. This category, while seemingly the simplest, results in problems of meaning unlike the other etiologies, because they all firmly fix the responsibility for the source of suffering on evil spirits or on human agents. Lacking such clear sources, the category of accident begs the question: Are these problems from God? Most respondents sensed this problem and many had already struggled with it. The majority felt that God is not the source of anything bad, but that He sometimes allows it in order to help humans grow. A few also mentioned that sometimes the Lord sends people trouble and suffering as a kind of test or trial of faith so they can grow in dependence upon Him. These theodicies of unexplainable suffering, then, serve to put some of the responsibility back on humans—the responsibility to use the experience for growth or to come through the trial with unshaken faith.

Definitions of Health

One neglected approach to understanding a group's definition of illness is to try to grasp its notion of health. This is, however, difficult, because it is often only in formulating responses to illness that people articulate their concept of the ideal (health) to which illness is compared. Indeed, this articulation is one of the most important functions of disease etiologies—to express a social norm which would otherwise be difficult to symbolize.[53] The idea of health is clearly a socially defined norm, and for Catholic pentecostals it serves to embody their distinctive ideals. Almost all respondents gave spiritual criteria for healing. Just as illness was typically defined as a condition which results from or contributes to a person's not having the right relationship with God, so too health was defined in terms of a good or right relationship with Him. The most frequently cited criterion of health was "oneness with the Lord."

Because members view health as primarily a spiritual quality, they were quick to point out that it is not necessary to be physically healthy in order to be truly healthy. One man stated:

> I think that a really healthy person has got to have a good relationship with the Lord. Or else I don't think that they're really healthy, totally. I suspect there are a lot of people, take for example, atheistic communists, they can appear to be strong people, forceful, leaders in the world. I don't believe they're healthy if they don't have a good relationship with the Lord. I think that some of the lives of the saints have proven that. They have not been physically healthy. A person's realization of who they are, as against the Lord, their relationship with the Lord, is a person who is healthy. A person who knows their relationship with the Lord and why they're here. They know what the purpose of life is or what the end result is supposed to be. Then they're healthy.

This quotation also illustrates the common opinion that many people appear to be healthy but in actuality are not truly healthy. The concept of real versus apparent health serves to distinguish the group's ideal from the norms of the larger society.

Because this ideal is so extreme, many members emphasized that achieving it is not possible in this life. The ideal of healthiness was equated with perfection. The promulgation of such a high ideal is an important factor in the meaning of faith healing; if all are so far from the ideal of health, then all require frequent, regular healing until the final "healing"—death. For this reason, many (approximately one-third) members conceived of health as a process rather than as a state of being. Healing ministers were especially likely to emphasize health as process. From this point of view, relative health (that is, growth toward ultimate health) is all that can be attained in this life. Thus healing (growth) produces health (growth toward ultimate health—one-ness with God). One prayer minister reflects this approach:

> I don't think we reach that ideal—not in this life, at least. It has to do with a wholeness, in which the spirit, mind, relationships, and body are all whole—well, the body doesn't matter as much, but it's part of it. Anyhow, in this life, we're all still growing, and things will keep happening until the day we die that will be things that will need healing. I mean, there'll be relationships that need mending and hurt feelings or spiritual difficulties. We never achieve that perfection, but it's the direction we should want to go. Actually life would be boring and stale if we just stood still; it's the growth that makes it interesting.[54]

This explanation also emphasizes the notion of wholeness: Because of sin, humans have broken lives, broken relationships with others and with God, and broken, imperfect bodies. Healing makes whole these fractured lives, the relationship with God being the highest goal of wholeness.

In characterizing the truly healthy person members interviewed emphasized spiritual criteria (being close to the Lord, good prayer life, going to the Lord with all problems, doing the Lord's will, growing in the Lord, pure, faithful). Other frequently cited criteria were emotional qualities or personal traits (relaxed, peaceful, joyful, "together," has no "hangups," positive attitude toward life, happy). Less frequent were criteria with a social component (outgoing, helping, giving, loving, understanding, tolerant, patient). Only one person mentioned a physical criterion (full of energy) but even that had a psychological component. It is interesting to note that people list relationships as very important among things which need healings, but their descriptions of the healthy person are primarily in emotional and spiritual (rather than social) terms. It is possible that even the healing of relationships is perceived as an individualistic experience and that the problems implied in the relationships are seen to be problems of the individual rather than the larger social situation. In this individualistic approach, Catholic pentecostals appear to be drawing upon psychological interpretations which emphasize adjustment rather than the problematic nature of social situations.

In general, therefore, health is equated with the Catholic pentecostals' ideal: health is holiness. This ideal is translated into everyday pragmatic terms, as exemplified by one member's description:

> I guess if you hold the Lord first in your mind, your whole world is healthy. And your mind is healthy and your body is healthy. If you get up in the morning and just ask His guidance and place yourself and all your dear ones around you in His loving care, it's just so beautiful. And He does take care of you. And He gives you the help and everything that you need and He gives you the strength to sustain you. And I think that's a pure and really healthy person.

An ideal of holiness is also inextricably intertwined with the moral norms of the group. Another explanation shows clearly the connections made between spiritual, emotional, and moral norms:

> I think to be truly healthy . . . well, I believe that if a person is healthy, they're one with the Lord. They're relaxed, relaxed in Him and resting in Him and always to be for the Lord. You know, waiting for the Lord to tell you what to do and where to go. I think that we have to fulfil our commitment, whatever job the Lord has given us in life. If you're a housewife, then you fulfil the promises that you made. Religious, or a single person, whatever. Just trying to lead the kind of life that the Lord wants you to lead. And to have a close relationship, a close personal relationship with the Lord and to be in communion with Him during that private prayer time every day for guidance.

The implications of these ideals of health is that, although all fall short —in this life, at least—and therefore need frequent healings, most of the time people are responsible for their shortcomings. The opposite of health is not merely illness; it is sinfulness.

Legitimation and Theodicy

Every belief system about healing (including that of the established Western medical system) contains a set of legitimations which serve to shore up plausibility of the core beliefs. Wherever there are points of inconsistency or problems in the system, these ideas are developed to answer the crucial question: Why? One critical legitimation for all systems of healing is how to explain failures. Each system will favor legitimations which adequately protect the power of the healing agent and satisfactorily give meaning to the event of failure. Another set of legitimations in all belief systems about healing addresses the questions: Why is there suffering? Why is there death? Modern Western medicine has highly truncated explanations of suffering and death and largely relies on the individual finding meaning in the private sphere (religion, family, traditions).[55] ·By contrast, most traditional medical systems address themselves directly to issues of meaning.

Legitimations of Suffering and Death

For Catholic pentecostals, the problem of suffering is particularly acute, because of their strong emphasis on a loving God who cares about each individual in a very personal way. How could such a God permit suffering? Their problem is further complicated by their belief that, through the power of prayer, God takes care of people's everyday wants and needs. Why do good Christians who pray regularly in faith for health still get sick and sometimes die "before their time"? It is important to realize that the legitimations with which any group addresses these problems are not mere rationalizing but rather important ways of structuring their world view to handle the potential threat of chaos. Suffering and death create problems of meaning, and challenge the order of the world view in which the believer operates. Only by creating a satisfactory way of dealing with such threats can any group support and retain its belief system.

The problem of suffering is directly linked with the problem of illness: Who sent it and why? The majority of members interviewed felt that God does not send suffering but sometimes permits it. The following explanation shows how problematic this issue is for many members:

> I've been getting bombarded with questions by people who tell me, "Well, you're charismatic, you believe in God. You tell me why there's so much sin, so much sorrow, so much suffering in the world. If God is good, why is it that we suffer, why is it that people die, why is it that . . .?" So I said, "Well, I don't know the answer to that right off, but I think it has to do with ourselves. I don't think it has to do at all with God." And I went before the Lord with that . . . The answer that I got from Him I could put quotes around; it was really beautiful. He said to me, "Do not look to Me for your sin. The sin which causes sorrow, suffering and death, I do not cause that." And I just stood there, stunned, because that [answer] just came like from nowhere.

Thus God's power to prevent suffering—if He wishes—is defended, while putting the responsibility for suffering on other agencies (mainly sinful humans or evil spirits).

This legitimation, however, creates another problem: Why does God permit suffering? Some healing ministers offered relatively complex and theologically elaborate answers to this problem. They explained that people lack the self-discernment to know which areas of their lives need healing, so the Lord permits them to experience discomfort in order to motivate them to do something about their condition.[56] The average member, however, often preferred a much more simplistic legitimation. For example, one woman stated, "The Lord gives you some suffering so you could find Him. You'll never find Him if you don't have anything to suffer, really. He gives you some suffering and I'll tell you this day, I always say, 'Lord, give me a little cross,' because when I have that little cross, I just feel His embrace." This legitimation adds the connotation that permitting suffering is a sign of the Lord's love and care; indeed, the individual even implied that the Lord was the source of the suffering—but for a good purpose.

Some members drew upon legitimations learned in their childhood Catholic socialization, which had become newly meaningful. For example, one woman said, "Small illnesses, small trials can be a stepping stone . . . or a stumbling block. It's the same way with illnesses. You can take this illness and you can offer it up for your sins or you can offer it up for someone else, or for anything you want to. In that way, you would be using it as a stepping stone." The idea of "redemptive suffering," another traditional Catholic legitimation, was used by several members. For example, one woman stated:

> I think He might allow suffering if He can get a lot of mileage out of it. There are times I didn't think He was so great. I used to say, "Why am I not healed? You say, 'ask'; You say, 'knock,' and I'm pounding on Your door and yet You're not healing me. I'm following You; I've turned my life over to You, I'm doing what You want, I'm trying to change, I've asked You to change me, to make me a good Christian. Why hasn't the healing happened? Why do I still have this pain?" It was shaking my faith, and my friends too. Because I was doing things that were difficult for me to do—like reaching out to people. I was definitely changing and I wanted my healing to be a reward. And it wasn't coming and I felt hurt. And people would say, "Isn't God great?" And I'd think, "He isn't so good." Really! And even though I'd come to prayer meetings and said, "Praise the Lord," I just praised Him for other people, but I felt hurt inside . . . I felt He loves other people, but He doesn't love me.

The fundamental function of such legitimations, as with all theodicies, is to assert meaning where events and experiences seem meaningless. Theodicies do not necessarily make the person happy or eliminate the suffering; they do provide meaning.[57] Thus the ultimate theodicy, when the others fail to satisfy, is that while humans might not know why, God does; meaning exists, but because we are human we are not always able to know what it is. For example, one woman stated, "You just have that confidence. You know that whatever goes wrong. . . . You know that He knows it. And that it is for the good and that we may not understand it right now, but perhaps later." It is satisfying for some persons to know merely that meaning exists, even if they personally do not know what that meaning is.

In some ways, the problem of death was less of a threat to the meaning system of Catholic pentecostals than was suffering. This is largely because the traditional Christian theodicy of death (specifically, the belief in an afterlife of union with God), together with their new-found experiential sense of what that union might be like, satisfied the need for explanations of the larger problem of death. On the other hand, the specific Catholic pentecostal belief system made them vulnerable to two other problems: one more philosophical, the other very practical. The first problem in need of legitimation was: If death means union with God, why should we pray for people to be healed and delivered from death? The second need for legitimation was the problem of why God sometimes apparently failed to answer fervent prayers for healing and the person died.

Several respondents expressed a conflict between their ideal and their personal inclination about praying for people to be delivered from death. One woman stated that one should pray that the Lord's will be done, and if that means that the person dies, the prayer group should be happy. Then she added that if the dying person were someone very dear to her, she would probably be hoping and praying for recovery up to the end. Several healing ministers pointed out that part of their prayer was to ask for discernment from the Lord as to whether to pray for a complete healing for the person. If the Lord were to show them that it was His will to "take" the dying person, then their prayer would be for the person to have a "good death" (that is, prepared for Heaven by having repented for sins and being reconciled with loved ones, etc.), to experience as little pain as possible, and for the family to be able to handle their grief and sorrow, and come to the Lord through it.

They felt comfortable with this approach for dying old people, but had great difficulty—both practically and theologically—when the person they were praying for was young and needed by others. Two of the groups studied experienced the deaths of people for whom they were praying fervently during the period of this research. In both cases, the persons who died were "too young to die." One group experienced both the loss of the wife of one of their most influential leaders, and the instantaneous death in an automobile crash of a teenage child of a member; another group experienced, within one week, the death of a young mother of three children and the death of a young girl. In three of these four instances, the prayer groups had poured intensive prayer and personal energy into the healings of the dying persons. These experiences were understandably very difficult and produced a crisis of meaning. In both groups the ensuing weeks were filled with witnessing about the events—at first, veiled and tentative, then more open and authoritative. In both groups this integration of the meaning-threatening events into their belief system culminated in prophecies (for example, God speaking to them about the need for faith) and in highly effective witnessing by key leaders during which many members were even moved to tears.

Members used two general types of legitimation of death. The first type is predicated upon the dominant notion of death—that it is a termination, an end of life as humans know it. Many of these explanations are commonly used by non-pentecostals, as well. For example, some members saw death as an instrument for bringing others (such as the immediate family) closer to the Lord. Others commented that often death was desirable, because the person's life was so miserable or painful. Others merely commented that "the Lord knows best." Many others gave traditional Christian legitimations, which imply that the person dies but something good follows (for example, one experiences the glory of God, can be with Jesus, or the Lord takes us into His arms).

By contrast, a few members asserted a different concept of death.[58] For example, one person explained that the "world" called it death, but that it is really life—true life (that is, union with the Lord). This distinction between the world's and the believer's meanings serves to distance the individual from the usual conception of death, reducing some of its fearfulness. Another legitimation goes a step further to identify death as the ultimate healing.[59] This legitimation represents a further explanation of the Catholic pentecostals' definition of healing. The logic of it is comprehensive: If illness is from sin, and sin means separation from the Lord, then healing means reuniting with the Lord. Therefore, since death precedes the ultimate union, it is the perfect healing.

Legitimations for Therapeutic Failure

In any medical system, the main function of legitimations for therapeutic failure is to explain failure while protecting the power of the therapeutic agent, or agents, and maintaining believers' faith in the truth of that medical system. Too often, people assume that these legitimations are merely rationalizations, trying to explain away the uncomfortable truth of failure. In this sense, all medical systems contain a self-perpetuating element: The belief system itself contains rationalizations for apparent contradictions. In his comparative study of psychotherapeutic processes, Frank notes that all psychotherapies (including modern "scientific" ones) are predicated upon a myth which explains health and illness, deviance and normalcy, and other normative definitions. He adds that the use of the term "myth" is appropriate for these explanatory systems because their rationales cannot be shaken by therapeutic failures.[60] Even modern biomedicine, with its presumably scientific reality-testing[61] is predicated upon a similar set of socially constructed definitions of reality.[62] As such, the established medical system presupposes a particular belief system, which also needs legitimations to shore up its plausibility.

These legitimations may appropriately be categorized by the degree to which they deflect responsibility for the apparent failure from the primary agent of healing, thus protecting and affirming that agent's power. The two main legitimations used by Catholic pentecostals are that (1) the failure is not really a failure but merely apparent, and (2) the therapeutic failure was not God's fault. One commonly used explanation is that human lack of understanding prevents the realization that God really did answer the prayer. Similarly, one woman pointed out that "healings are always successful" but that one might be praying for one person to be healed and another person received the healing. The failure is believed to be only an apparent failure, due to observers' lack of understanding. Also, many members pointed out that healings often take a long time, and lack of immediate results does not mean that healing is not occurring. Another explanation is that the healing has occurred, but because the individual has not claimed the healing, it cannot yet be experienced.

The legitimations which acknowledge that people have not been healed typically assert that responsibility lies with the individual, the prayer ministers, or the larger social group—but not with God. None of the prayer ministers in the groups studied were believed to have received any special "gift of healing" (although a few felt that they were being prepared to receive one). Therefore, they did not assert any individual power which needed to be protected in the event of failure; this is in marked contrast with many folk healers and some classical pentecostal healers. It may be hypothesized that, as these prayer groups develop members with specialized "gifts of healing," the exercise of those gifts will become a field for the assertion of power, just as the exercise of prophecy is. At present, however, the main power to be protected is God's power. Thus the prayer ministers can afford to be self-effacing in order to support that healing power.

Prayer ministers attributed therapeutic failure to their own or the sick person's failures; by contrast, the ordinary members were more likely to attribute the failure entirely to the sick person. For example, prayer ministers cited the following reasons not mentioned by ordinary members: lack of discernment about the correct cause of the illness (faulty diagnosis); not knowing or understanding the exact problem to pray for (not being able to discern which specific memory needs healing); and lack of faith on the part of the prayer group or prayer ministers themselves. Prayer ministers and regular members alike gave the following reasons for failure: lack of faith of the person being prayed for; sin that has to be dealt with before the healing can take place; the person does not really want to be healed (enjoys being dependent on others); other healings have to take place before this one can.[63]

It is useful to point to parallel legitimations used by the medical establishment in order to belie the notion that such legitimations are peculiar to religious believers. The primary difference between the Catholic pentecostals' legitimations and those used by the established medical system is that the latter protect the power of the medical profession and individual doctors. The following legitimations illustrate how the medical establishment also deflects responsibility for failure from itself: the illness was too advanced or the person was not brought for treatment in time; there was inadequate preventive medical care; the person's illness resulted from self-inflicted problems (for example, obesity, alcoholism, drug addiction)—you can't help those who won't help themselves; the person lacked the will to live; the patient was too weak to fight the illness; the patient did not cooperate with the therapeutic regimen. The responsibility is deflected not only to the sick person but also to the realm of "things" that are outside of possible human control—nature, fate, accident (for example, "complications" set in that made it impossible to do anything for the patient). Therapeutic deficiencies that are admitted are attributed to larger problems for which the healer is not personally responsible (for example, medical science has not discovered a cure for that yet). A study of a hospital's "Mortality and Morbidity" inquiries showed that these sessions served primarily to justify doctors' actions and to certify their non-responsibility for therapeutic failure, rather than to open the broader issue of why the patient died.[64] It is ludicrous to imagine a highly paid surgeon telling the next-of-kin, "I was not capable of saving him because I didn't have the skill for that surgical operation." By contrast, a pentecostal prayer group is likely to explain that "our lack of faith resulted in the failure of that healing." The difference is that the pentecostals' legitimation serves to protect the healing power of God; the medical doctor's protects his own power and that of his profession.

Summary

The descriptions presented in this chapter illustrate the dramatic distinctiveness of Catholic pentecostal beliefs about health and illness. A sociological understanding of faith healing requires an appreciation of their alternative definitions of healing, health, illness, and death. Part of their belief system is a set of explanations which support the plausibility of the whole system, so that an awareness of their legitimations for suffering, death, and therapeutic failure is especially important for a sociological interpretation. Every medical system (including the dominant "scientific" Western one) includes similar socially constructed definitions of health and illness, healing and dying, and legitimations for therapeutic failure.

Although these descriptions of Catholic pentecostal healing rituals and beliefs are interesting in themselves, they are also rich in sociological significance. They reveal a great deal about the nature of the group and how it symbolizes itself. They are concrete expressions of the ways the individual relates to the prayer group; they embody group norms and sanctions—often formulated in the very process of being ritually articulated. The use of healing in prayer groups illustrates the interweaving of issues of power, authority, responsibility, and meaning. The following chapter examines the implications of these healing rituals for a theory of health and illness.

Seven—
Healing:
Conformity,
Community,
Order,
Power

As the preceding chapter shows, the Catholic pentecostals' very definitions of illness and healing differ dramatically from
those of the larger society. In order to understand the functions of
their healing rituals, however, it is imperative to recognize the social
construction of *all* medical reality. A common assumption is that diseases are "things," objective conditions independent of societal ways
of making sense of the world. This idea is fallacious; diseases are socially constructed realities and vary considerably from one culture to
another.[1] Medical sociology has been remarkably slow to recognize the
full implications of the social nature of illness, and much of the literature from this field reflects a general acceptance of the medical profession's definitions. Theories from anthropology, where cross-cultural
differences have encouraged researchers to question their assumptions
about the nature of illness, provide a better foundation for a sociological interpretation of faith healing.

Four interpretive themes emerge from these empirical data, and these
themes have important implications for a broader sociological theory
of health, illness, and healing. First, illness may be analyzed as a
form of deviance, and healing is the corresponding form of social control. Second, healing may have metaphorical significance, by which
wholeness is symbolically produced. Third, illness may be interpreted
as dis-order; healing constitutes re-establishing order. Fourth, and
closely linked with the other three interpretations, is the theme of
power—the loci of the power to produce or heal illness, the manipulation and communication of power by healers, and the relative power
or powerlessness of the sick person. These four themes not only organize a sociological interpretation of faith healing, but also suggest

categories for a sociological analysis of corresponding practices of other medical systems, including the dominant Western system.

Illness as Deviance; Healing as Social Control

Sociological analysis of illness has focused mainly on the concept of deviance. Individuals who differ significantly from the socially established norms have to be dealt with; whether the society punishes the individual or not depends largely upon its determination of who is responsible for the deviant behavior. The sick role is permitted for deviant individuals under the following conditions: (1) the individual is not considered responsible for the deviant behavior; (2) the sick person is exempted from normal obligations; (3) thus, although the individual is allowed to deviate legitimately, there is an implicit obligation to try to get well; (4) to the extent that the individual cannot get well without help, there is an obligation to seek and cooperate with competent help.[2] Other authors have expanded upon this analysis, qualifying the criteria of imputed legitimacy and seriousness of the deviance,[3] and pointing out the contrast between the medical profession's and patient's labels of the condition.[4]

While useful for its emphasis on the issue of responsibility, this analysis needs to be combined with a recognition that the norms by which deviance is defined in the first place are themselves socially constructed. Deviance is, at root, contingent upon that social group's definition of the norm.[5] Deviance is a product of the group which so labels it. Thus, the concept of illness, far from being a neutral scientific concept, is ultimately a moral one, establishing that group's evaluation of normality or desirability.[6] From this perspective, diagnostic actions may be seen as labelling deviance; therapeutic actions, as social control.[7] The role of healer, therefore, may be viewed as the moral entrepreneur;[8] that is, the medical profession creates the domain from which it subsequently reaps rewards. In fact, a prime consequence of medical activity is to increase the scope of what is defined as deviant by "finding illnesses."[9]

The process of reintegrating the deviant individual into the social group is "therapy," which for even relatively minor deviance entails a form of social control (for example, getting a young mother "back on her feet" so she can resume her family responsibilities). The social control functions of therapy are clearly evident in its grossest forms, such as the Inquisition or—more recently—mental hospitalization of political dissidents.[10] Social control may seem more pleasant when the deviance is treated as illness rather than crime or sin, but the potency of the agencies of control is just as great.[11] This apparent pleasantness toward illness makes it especially suitable as a focus for social control in modern societies which consider themselves too humane to employ heavier-handed tactics.

The sociological perspective which views illness as deviance is, indeed, applicable to the situation of Catholic pentecostals. Although they participate in the larger society and are subject to its definitions of deviance,[12] their concept of illness implies a much broader definition. The norms promulgated incorporate a wider scope of behaviors than those of the larger society; there is greater need for healing, because all members fall short of the normative expectations. For example, in the area of physical norms, Catholic pentecostals expect a high level of energy, vitality, and activity, together with low levels of pain, discomfort, and "inability" (in the fullest sense of the word). Similarly, in the psychological sphere, theirs are exceptionally difficult norms, because spiritual well-being is supposed to produce psychological states of joy, love, peace, and other related positive feelings. Experiences of stress, anxiety, fear, and anger are highly deviant. By extension, social areas are also subject to extreme expectations; personal psychological states are supposed to result in smooth, satisfying, and effective interactions with others. Disrupted interpersonal relations are, therefore, seriously deviant, especially if they are relations with others in the prayer group itself. Furthermore, Catholic pentecostals also include thoughts and attitudes, as well as overt behavior. For example, resentment, greed, jealousy, and thoughts of lust or violence violate the norms.[13]

The medical system of Catholic pentecostals also differs from the dominant medical system of the society in the imputation of responsibility. Like Western medical diagnosis, the pentecostal practice of discernment functions as a form of labelling deviance. Depending upon which label is attached, different degrees of personal responsibility are imputed to the ill person.[14] Unlike Western medical diagnosis, however, discernment frequently points to root causes of illness that imply a very different conception of human responsibility. For example, if the root of the illness is discerned to be sin, the person is believed to be highly responsible for the condition of illness. Appropriate therapy consists of confession, repentance, and reform on the part of the ill person, prayer and forgiveness (and sometimes confrontation and counselling) on the part of the group. By contrast, if the illness is discerned to be the result of accident or evil spirits (lower responsibility for deviance), the ill person is still viewed as too weak to rectify the condition without help. Thus the appropriate therapeutic response on the part of the group and the individual is to call upon God's power through prayer. The function of imputing responsibility is similar to that of Western medicine, but the process and interpretive categories are very different. The strong relationship which Catholic pentecostals see between responsibility and healing is exemplified by the following explanation which one woman gave about sickness and suffering:

> Man must accept his own responsibility for sin and not be shoving it off on other people or other things. But the idea is that when we sin, not to overlook it. But go to Jesus and ask forgiveness, and ask to be healed. Even if that healing is going to take us back into the painful past and show us the root of the sin, to be willing to do that [is what is necessary]. And if everyone was willing to do this in the world, I personally feel that a tremendous amount of healing . . . will come about.

The deviance/social control model, therefore, suggests a number of social functions that are fulfilled by faith healing. First, one of the most important functions is that the healing rituals give symbolic form to group norms. In the construction of disease etiologies, people are compelled to reflect on various aspects of the group's basis of moral order. For this reason, etiologies resemble "socially important myths" in providing symbolization of wider meanings for the whole social group.[15] Part of the process of crystallizing group norms is naming the deviance; the very process of articulation is meaningful for the group. Furthermore, identification with the social group is promoted through absorption into the ever-widening net of pentecostal norms. It is basically a learning process: The more the individual participates in the group's healing rituals, the more norms are learned; having learned more, the individual perceives more deviance and feels the need for further healing.

Secondly, the belief system surrounding faith healing provides legitimations for non-achievement of group ideals and exculpation from some deviance. For example, the interference of evil spirits can help explain the believer's lack of successful achievement of the group's norms. Healing rituals themselves provide mechanisms for the relief of guilt and stress and other byproducts of the difficult group expectations. These rituals also give the individual who is prayed for a sense of greater power because of his attempts to conform (in this sense, the members view healing as growth toward the ideal). Furthermore, faith healing provides a set of roles and relationships within the prayer group which are based upon group norms and social control mechanisms. These roles are part of the general stratification of the prayer group; the gift of healing is prestigious.

The belief system surrounding faith healing also suggests a number of social control mechanisms for preventing and handling deviance (for example, exorcism or confession). The sick role is allowed and the person's dependency is encouraged; however, the healing requires the person to transfer dependency to an acceptable agency—God. Finally, healing serves to reintegrate the deviant individual into the social group; in the context of the group, confession and other mortification processes, together with repentance of one's former self, help to produce a "new self" which is more consistent with group norms,[16] and the individual is reintegrated into the social world of Catholic pentecostals. This raises the question of whether membership in the Catholic pentecostal movement and participation in such practices as faith healing are ultimately integrative relative to the larger American culture. In other words, does membership in movements such as Catholic pentecostalism encourage effective functioning in the larger society? Does the prescribed behavior enable members to achieve what the dominant culture defines as success? Does membership in such a movement enable some individuals, who would not or could not previously embrace the larger society's values and operations, to "fit in"? Does the movement, therefore, provide effective therapy for deviance, according to the larger society's norms, as well? The evidence of this research points to a qualified "yes," as discussed in Chapter 9.

Although the illness-as-deviance perspective yields a number of insights into the social functions of faith healing, it fails to explore adequately the immense symbolic significance of healing, nor does it account for the problems surrounding Catholic pentecostals' alternate definition of deviance. The sociology of religion has long appreciated the immense significance of ritual and symbol in a group; medical sociology has generally regarded this approach as inapplicable to modern medicine. The continuities between traditional and "scientific" medicine are, however, probably greater than recognized, and specific analysis of ritual and symbolism in modern medicine would be fruitful.

Healing the Metaphorical "Body"

One of the characteristics of the Catholic pentecostal movement is the renewed salience of body symbolism. The human body serves as a vital symbol of the social body, reflecting the re-union of the individual's being with the system which orders one's existence.[17] Healing ritual is particularly significant as an expression of the social body. Although the term "body" has a number of referents in Catholic pentecostal usage, its main significance is the particular prayer community of which the individual is a member.

One of the most important functions of body symbols is cohesion of the prayer group. The idea of re-birth through baptism in the Holy Spirit (the sense of self as a "born-again" Christian) symbolizes not only the process of conversion, but also the transition from a mechanical to an organic metaphor. The identification of healing as continual growth fits into this metaphor. The cohesion of the community is based upon person-to-person bonds, rather than on obligations and constraints of formal commitments.[18] Body symbolism, especially the symbolism of healing, represents the incorporation of the individual into the group. Sociologically, therapy (healing) means eliminating those things that prevent the individual member's total commitment.[19] The range of healings prayer group members sought illustrates how healing and commitment are interrelated; and the controversial "breakthrough ministry" of some Catholic pentecostals (see Chapter 8) sought a "healing" for the purpose of enhancing the commitment of already highly involved members.

The symbolism of healing also represents the incorporation of the group into the individual. This can been seen in the movement's encouragement of a renewed respect for the Eucharist, in which the "Body of the Lord" is ritually ingested. For example, in an article recommending that members pray for healing, specifically, when receiving Communion, one spokesperson emphasized this connection:

> A major condition for experiencing the healing power of the Eucharist is recognizing the body of the Lord. . . . Isn't it true that many of us do not experience the healing power of the Eucharist because we do not recognize the body for what it is? It is both the flesh of the Lord and the Lord's people assembled. If we have resentment against one another as we come to the Eucharist, we do not recognize the body of the Lord for what it is; this keeps us from asking for forgiveness and healing and receiving it. The Eucharist is intended for our healing.[20]

The frequent references by Catholic pentecostals to the dual themes of repentance and healing, as suggested in the above quotation, are partially explained by theories of health and illness that identify sickness as the eruption of conflict and divisiveness of the social system; the condition of the sick person is only symbolically an individual expression.[21] Thus the healing is the symbolic healing of the larger social body. This interpretation is somewhat useful in explaining some of the functions of faith healing, but it begs the question: What is the larger social body? In the simpler societies studied by anthropologists, the social group experiencing conflict is clearly identifiable. In the case of religious movements in modern Western society, however, the social body could be the local group, the larger movement, the church of which the group is part, the society or the whole world. While Catholic pentecostals' conceptions of illness clearly include conflict and divisiveness in the society and world, it is probable that their rituals of healing do not have the potency of symbolizing the healing of such large social bodies. The social body healed in faith healing is the immediate prayer community.

Another important function of body symbolism is boundary maintenance. The social concerns of the group are reflected in their sense of pollution—"matter out of place."[22] As discussed in Chapter 2, Catholic pentecostals have a serious concern for order and perceive the world to be a place of grave dis-order. The prayer group must be protected from pollution of the world. The etiologies of illness employed by Catholic pentecostals reflect two sources of pollution: external and internal. External pollution is from the chaos of the world and from evil spirits. The group must protect its boundaries from attacks by these forces. The practice of informal exorcism, the deliverance ministry, and official exorcisms are all dramatic ritual expressions of this threat. As one woman said, "Community gives strength and you're invincible [against Satan] in a group." Through faith healing the individual participates in the mythic battle of dualistic forces, allying with God to fight the powers of Evil. This temporalization of a cosmic battle may be one further expression of the millennial hopes of the groups' belief system.[23] On the other hand, it may be that faith healing will come to replace the expectation of imminent doom as the concrete expression of dualism in the movement. In other words, to the extent that the imminence of the Millennium seems less salient to members, their dualistic focus may find a more satisfactory expression in the increased practice of faith healing.

Internal pollution refers to disorder within the social group—"the system at war with itself."[24] This problem is seen as the result of human imperfection—sin. All out-of-order behavior, thoughts, emotions, and relationships are threats to the "body" and, therefore, require healing. Purification rituals, such as confession and "inner healing," are ways Catholic pentecostals address these concerns. Similarly, purging sometimes involves symbolic physical purging, as described by one man who had received an inner healing, "I felt a very strange sensation in my body and I just felt all that garbage going out of me" [gesturing upward from the abdomen with both hands and outward through the mouth].

Not only does the body metaphor refer to the social body, but also it can refer to the individual's identity. This reference is sometimes used in conjunction with the rituals of internal purification. The concept of one's body is connected intimately with one's concept of self. The individual's experience is of both being a body and having a body.[25]

On the one hand, the body is the locus of many subjective experiences; on the other, it is perceived as something separate from one's real self (thus, for example, supporting the legitimation that the body's death is not really the death of the person). The intertwining of these aspects of the individual's experience of body allows for metaphorical interpretations. One of the metaphorical uses of the body among Catholic pentecostals is the idea of consolidation of one's identity through religion.[26] The healing consists of the individual being brought to an experience of a unified personal identity. For example, one woman witnessed to the prayer group:

> I used to be like all bits and pieces. I was one person with my family, and another at church, and another at parties, and another when I was alone, and there was no real me holding it all together. Like, just being different people, except outwardly looking the same, you know. Now that I'm in the Lord, I'm together—nothing phoney, just me. It's a real healing.[27]

A further metaphorical significance of healing of the body promotes social control and lines of authority in the group. As described in Chapter 8, the imagery of the "head" (proper authority) is directly connected with the health of the body (group). If the group experiences problems of social control and lack of authoritative leadership, healing consists of the body coming into proper alignment with the head— namely, submission. Thus a number of healing rituals—especially in intensive communities—include rituals of submission and deference. A similar idea is extended to the family; healing of the family unit consists of the husband/father assuming real headship, while the wife and children are appropriately submissive.

To describe the metaphorical significance of healing the body is not, however, to imply that this function is less than real. Through ritual and other metaphorical expressions, collective representations come to invoke powerful sentiments. Durkheim states, "Yet the powers which are thus conferred, though purely ideal, act as though they were real; they determine the conduct of men with the same degree of necessity as physical forces."[28] Thus the power of such symbols is a real power; healing rituals can have real effects (including physical effects) on the groups for which they have meaning.

Healing can metaphorically signify the cohesion of the group and incorporation of the individual into the group. The healing thus refers to the larger social body being made whole. Healing also has the potential to symbolize boundary maintenance of the group—especially important for a cognitive minority such as Catholic pentecostals. Through healing, the group protects itself from external pollution (for example, "the World" and evil spirits) and from internal pollution (especially sin). The body metaphor also can signify the experience of a unified personal identity of the individual, as well as the consolidation of authoritative leadership and social control within the group—the prayer group or family unit. Many of these metaphorical functions of healing refer to the symbolic re-ordering of relationships. For heuristic purposes, however, it may be useful to examine the problem of dis-order and order separately.

Illness as Dis-order; Healing as Re-establishing Order

Consonant with a number of theories about the metaphorical significance of healing are those perspectives which focus on the problem of order. This problem is especially acute for Catholic pentecostals, for whom order is an important reason for belonging to the group in the first place. Disorder threatens the new framework and undermines the ability of the group to structure the individual's world into a meaningful entity. Yet problems of disorder swirl around the group; the members are exposed to and are only partially able to avoid the seemingly chaotic influences of "the world" in their daily lives. A number of theories of conversion imply that, having adopted the meaning system of the group, new members will find a resolution of all the stresses, tensions, and crises that had initially propelled them to change their belief systems and allegiance. Although the new members may have initially experienced a sense of total resolution, their new-found sense of order is typically primarily at the level of meaning. That is, they continue to experience tensions and conflicts, but their belief system now gives meaning to their experiences and enables them to cope with problems. Their new belief system also, however, makes them more keenly aware of disorder.

Threats of disorder—resulting from rapid social change, personal or group crises, and the like—are integrated into the new order through healing. In other words, chaos-threatening experiences which may have initially propelled the individual to conversion are not qualitatively different from the problems that subsequently the group member resolves by a healing. It is not necessary, therefore, to elaborate on the possible multiple sources of threats of disorder; they are essentially the same sources as before conversion—except that now they are interpreted by members in terms of their distinctive new belief system. Whereas before conversion, for example, the individual had a sense of being surrounded by undefinable dangers, now the threat is attributed to evil spirits.[29] Especially threatening, however, are experiences of disorder that cannot be readily managed by the new meaning system, as the believer understands it. Healing ritual serves as an important part of the group's plausibility structure. The reintegration of the experience of disorder into the meaning system of the group serves to confirm these beliefs for both the individual and the group. Chaos is transformed into order.[30]

One important ordering function of the healing process is merely naming the problem, thereby reducing anxiety and fear.[31] Sharing the discernment of the root causes is one way this naming is done. For example, learning that one's problems are due to hurtful experiences embedded in one's memory is itself helpful, by giving a sense of order to previously ill-defined feelings and implying a course of action consistent with the belief system. The link between naming something and the course of action implied is crucial for the individual's sense of being able to change the unpleasant situation (that is, hope), because it gives the individual a "handle-hold" on the problem. Naming the problem may enhance the sick person's ability to mobilize personal resources against the illness.

Furthermore, the order asserted by the group's belief system does in fact structure the experience of illness and/or healing.[32] There is a sense of reassurance in knowing what to expect to experience—such as feeling pain when one is supposed to feel pain.[33] The therapy consists not only in the various means for curing illness but also in the means by which the illness is named and given cultural form.[34]

The order-restoring function of any healing practice is directly related to the function of power, discussed more fully below. The healer gains power over the sick person through his ability to manipulate the patient's definition of the situation—especially at those stages when the sick person is desperately uncertain about what is happening and, therefore, most vulnerable. Studies have shown how physicians enhance their power by manipulating the giving of information to patients.[35] Similar power is gained in other medical systems by the healers' skillful control over the uncertainty of the sick person. Even the healer who has no self-serving motives can produce a sense of power and awe in the patient by the timing of the resolution of uncertainty.

Faith healing serves to restore a sense of order—of meaning—for both the individual seeking the healing and for the larger prayer group. Although all therapies (especially psychotherapies) require the recipient's general acceptance of the premises of that therapeutic system's ability to heal, in the case of faith healing (and most other traditional healing systems) those premises encompass the group's beliefs about all other aspects of the community's life.[36] A person going to an internist, for example, would need to believe in the doctor's ability to read X-rays and in the ability of X-rays to illustrate certain internal disorders, but would not need to share the doctor's perspective on the problems of society or on religious experience. By contrast, all areas of belief and practice are relevant in faith healing. This comprehensiveness is because one function of faith healing is to reaffirm the members' belief system and their style of life.[37] Healing is, therefore, the ritual reassertion of the meaning system for the individual who is experiencing problems of meaning and for the group.

Important parallels to faith healing are found in the analyses of shamanism in other cultures.[38] A number of authors stress that the acquisition of shamanic gifts (such as healing) follows the resolution of a psychic crisis.[39] Some suggest that this crisis is essentially a psychotic episode, except that the shaman's culture positively values shamanistic abilities and therefore allows the crisis to be resolved through that specialized role; whereas, in Western society the behavior would be disvalued, defined as "mentally ill," and the individual could not achieve a positive integration.[40]

Studies of shamanism sometimes emphasize the individual's experience of chaos (for example, feeling incapable of personally exercising any effective control over one's life situation);[41] others emphasize the instability or chaos of the larger social system.[42] The shaman's role in healing is to mediate power in order to restore balance and harmony.[43] Disorder is dangerous; the shaman must have the power to counterbalance disorder. Note, too, that in many cultures shamans are believed also to have the power to cause disorder; they can harm as well as cure. This belief is comparable to the distinction made by Catholic pentecostals that Satan can give the power to heal, as well as to harm, because he can counterfeit the gifts of the Spirit. For example, if a sick person had previously been taken to a healer whose gifts of healing were not "of the Spirit," then the healing ministers would immediately suspect the evil influence of the Devil in causing this illness. By contrast, Catholic pentecostal healing ministers claim only the power to heal, not to hurt, because "all of the Lord's gifts are good."

The shaman mediates power from a superhuman source to the social system. The basis for the shaman's power is the ability to distinguish key structural symbols and to move them into a proper relationship (order).[44] This manipulation of symbols produces power. Thus the power to produce order is at the root of the healing process. This interpretation, therefore, goes beyond the understanding of order applied by a structural-functionalist approach. It is the ability to produce/

manipulate ordering or re-ordering within the social system that is the basis of power in healing.

Healing and Power

To explain faith healing as a function of power would appear almost tautologous to Catholic pentecostals. Indeed, it was their discovery of a new source of power in their lives that led them to the practice of faith healing. Almost every member interviewed emphasized the notions of "God's healing power," "God's powerful gifts of healing," the "power of prayer," and so on. Experiences of power have been central to sociological definitions of religion, at least since Durkheim's analysis.[45] Yet few sociologists have appreciated the full implications of the significance of power for understanding illness and healing.

Studies of medical systems should examine the loci of power in that group according to its medical belief system, and ways of controlling power in that system. Etiologies of illness yield information about the group's ideas about disease-causing power, and therapies embody ideas about how that power can be overcome. From this perspective, the treatment of illness is essentially the restoration of the balance of power—by weakening the antagonist's (disease-causing) power or by strengthening the victim's power.[46] This perspective can be applied to all medical systems, including modern Western medicine, which includes, for example, ideas of germs, viruses, pathogens, antibiotics, X-rays, hormones, etc., all of which are believed to have power to help or harm humans; the healer is believed to have power by virtue of knowledge and skill to manipulate the helpful forces to counteract the harmful.

The Idea of Power in Faith Healing

The idea of power is explicit in Catholic pentecostals' beliefs about healing. One movement spokesperson stated that the reason some are not healed is that Christians do not yet have enough power to perform the healings God desires.[47] The etiologies of illness (described in Chapter 6) clearly outline a concept of a hierarchy of powers. Illness is believed to occur when (1) human powers are weakened (such as by sin, unpleasant biographical experiences, or natural causes), and/or (2) external evil powers overwhelm the person. Most members interviewed articulated a model of power in which humans are seen as having no power of themselves; a few members, however, felt that there exists a natural power to keep healthy or to get well, but that it is not very great. All believed that it is God's superior power that enables people to heal and be healed. Furthermore, according to them, God's power can be mediated to others; the Lord selects certain believers to receive His gifts of power. The imagery used by members to describe this mediation is interesting in its evocation of technological similes: The power is likened to an electric current flowing from God through the mediator to the sick person (other images invoked were the sense of heat, electric tingling, and gentle light); it is like X-rays being transmitted into the sick person and going straight to where the healing is needed (other images—it "pierces," "zaps," "emits").

Figures 3 and 4 are models of power implicit in respondents' healing beliefs. In Figure 3, forces of differing potency are seen as warring with each other; the outcome for the sick person depends upon allying with the right forces. Figure 4 does not rely upon the explanation of external powers in the causation of illness (although many members used the two models together). Illness is the result of the individual being weakened through natural causes, personal sin, unhealthy relationships, and so on. Healing is achieved through obtaining power from God, directly or indirectly, because the person is so weakened as to be unable to help him or herself. The individual's sin (separation from God) is seen as a barrier between the sick person and the source of help—God; it also separates the individual from other humans who could otherwise mediate that power in order to heal. The implication of this barrier of sin is that the person must seek God's healing

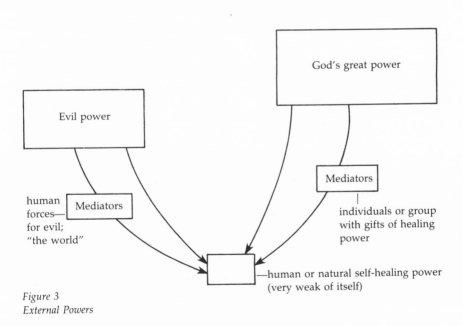

Figure 3
External Powers

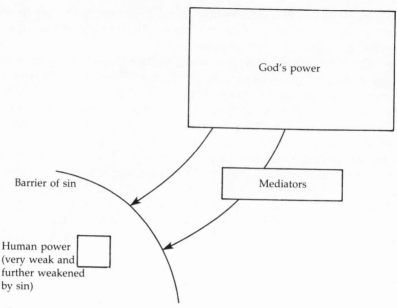

Figure 4
Sources of Power For an Otherwise Weak Person

power through prayer; the power does not flow unwanted. This model (Fig. 4) emphasized strengthening the sick person; the previous model (Fig. 3) emphasized counteracting the power of the sickening agent or agents.

Powerlessness and Illness

The individual's sense of powerlessness is central to understanding the functions of faith healing. Studies of traditional medical systems link this sense of powerlessness to the problems of anomie;[48] other studies suggest that the problems of disorder accompanying rapid social change are also related to a sense of powerlessness that is expressed as a need for healing.[49] As suggested in Chapter 3, the experience of rapid change can result in a sense of power-deprivation even for those social classes which are ordinarily relatively powerful; people sense that change has "robbed" them of the power to control the future, to effect their wills on their environment, to know what to expect and to act accordingly.[50] The recent expansion of non-scientific medical systems (including faith healing) may be closely related to this source of powerlessness.

This study has generally bracketed the question of whether faith healing works in the biophysical sense of the word, because the documentation of this aspect is outside the expertise of a sociological researcher. At the same time, however, it may be productive to speculate on the probability of the biophysical effectiveness of such healing. Other authors have suggested that there may be more to traditional medical therapy than merely psychological help or placebos for suggestible patients;[51] some propose that faith healing enhances and speeds up the body's natural self-healing capacities.[52] There is a growing literature pointing to the likelihood that biophysical conditions are intimately intertwined with a sense of well-being, mastery, and harmony in one's social environment.[53] Calling an illness "psychosomatic" is not helpful, because the term has come to connote illnesses which are less-than-real ("all in the head"). Much of both the Western medical professional's and laypersons's conception of illness hinges on a basically dualistic scheme, in which a condition is believed to be either biogenic or psychogenic (body versus mind);[54] it is interesting to note that, unlike many traditional medical systems, this scheme pays little attention to the idea of sociogenic illness. Nevertheless, there are probably few or no illnesses that are purely one or the other; all illnesses involve physical, psychological, and social components.[55]

Increasing evidence in Western medical terms suggests that illnesses previously thought to be purely biogenic are related to social and psychological states such as stress, conflict, sense of "threat," rapid social change, and sense of powerlessness.[56] If this is the case, it is plausible that non-scientific healing methods such as faith healing may be able to address those problems as well as, if not better than, the dominant scientific medical system. Believing oneself to be in touch with a great power which can direct one's life, solve one's problems, and authoritatively forgive one's past mistakes, may very well literally empower the individual believer to be more effective in daily life, or at least to cope more adequately. For example, "handing it all over to Jesus" may result in gaining a sense of control over forces in one's life that formerly seemed out of control. At the same time, the individual feels freed from having to take responsibility for the outcome.[57] A sense of control without responsibility could, indeed, reduce anxiety and worry. Other curative factors indirectly linked with healing in the context of the Catholic pentecostal prayer group include the supportive atmosphere of a warm and caring close-knit group and the material support of the community (such as child care, preparation of food, and cleaning for the family, etc.). The sense of being truly cared for (rather than being perfunctorily "tended") and the reduction of worry about the well-being of one's family may also contribute to the successful recovery of the sick person. These concrete expressions lend strength to the individual's belief that problems have been brought "under control."[58]

Another basis for a sense of powerlessness is that many people had such great faith in science and technology that, when it began to appear that maybe medical science could not solve all problems, those who had counted on that power to protect them felt doubly powerless. It is relevant to this point that many respondents had included, as part of their stories, statements such as: "The doctor could not find out what was wrong with me," "Doctors could do nothing for me," or "I felt I just wasn't being helped in the hospital." These statements are not only expressions of subjective feelings of helplessness, but may also objectively describe the powerlessness of Western medicine to deal with a certain range of healing which people seem to require. In earlier times, much of medicine focused on acute illnesses, which were either self-limiting or amenable to dramatic improvement through antibiotics and the like; many medical problems now are chronic illnesses in the face of which medicine is not nearly so awesome and powerful. Similarly, Western medicine has little conceptual capacity to deal with non-specific complaints, and practitioners are tempted to dismiss patients with these problems as neurotic or mentally disturbed.[59] Thus when respondents complained of the inability of medical professionals to help them, they were partially correct in assessing the dominant medical system's powerlessness in certain areas in which they felt need for help.

The successful treatment of many illnesses is related to the patient's hope or expectation of getting well. Yet, much of this hope is born of the person's belief in the power of the healing agent or agents; if one feels personally powerless, there is hope in allying oneself with the powerful. One respondent said, "It is not enough to hope in hope itself; we have the power of the Lord to count on." Hope engendered by belief in a strong supernatural power may, indeed, be more successful than hope in purely human powers. Furthermore, there is evidence that hopelessness and helplessness are themselves factors in the development of illness.[60] In both cases, the sense of powerlessness on the part of the individual is critical. The individual who "gives up" becomes more vulnerable to illness. If this is so, then, Catholic pentecostal conversion with its continued "healing" has the potential to prevent illness by allowing the individual to "give up" and then to transform that resignation into "giving over" one's life, hopes, and will, to the Lord. The believer gains hope and help, not by a new self-assertion but rather by submission and dependence. This experience may, indeed, account for the fact that many respondents evaluated "being brought to your knees" in a health crisis to be a healing, because it showed them how much they needed the Lord.

Furthermore, a secular medical system is incapable of providing the ultimate healing power sought by most people—everlasting life. Although medical systems are called upon to improve the patient's everyday functioning (alleviate discomforts, or ameliorate conditions which hamper full activity), one of the foremost desires of people is to prolong life. Although most people will philosophically agree that everyone has to die sometime, they still want to be healed of potentially fatal illnesses. A secular medical system may approximate this goal by increasing the longevity of the populace, but it cannot provide any healing for the condition of death itself. By contrast, Catholic pentecostals and similar groups assert a final healing; death is congruous with their medical system, because for them perfect health is attainable only in full union with God. Thus the power of faith healing is not diminished by a failure to heal the dying person; indeed, that death is the ultimate healing.

Power and Stratification

Another area in which the relationship between healing and power is significant is the microcosm of the prayer group itself. Like the other "gifts of the Spirit," the gift of healing is related to stratification within the prayer group. The key variables in the relationship are the existence of specialized gifts of healing, and the relative centrality of the healing ministry to the prayer group as a whole. On the one hand, the practice of faith healing among Catholic pentecostals represents a democratization of the power to heal. Members contrasted their new beliefs about healing to their previous notion that only very holy persons, like the saints, could heal. Several groups had occasional prayer meetings in which all members prayed with each other for healings. The goal was that prayer for healing should be a normal part of everyday life of the individual member and prayer group.

On the other hand, in those groups in which the healing ministry was an important aspect of the whole group, members of the ministry team were prestigious members of the prayer group. Even though these roles were powerful, the healing ministers did not challenge the power of the main leaders of the core group, because their roles were usually conducted in private. Even in groups in which women were not allowed on the leadership team (see Chapter 8), they were predominant on the healing ministry team. This fact is understandable, because healing is consistent with the nurturant role of women advocated by Catholic pentecostal ideology. Furthermore, of those persons who were believed to have received specialized gifts of healing, a disproportionate number of men were prominent. For example, four of the five large-scale healing services attended during the research featured male healers. Similarly, among the nationally prominent healing ministers in the Catholic pentecostal movement, only a few were women (although this is partly due to women's lesser freedom to travel away from home to conduct services, etc.). There is some evidence that certain gifts of healing are more likely to be claimed by women than men, although not enough data are available to firmly support this. It appears that men are more likely to claim to have received the general gift of healing, especially gifts of physical healing and deliverance, and the powerful gift of discernment, especially that of discerning evil spirits. By contrast, women are more likely to claim gifts of knowledge and inner healings—gifts which are less powerful in the stratification system of the prayer group. Although these generalizations are mere hypotheses, they are consistent with the overall stratification patterns of the groups studied.

This contrast between the democratization of healing, on the one hand, and the development of prestigious roles, on the other, is not surprising. Faith healing is an assertion of power, but the power is borrowed from a source outside oneself. In pentecostalism, Catholics have discovered a sense of personal communication with that source of power; all members share, to some extent, in this experience. At the same time, however, the belief system explains that certain members receive extra gifts of power for the good of the group; stratification is based not only on different roles but also on differences in assertion of God-given power. These specialized roles can be compared to those of shamans in other cultures. Such stratification enhances the group's sense of the miraculous and promotes the re-mystification of the world.

The assertion of power is not merely in the context of the prayer group—although it is significant there, too. It is directed primarily at the society and the total environment of the individual.[61] The assertion of power in faith healing and other pentecostal practices is the alliance with the power of God in the face of the instability, uncertainty, and conflict of a threatening socioeconomic and physical environment, in the face of which the individual would otherwise feel helpless and afraid.

The assertion of healing power by Catholic pentecostals and other traditional medical systems is fundamentally in conflict with assertions of power by the dominant medical establishment in this culture, token accommodative gestures notwithstanding. For this reason, it is useful to examine the function of power in the dominant medical system in order to understand better the points of conflict between the two. The slowness of medical sociology to appreciate the power functions of medical systems is due to the assumption that the modern secular medical situation is totally different from supernaturalist medical systems, and also that the medical profession has largely "sold" medical sociology on its definitions of reality—the "medical model."[62] Sociology has begun to question the medical model in the area of mental illness.[63] What is still needed, however, is a radically sociological approach to the entire sphere of Western medical beliefs and practices.

It is necessary to analyze the medical establishment as claiming and exerting power in several areas, including: the definition of deviance, monopoly over healing practices, certification and segregation of causes of illness, and cultivation of the public's faith. Several authors have noted the power of the dominant medical system in the definition of deviance; in this area, it has largely replaced the functions of religion and law as the means of defining and sanctioning deviance.[64] An ever-widening scope of behavior is being defined as illness (for example, alcoholism, gambling, drug addiction, child abuse, and homosexuality). Furthermore, the medical establishment successfully asserts its power to certify (to certify that smoking is bad for one, to certify that a person had a bona-fide excuse for drawing sick pay or insurance, to certify that an employer was not negligent in providing a safe place to work, to certify that a disruptive person should be hospitalized as insane, or that an alleged murderer was not sane at the time of the crime, and so on).[65] This gatekeeping function is one of great power in this society. It distinguishes between who is responsible and who is not responsible; however, one of the byproducts of the medical model is the tendency to find the problem located in the individual rather than the social system.

The power of the medical establishment to maintain a monopoly over healing practices is significant for an understanding of the place of faith healing in society. In contrast to established religion, the dominant medical system has the power to sanction strongly or to eliminate competing systems. Pluralism on the religious scene is primarily a result of the lack of power of any single religious system to effectively suppress its competitors; no such pluralism exists in Western medicine. The history of American heterodox medical practice, such as homeopathy, osteopathy, naturopathy, chiropractic, Christian Science, and faith healing, shows the high degree of success of the dominant medical system in suppressing its competitors.[66] Indeed, although society is increasingly tolerant of most cultic behavior, medical practices are the main area where it is strongly attacked.[67]

This power of the medical profession has direct implications for the patient. The institutional specialization of medicine in Western society has resulted in the delegitimation of the power of other possible agents of healing, such as the family of the sick person. The professionalization of Western medicine results in transferring the power to articulate models of reality from the sick person to the professional. The model in Western medicine is that of an active and powerful healer affecting the condition of a passive and objectlike client.[68]

The practice of faith healing and other heterodox methods may be a political statement—a counter-assertion of power—against the dominant medical system. As practiced by Catholic pentecostals, faith healing represents the affirmation of the role of the patient and the whole community in the process of healing; it puts forth alternatives to the definitions of deviance promulgated by the dominant system, and—most important—asserts a different source of the power to heal.

Summary

A sociological approach to the phenomenon of faith healing shows clearly that it is far more than merely an alternative technique. In the context of the Catholic pentecostal movement, faith healing includes dramatically different definitions of health, illness, healing, and healing powers. The diversity of these meanings suggests that a wide scope of functions may be served. The interpretive themes suggested by these functions are also applicable to other systems of health, illness, and healing.

One such function is the definition, labelling, and control of deviance—a function fulfilled by all medical systems. Critical to this function is the establishment of responsibility for deviance from social norms. Furthermore, rituals of healing give symbolic form to group norms, communicating them to the whole group, and, finally, serve to re-integrate the deviant individual back into the social group. Another set of functions of faith healing relate to the metaphorical significance of the body and its health. Healing represents the incorporation of the individual into the group. It also signifies the healing of the larger social body—in this case, the prayer group. Another important function is that of boundary maintenance; the social concerns of the group are reflected in their notions of pollution, both from within and without. Healing sometimes reflects metaphorically the consolidation of personal identity. It also can signify the establishment of social control and lines of authority in the group; the stratification system of the prayer group itself is expressed in body imagery.

Two key functions of faith healing are the re-establishment of order and the assertion of power. Threats of dis-order are integrated into the group's meaning system through healing. Furthermore, the group's belief system structures the experience of illness and/or healing and reassures the person that there is meaning in the experience. The power to produce order is at the root of the healing process. Fundamental to every medical system is a set of beliefs and practices about power. The distinctive belief system of Catholic pentecostals contains several related conceptions of disease-causing and healing power. The transmission of divine power through human vehicles is central to their notion of healing, and although their healing practices have generally resulted in the democratization of the power to heal, recognition of specialized gifts of healing and specialized healing ministries promotes stratification within each group and the movement as a whole.

In spite of their avowed use of regular medical procedures, the Catholic pentecostal belief system and practice of faith healing are, at root, in conflict with the beliefs and practices of the dominant medical system. The spread of faith healing may even represent a political statement against the power of the medical establishment—especially its monopoly over the definition of deviance and its unwillingness to include spiritual values in the definition of health.

Eight—
Community
and
Authority

In studying religious movements, sociologists often address themselves to the question of typology. Typologies can be argued endlessly, and numerous categories could be applied to the Catholic pentecostal movement. It can be analyzed as to where it fits on the church-denomination-sect continuum (or refined variations of this); it could be fitted into categories such as "chiliastic," "gnostic," "revitalization," "cultic," and "reactionary." Typologies validly serve the purposes of (1) refining the description of the movements, and by extension, clarifying comparisons with other related movements, and (2) insights which conceptualization in terms of these categories can give into the relationship between the movement and the larger society. In the case of the Catholic pentecostal movement, it is useful to apply the typological concepts of "sect" and "cult" to meet these ends. Both categories describe the movement and imply significant qualities of the shape of religion in contemporary society.

In analyzing the sect-like and cult-like qualities of the Catholic pentecostal movement, this discussion explores the distinctive characteristics of core groups within the prayer group. It further examines the qualities of "covenant communities"—highly involved individuals who have vowed (covenanted) special commitment to their group, usually living communally and serving the covenant community according to the direction of the religious leaders of the group. While these communities are not the focus of this study, their practices are important because they have become idealizations for the larger movement, filtering down to ordinary, less-specialized prayer groups. It is difficult to understand the development of the Catholic pentecostal ideals of order and authority, without first appreciating the articulation of these ideals within such distinctive communities. By extension, the roles of women and the image of family life within the movement are best interpreted by reference to the ideals and practices of covenant communities. These communities should not be seen as a separate phenomenon, however; they are only the logical extension of the sectarian tendencies characteristic of the larger movement. These sectarian qualities—especially the commitment mechanisms—are examined. Finally, the sectarian forms of social organization within the Catholic pentecostal movement are interpreted in terms of its status as a cognitive minority, relative to the dominant society.

Sectarian and Cultic Qualities of the Catholic Pentecostal Movement

The concept of "sect" and "cult" apply to forms of social organization, as well as to the nature of concomitant personal allegiance to each type of organization.[1] Certain types of social organization are conducive to or required for the maintenance of different kinds of belief system. The following analysis outlines a model of sectarian and cultic forms of social organization and personal allegiance, and applies this model to the Catholic pentecostal movement. Unfortunately, popular culture—especially mass media—has recently used the term "cult" pejoratively to refer to new religious groups which are outside the mainstream Western religious traditions. The term "sect" once had a similarly pejorative connotation. The terms "sect" and "cult" are used here purely in their sociological sense; that is, they describe certain characteristic patterns of group organization and certain modes of adherence of individual members.

The foremost characteristic of the cult is a particular type of individualism.[2] Wallis terms this feature "epistemological individualism," meaning that there is no clear locus of final authority beyond the individual member, and thus no way to legitimize the attribution of heresy. As such, cults are precarious social organizations; there are no clear boundaries between the cult ideology and that of the surrounding milieu, and therefore, no clear boundaries between members and non-members.[3] The accompanying form of personal allegiance to this type of social organization might be characterized as "seekership." The cult seeker wants an eclectic selection of particles of truth; individual members decide what components of the belief system they will accept and then synthesize these with other beliefs from a variety of sources.[4]

By contrast, the sect is characterized by "epistemological authoritarianism." There is an authoritative locus for the legitimate attribution of heresy, a belief in the group's privileged access to truth (and by extension, a clear distinction between members and non-members), and strong control is believed necessary to protect this truth.[5] Personal allegiance in the sectarian mode is more total; the adherent is looking for a system for salvation, a coherent whole.[6] Furthermore, the social organization of the sect is designed to protect the members, who constitute a cognitive minority within a dominant society which is perceived as hostile or opposed to the aims and beliefs of the sect.[7]

The classical formulation of the concept of the sect includes a number of historically bound features, such as the specific content of sectarian beliefs, and the sect's relationship with a church-monolith. If these features are eliminated, however, the general features of the sect include its self-concept as an elect or elite, totalitarianism, a belief in the right to exclude persons from membership, and a hostility toward or separation from society. Sectarianism may constitute a conscious organizational strategy, as cult leaders may try to guide the group toward sectarianism as a way of trying to overcome the cult's inherent organizational and doctrinal precariousness. The transition from cult to sect involves the arrogation of authority.[8]

The model below emphasizes the type of personal commitment of members:[9]

	SECT	CULT
Quality of personal allegiance:	(1) the group and its ideology are the primary object of member's allegiance	(1) member has multiple personal allegiances; eclectic ideology
	(2) defines the totality of the person's life	(2) defines a limited area of person's life
Perceived relationship with dominant society:	dominant society perceived as in opposition, hostile	dominant society perceived as wrong, but accommodative, neutral, or irrelevant
Group structure:	internal elitism, purism, emphasis on order and authority	internal diffuseness or pluralism

Several observers of the Catholic pentecostal movement have noted its cultic qualities. Fichter categorizes the movement as a cult, and states that demand for total commitment would be alien to the movement "which sees itself as an instrument for helping people to lead better family lives and perform effectively their occupational and other social roles."[10]

In the prayer groups studied and the movement as a whole, however, cult-like social organization characterizes only the earliest stage of development. In the early stage the primary experience is the discovery of the immediacy of God and His personal communication with the individual. The main function of the group at this stage is somewhat similar to that of a gnostic cult; the group serves as a source of information for attaining this experience. Individual members at this point were experiencing God's revelation of Himself to them personally—by definition, a highly individualistic focus. More importantly, in the early stages of the movement and in the early stages of most prayer groups, there was no objective basis for order and authority that was capable of delineating group ideology and normative behavior. The development of prophecy and discernment, along with other "gifts of the Spirit" contributed to an identifiable locus of authority within the group, thus making a sectarian form of social organization possible.

The transition to a predominantly sectarian social organization began very early in the history of the movement and had become typical by 1971. The arrogation of authority occurred at both the national and the local levels. At the national level, this primarily took the form of control over the movement's official teachings—through the Word of Life publishing house and the Communication Center (which markets books, records, cassette tapes, and so forth). The same national leaders also edit and publish *New Covenant* magazine, which is regarded as a teaching tool rather than as a forum for discussion and disagreement about ideas. They have also developed the Life in the Spirit seminars and related instructional seminar curricula and teaching materials, and they organize and control national and international conferences for Catholic pentecostals.[11]

At the level of local prayer group, the arrogation of authority has been mainly in the form of control over the prayer meeting, especially prophecy, interpretation of tongues, and discernment, as described in earlier chapters. Three of the groups studied (the small and large closed groups and the large medium-to-open group) were already more sect-like at the beginning of this study. All of the groups, however, were grappling with the ambiguity inherent in the highly individualistic revelation and style of prayer meeting religiosity, and were moving toward greater control and authority. Authority was eventually institutionalized in the prayer group's form of leadership—the pastoral team, and in an ideology of leadership responsibility, namely the exercise of headship (discussed further below). These latter terms, however, represent merely a conceptual consolidation of the sectarian patterns which were developing in the groups from their inception.

The sectarianization of the Catholic pentecostal movement does not appear to have been strategy, because the deliberate manipulation implicit in the concept of sectarianization-as-strategy, does not seem characteristic. The belief system already provided for the possibility of arrogation of authority, and the participants were comfortable with (if not, indeed, attracted by) strong claims of authority (as noted in Chapters 2 and 3). The central self-conscious strategy was one of boundary-creation and maintenance. Very early in the movement's development the leadership sought to distinguish it from classical pentecostalism and to define the proper roles for participating Protestants. Gradually other boundaries were defined, notably in strong denouncements of competing cultic meaning systems. For example, the *New Covenant* has featured articles attacking Transcendental Meditation and other "consciousness movement" techniques, Yoga, and the teachings of Edgar Cayce.[12] An increased sense of opposition toward the "world," is illustrated by prophecies of coming "days of darkness" and the necessity for "spiritual combat" (heard by some 10,000 pentecostals at the 1975 conference in Rome). This sense of opposition further solidified the sectarian tendencies of the movement.

Catholic pentecostalism is both cult-like and sect-like in its characteristic modes of personal allegiance. The findings of this study corroborate the observations of Harrison that, while general participants are allowed some latitude, the "elite core" exhibits a highly sectarian pattern of involvement.[13] A sectarian form of allegiance is being increasingly defined as normative by group leadership, so a certain proportion of the general membership is also moving in this direction. The difference between their involvement and that of the core is a matter of degree: They are in the process of being socialized into a sectarian pattern of involvement, gradually shedding competing allegiances and becoming absorbed in the group's totalism. They share the sectarian ideal, but may not fulfill it as well as the elite core. Other participants, however, may remain on the fringes indefinitely, unless specifically excluded by the core. Their allegiance to pentecostalism is just one among many, and they find eclectic bits of meaning in a wide variety of contexts. For example, some participants interviewed indicated that they also found valuable such diverse sources as horoscopes, articles in *Reader's Digest*, Silva Mind Control, popular psychology books and articles (such as those dealing with "coping" and "anger" in women's magazines), popular versions of parapsychology, Alcoholics Anonymous, religious shows on radio and TV (Kathryn Kuhlman's show was mentioned by many), and so on. Several participants, especially in middle-sized and large groups, indicated that they attended two or three different prayer meetings regularly, a practice severely discouraged by the leadership because it inhibits strong commitments to a single prayer group. Thus while the group as a whole may be moving in the direction of a sectarian form of organization, a segment of the membership may participate with a cultic pattern of allegiance.

This cultic pattern of personal allegiance is tolerated within the movement to some degree, because it seeks to identify itself as a "normal" way of being Catholic. In other words, to the extent that the movement legitimates itself as being part of the renewal of the Catholic church, it is constrained to tolerate the cultic forms of allegiance alongside the idealized sectarian mode. Such tolerance is not without its negative effects; the main problem posed by the coexistence of sectarian and cultic modes is one of boundary maintenance. The sectarian ideal of the movement holds that there is a clear distinction between one who is "in the Spirit" and one who is not; that there are clear differences in commitment and daily behavior between one who is "born again" and one who is not; and that there is no ambiguity or uncertainty of belief or moral norms for one who is charismatic; and so on. The eclectic, non-authoritative selection of meanings characteristic of the cultic mode is, thus, threatening to the neat boundaries of Catholic pentecostal identification. Some groups encourage an even higher level of elite involvement, such as covenant communities. The main difference between these covenant communities and ordinary core groups is that the former have adopted specific social arrangements that enhance their separation from the "world" and increase reliance upon each other for total support of their world view and daily actions as charismatic Christians.

Sectarian and Cultic Forms in Contemporary Society

While the concepts of "sect" and "cult" are useful for describing the development of patterns of social organization and personal allegiance in the Catholic pentecostal movement, they are more important for the understanding they provide of the place of religion in the larger society. The significance of sect-type and cult-type religious organizations in contemporary society is due to the impotence of the dominant religious orthodoxy to control societal beliefs. Troeltsch's analysis of sect and church in medieval Catholicism was predicated on a situation where the "church" was a powerful arbiter of societal values and beliefs and had the ability to define what elements were deviant.[14] Sociologists who agonize over the inadequate explanatory value of the sect type to modern religious movements may have overlooked the historical and culture-bound assumptions of Troeltsch's typology. In contemporary society, the church simply does not have control over societal beliefs or the ability to define and sanction heresy in the dominant society. Any religious group—including a recognized church—which attempts to assert a religious orthodoxy, a comprehensive system of truth, and to wrest the allegiance of its members from the claims of competing sources, will resemble the form of social organization historically characteristic of the sect.[15] As such, the group will need to establish social and psychological devices for protecting itself as a cognitive minority. Some Catholic pentecostals are quite explicit about the believer's status in a non-believing social order. One national leader states, "The problem is that we are in a post-Christian society, and in some ways we are Christian exiles in it."[16] The sectarian response to the felt opposition of the world is to exaggerate the group's marginality.

While many religious groups will continue to assert the ideal of religious commitment, increasingly the dominant form of religious allegiance in Western societies approximates the cult-type (if, indeed, there is a group affiliation at all). The increased prominence of cult-type religiosity is also related to the decline of power of the traditional religious systems.[17] Campbell, commenting on beliefs traditionally identified as part of a cultic milieu (for example, ESP, flying saucers, astrology, Rosicrucians, witchcraft), notes that structural changes—secularization and pluralism—have benefited the status of cultic culture. He suggests that, "The very processes of secularization which have been responsible for the 'cutting back' of the established form of religion have . . . created the circumstances for the emergence, not of a secular scientific society, but a society centered on a blend of mysticism, magic and pseudo-science."[18] Present-day cult-type religious allegiance is not strictly comparable with traditionally cultic beliefs. Luckmann's analysis of the relationship between religion and personal identity in modern society is particularly useful in explaining the cult-like quality of much contemporary religious affiliation. Luckmann characterizes modern society as having a fairly sharp division between primary public institutions (for example, political, juridical, and especially economic) and secondary institutions, which are located in the private sphere and cater to the private needs of individual consumers (religion, family, art, popular psychology, sports, music). The sense of autonomy in the individual's freedom to choose meaning from themes in the private sphere is directly proportionate to the loss of freedom, meaning, and self-determination in the public sphere. Luckmann states:

> Individual religiosity in modern society receives no massive support and confirmation from the primary public institutions. Overarching subjective structures of meaning are almost completely detached from the functionally rational

norms of these institutions. In the absence of external support, subjectively constructed and eclectic systems of "ultimate" significance will have a somewhat precarious reality for the individual.[19]

The social organization supporting this type of religiosity would be, therefore, the "ephemeral support of other 'autonomous' individuals," and would be located primarily in the private sphere.[20]

These interpretations point to the larger significance of applying the concepts of sect and cult to religious and quasi-religious movements in contemporary society. To the extent that group expressions of religiosity survive—and there is every indication that they will not only survive but even multiply—it is probable that the characteristic form of these groups will be either sectarian or cultic (or both). To the extent that they are pluralistic, flexible, and eclectic, group expressions of religiosity will tend to utilize the cult-type form of social organization. To the extent that the groups are internally orthodox, totalistic, and in opposition to "the world," they will tend toward a sectarian pattern.

Order, Authority, and Commitment among the Core Membership

The preceding discussion shows that there are different levels of commitment and involvement in the prayer group; indeed, these levels are so different as to constitute qualitatively distinct modes of participation: cultic and sectarian. This section analyzes the interaction of the sectarian core of the prayer group, as well as the influence of sectarian patterns on the larger membership. This research has not focused primarily on this aspect of Catholic pentecostalism, but rather emphasized those areas of belief and practice readily accessible to the average participant. Understanding the actions of core membership is, however, significant for a comprehensive treatment of the larger prayer group; the core group shapes the direction of the whole.

In addition, the actions characteristic of the sectarian core are the most frequently cited by critics of the movement.[21] Apparent aberrations within the movement, such as the scandal over practices in True House (which reached such proportions that they were reported in *Newsweek*)[22] can best be understood as logical—albeit extreme—extensions of sectarian patterns of involvement. For these reasons, it is necessary to discuss the significance of distinctive core group interactions. This analysis rests mainly on descriptions by members of several groups, media from the national movement, and reports of other researchers. Several types of core groups are described, focusing especially on the qualities of covenant communities. The idealizations of order and authority that have developed in these communities follow, showing their extension to norms for women's roles and family life. Although these beliefs and practices are interesting in themselves, they are especially significant because they have become ideals for the larger movement, not merely the sectarian core.

Types of Core Group

Core groups vary considerably in their internal structure and their relationship with the wider prayer group. The most common situation is an ordinary prayer group with a highly committed core of member-leaders. Whether or not they are formally organized into ministry teams, these members are extremely active in prayer group activities (especially in such elite activities as teaching Life in the Spirit seminars, organizing conferences, giving teachings, running prayer meetings).[23] They spend sizable amounts of time with each other, not only accomplishing leadership tasks, but also providing much mutual support for their extreme level of commitment. Even in small and medium-sized groups, the core leadership is likely to be distinctive—not merely in the amount, but (more importantly) in the sectarian pattern of their involvement.

A second type of sectarian core evolved from the creation of "covenanted communities" of Catholic pentecostals. These groups are typically, but not necessarily, residential communities organized into households and often economically communal as well.[24] Communal living is not characteristic of older-style pentecostalism and this pattern of involvement more closely resembles some counter-cultural groups, such as the Jesus People. While it is possible for an entire prayer group to constitute a covenant community, often the covenanted body is the core or sponsor of a larger prayer group. This latter situation presents some unique structural issues, especially: Is the prayer group an operation of the covenanted community or is the community a sub-unit of the prayer group?

A similar arrangement is a third type of core group: one in which a religious house (for example, nuns or monks) is organized as a charismatic community.[25] Although these often function as self-contained prayer groups, many times the religious house serves as a focus for a larger prayer group, attracting lay people as well as religious living outside the sponsoring house. Members of the house would provide much of the core leadership of that larger prayer group. Groups with these second and third types of core groups were visited and some members interviewed, although this aspect was not central to this study. Other contexts for sectarian involvement are possible but not common (for example, a place of work hiring only fellow pentecostals).

The sectarian pattern of involvement and social organization was evidenced by a core of members of all nine groups studied and is encouraged by much of the teaching of the national leadership. This pattern fulfills several functions: providing leadership, insuring effective organization, and embodying the movement's ideals.[26] The pattern is also functional in more basic ways: maintaining belief, and promoting commitment. For these reasons, the sectarian pattern of involvement is held up as an ideal for members, and the movement as a whole is moving in this direction.

The special form of the covenant community is particularly important in the development of these ideals. The development of communitarian living is relatively new in pentecostalism; it was not practiced in classical pentecostalism. Although the communal living of the counter-culture of the 1960s may have provided some impetus for this development, it is probable that the model of older pietistic sects, such as the Bruderhof, was more influential.[27] The following excerpt is an example of an agreement signed as a covenant by members forming one such community:

> We submit to the agreements, pastoral guidance, and organization which the community is always developing and re-evaluating through the guidance of the Holy Spirit.
>
> We serve the brethren through: the charisms which the Spirit gives to each of us; prayer and penance for the love of one another; the ministry of reconciliation; and waiting upon the personal needs of one another. We reorder our priorities, especially time and finances, according to our community responsibilities.[28]

This type of agreement is believed to be not only a commitment among members, but also a special agreement between the group and God, whom they believe to have called them into this special relationship.

These covenant communities are important both as "power-houses" for work done in the movement and as a concrete expression of the ideals of Catholic pentecostalism. They epitomize the fullest embodiment of charismatic community. As such they are more influential in the movement than their numbers alone would indicate. They frequently become centers for teaching and leadership training in their area; their members sometimes adopt a program of "outreach" to encourage the formation of new prayer groups in areas lacking local initiative; they often coordinate the regional and national movement organization, write the media, and plan the conferences. Although there have recently been cautionary statements against groups becoming covenant communities without adequate preparation and leadership, it is clear that most members consider them to be the epitome of Catholic pentecostal life.[29]

In many respects these communities are very un-representative of the larger membership. The self-selection factor in the membership makes them more likely to consist of·students, young-married couples, and celibates (celibacy is gaining as an ideal for lay members as well as "religious" people). Although older people and families with children are also involved, the amount of time and energy, and undivided commitment required in many covenant communities, makes this style of life less feasible for them. Also, the fact of living together means that more areas of their lives are subject to distinctive pentecostal patterns of decision-making and conflict-resolution. Such patterns, growing logically out of the belief system of the movement, are turned into everyday usages. In fact, ideals and practices formulated by covenant communities might very well never have been conceived by ordinary prayer groups, even though these ideals and practices were consistent with the ordinary groups' belief system and have subsequently filtered down to their level of involvement. In summary, the process of formulating ideals and practices is as follows: the sectarian cores of ordinary prayer groups sought a more perfect expression of their commitment—the intensive community; the intensive communities had experiences and needs requiring a more detailed set of practices and a more thorough ideology; these ideals and practices then were adopted in a milder form by ordinary prayer groups. This elaboration of movement ideology by the sectarian core, especially communal core groups, can best be seen in the fundamental issue of authority.

The Idealization of Order and Authority

The idealization that has evolved is well expressed by a movement spokesperson:

> The relationships we are forming with each other—laying down our lives for one another in committed service—need order for peace and real freedom. . . . We know that the Lord wants to establish his order in our prayer groups and communities. The Lord also wants to establish his order in our living situations: our marriages, our households, our convents, our rectories. When we are baptized in the Spirit, the Lord inspires in us a desire to put things right, by the power of his Spirit. We need some instruments to help that work, and the Lord has given us those instruments.[30]

The two most commonly used instruments which he then describes are (1) agreements and covenants, and (2) "headship" and "submission." The concept of headship and submission in a community setting is described by another national leader:

> Being part of a body means that none of us can make decisions about our lives on our own. There is an order to the

life in a body. Part of that order means that the members have to be subordinate to the life of the body as a whole, and to the direction of the head. . . . Effective authority and subordination is crucial for a successful community.[31]

In elaborating the ideal of headship and submission, leaders emphasize that this does not mean that the head should be authoritarian and domineering and that the submitted should be passive and subservient. The ideal holds that the head is performing a service for the whole body in assuming responsibility and care for those under him, and the submitted should be obedient, loyal, supportive, and encouraging.[32] According to another national leader, the advantages of headship-and-submission are threefold. First, the arrangement eliminates power struggles ("It's a very liberating thing. . . . It clarifies who's responsible for making the final decision"). Second, headship allocates responsibility for getting things done. Third, it gives proper "deployment" (that is, arranges group personnel for effective functioning).[33] He gives three reasons for the headship-submission relationship for individuals. First, it provides a context for Christian "formation" ("By agreeing to submit to the person who is doing the formation, the disciple's growth in the Christian life can take place more quickly and effectively"). Second, it promotes the ascetic goal of giving up one's will ("A person can more effectively do so when he is called upon to obey in concrete ways"). And, third, the head shows the submitted what his or her "problems" are ("Simply having someone other than yourself offer you strong input about the direction of your life protects you from overlooking certain areas").[34] Some leaders are conscious of possible abuses of this kind of authority structure; they recommend "collegial headship" (that is, shared by several leaders) and relationships among a number of communities, as the two best protections against such abuses.

At the same time, however, ideal obedience extends even to submission to heads whom one thinks are wrong. For example, one pentecostal leader urges members to be clear about who their heads are—in the church (recognizing the headship of bishop and pastor), in the prayer groups and communities, and in the home. He urges submission to the proper heads (that is, authority of office) in all arenas, whether the heads are Spirit-filled or not, whether their decisions are right or not. He adds that such submission does not extend to obeying directives that are morally wrong, but that such issues of conscience are rarely involved.[35]

The concrete application of these ideals depends upon the nature of the group, and the personalities involved. In general, ordinary prayer groups do not extend the headship-submitted relationship into the everyday lives of their members; covenanted groups do. On the other hand, several of the ordinary prayer groups studied in this research held the extreme form of submission to headship as the ideal toward which they hoped to move. For example, the group characterized as small and closed had, from the beginning—even before the ideology of headship was articulated in movement literature—adopted a highly authoritarian structure, largely due to the personalities involved. By contrast, one large group (more toward the open end of the continuum) held a loose concept of headship in which the heads of various prayer group functions were comparable to committee chairpersons (for example, there were heads of the refreshment ministry, the music ministry, and the maintenance ministry).

One important extension of these beliefs about authority results in an acceptance and even idealization of the authority structure of the dominant society. In Chapter 2, the analysis of the Catholic pentecostal belief system explained their very low level of involvement in social action. Belief in the imminence of the Millennium and focus on voluntaristic approaches to social problems are especially significant. Members' attitudes toward authority were also found to be strongly related to their lack of involvement in social action. Not atypical is one member who said, "I think Christians have to support the authorities, from the President all the way down, because the Scriptures tell us to be submissive to those in authority over us, and because without authority and all there wouldn't be any order in society, and God wants things to be in order."

This embracing of secular headship is the position of many, but not all, movement leaders. Those leaders who have had first-hand experiences of the third-world or other areas where problems of poverty and injustice are evident are the most sensitive on the issue of obedience. One such leader urged Catholic pentecostals not to be uncritically obedient, "A new-found obedience to God may lead to submission in areas of life where Christian freedom is needed. . . . A spirituality that stresses submission to authority somehow must contain room for those who proclaim against the injustice found in the society or the nation or authorities and officials."[36] He identified the problem for most Catholic charismatics: obedience to human authorities is seen as obedience to God. Thus not only the ideal of headship-submission but also the day-to-day practice of submission to authorities mitigate against fighting injustice and socio-political ills.

The Order in Family Life and the Role of Women

Another major extension of this ideology of headship is the belief that, under most circumstances, women should not be heads. One national figure asserts, "God's plan for function within his people places the roles of authority, of direction, of headship, of governance upon men. Women are called to be in a great variety of ministries which support that leadership, are responsive to that leadership, which are submissive to that leadership."[37] Stratification according to gender in the community—especially covenant communities—thus becomes somewhat of a caste system in which women operate and have some power in a women's world (caring for children, preparing meals, caring for the home, educating children and neophyte members, caring for the sick, being supportive of men), but ultimate power and authority belong to the men of the community.[38]

There is some softening of this notion as it applies to the ordinary prayer group. Sharing authority with women has somewhat greater acceptance in that setting, because the authority is over few areas of life, the group may not have enough men who can assume authority, or the leaders may wish to have a woman on the pastoral team to represent and supervise women's areas of concern. The ideals provide for women having headship over other women, but men should have ultimate headship. Thus women's roles in the prayer group are considered very important, but typically embody the relatively powerless nurturant and domestic tasks assumed to be appropriate for women's work. Women in the core group are likely to be concentrated as members of teams providing music, refreshments, child care, literature sales, induction of neophyte members, and care of the sick. Women held important leadership positions in only two of the groups studied; in the other groups women were, at most, in authority over other women.

This ideal of women's submission is applied not only in the prayer meeting, but also in the home. A member of a covenant community and wife of one of *New Covenant*'s editors states, "No matter how deep her insight may be, a woman must be in submission to her husband just as Christ is submissive to the Father, perfectly obedient in all things . . . when a woman submits to her husband and acknowledges his headship, she is submitting to the will of God."[39] Women are encouraged by movement media to come to a sense of higher self-esteem which is not based on the tasks they perform but upon their being "beloved of the Lord." The domestic tasks assigned to women are promoted as ways of serving the Lord, "The world we live in has such a low regard for 'just a housewife' that it is easy to begin to accept the lies and delusions of those who deny the possibility of this being meaningful to the Lord. Liberation for a wife and mother is not found by relinquishing that role, but by discovering how beautifully and richly one can grow as a Christian by being the Lord's own dependable servant in that role."[40] In a less positive tone, one respondent connected "women's lib" with temptation by Satan:

[She had described the job she had recently quit] I didn't see I was neglecting my children, neglecting my family's meals, neglecting my housework. I didn't see all of that then. But anything, like a mother going to work, for example. . . . This women's lib where the women want to be out in the world and working in the world and equal to the men and doing this job and doing that one. And that all seems very good, but if you take each individual and maybe trace back . . . where that need to be a part of that women's lib and to do that work out in the world is coming from, we're going to find that need is not really a good one . . . that's where Satan comes in, urging some of these people on in what appears to be a good thing, but then when we trace it back, we find that it's not so good.

The headship of the husband extends also to his role as head of the family, the ultimate authority over all members. The ideal holds that this order is God's will and is the only way the whole family can come to fulfill its potential. One woman, a member of a covenant community, states, "Most of my effort to counteract the work of Satan, the pressures of worldly status, and the strong self-will in the children has been fruitless. Even though the words I said were correct, their hearts were not changed. My husband began to take a more direct headship role in each child's life, and, as I submitted to his headship, things changed."[41] Much of the literature on headship in the home is aimed at the husband/father, urging him to take greater responsibility in the home—spending time with his family, directing and correcting them, supervising their spiritual and emotional development. One author suggests that mothers come to dominate the home because they try to fill in the void left by busy husbands, but that this usually produced "rebellious, frustrated, emotionally immature, insecure, anxious children."[42]

Applications of this ideal of headship-submission varied in the nine groups studied, but the ideal was clearly operant in all. Two groups sponsored special programs for men to encourage them to be stronger heads in their homes. Many women whose spouses were not in the movement witnessed that they had difficulty submitting when they felt their spouses were wrong. Members in various groups witnessed to how their family relations had changed since practicing headship-submission. The ideal was extended to children, who were to be submissive to both parents, but especially to the father who was to be in charge of their discipline. One couple witnessed that they had established a special "Jesus room" for their five and eight-year-olds, where the misbehaving children were sent to think about how sad Jesus is when children disobey their parents; the parents made a point of praying with the children after allowing them out and assuring them that

Jesus forgave them. Another woman witnessed that, as a single parent of teenagers, she felt great difficulty in administering proper headship; on several occasions she had asked the Lord to give them spiritual beatings, because she could not physically punish them as a father should. Although familial relationships figured importantly into all of the groups' concerns, relatively closed groups were much more vigorous than others in asserting the headship-submission ideal.

The pentecostal idealization of gender roles in the family and religious community serves a number of functions for the group, as well as the individual member. The gender role structure serves as a religious legitimation of the group's authority structure and contributes to the simplicity of the organizational structure.[43] The structure is directly linked with the larger ideal of order; relationships of God, man, woman, and child, are all neatly articulated. The idealization of order of relationships is seen as a reflection of cosmic order; dis-order, ambiguity and chaos are interpreted as works of the Evil One. The structure fulfills functions for the individual, as well. This set of role-definitions accomplishes the merging of the individual's identity with the meaning system of the group into a master role. Fulfilling the group's ideal of "being a woman" becomes identical to what it means to "be a Christian." Such consolidation of identity is consistent with the totalistic ideal of the sectarian mode.

Sectarian Involvement and Commitment Mechanisms

That greater commitment to a dissonant religious group should produce a more sectarian pattern of involvement is almost a truism. Many religious and secular groups adopt practices which enhance commitment, thus promoting the longevity of the group. Coser indicates a still wider category that he calls "greedy institutions":

> These institutions concentrate the commitment of all of their members, or of selected members, in one overall status and its associated central role relationships. Being insulated from competing relationships, and from competing anchors for their social identity, these selected status-occupants find their identity anchored in the symbolic universe of the restricted roles-set of the greedy institution.[44]

Although such commitment is typically voluntary, it gives the group great power over individual members; once committed, individuals are unlikely to want to withdraw, since their very identities are involved. Saying that members stay on voluntarily is rather like saying that a forty-five year old woman, who sacrificed obtaining job skills and personal money in order to care for her husband and four children, is "free to leave" an unhappy marriage.

An analysis of historical communal groups highlights a number of successful commitment mechanisms which are also used by Catholic pentecostals. One such mechanism is "investment." Individuals who invest their time and resources in the group become further integrated into it. Their investment gives them a stake in the group's successful operation. Renunciation, such as the cutting of ties with former associates or the renunciation of allegiances to alternate belief systems, constitutes another commitment-promoting device. Getting together frequently, especially for work and ritual activities, also promotes cohesion and commitment. Adherence to group values is aided by a stratification system in which differentiation is made according to the special spiritual or moral values of that particular group rather than the values of the dominant society.[45]

The most crucial commitment process is mortification of the "old self" and surrender; this process is probably most comparable to what charismatic communities call "formation," following obvious parallels in monasticism. "Mortification" refers to any number of practices designed to dismantle the self that was based on the "old" values, in order to replace it with a "new" self embodying the "new" values. By this process, the individual's self-esteem comes to depend upon the group's evaluation. Such processes are sometimes perceived as a sign of the members' care for the individual and serve to develop a sense of trust. Mortification practices range from little things, like forbidding use of cosmetics or certain styles of dress (because they express the old values and not the new), to more personal areas, such as mutual confession.Confession is a very potent method of undermining the "old self" as studies of so-called "thought reform" have shown. Such group-induced self-exposure is highly threatening to the individual; for the same reason, it can therefore be an expression of trust within the group.[47] In other words, it symbolizes that the individual trusts other members enough to risk dramatic self-exposure. Mortification thus prepares the way for surrender.

Especially relevant to an appreciation of Catholic pentecostal practices, particularly those of core members, is "institutional awe." Kanter explains, "Institutional awe, then, is a means by which surrender to the greater power of a social system can be effected. . . . Such systems with great ordering power not only satisfy the individual's need for meaning, but they also provide a sense of rightness, certainty, and conviction that promotes transcendence and surrender to the source of power."[48]

One mechanism for providing institutional awe is ideology, a coherent system of beliefs which legitimates demands made on members in the name of a higher principle—in this case, the will of God. A second source of institutional awe is power and leadership, made especially effective by increasing the distance of the final decision-making from the ordinary members, thus promoting a sense of mystery.[49] This mechanism is also clearly evidenced in the charismatic renewal, especially the uses of prophecy and discernment. These commitment mechanisms, among others, effectively promote group cohesion. Carried to their logical conclusion, they also result in a highly sectarian form of social organization.

Several of these commitment mechanisms, if applied in their more extreme forms, parallel mechanisms of "thought reform." Lifton's concepts of "milieu control," "mystical manipulation," "demands for purity," "cult of confession," "sacred science," and "loading the language," in particular, do apply in some degree to practices of the sectarian core of the Catholic pentecostal movement, as they probably do to most sectarian groups, religious or nonreligious alike. Various authors have applied Lifton's framework to such groups as the Jesus People, the Bruderhof, and the Unification Church.[50] Some critics of the Catholic pentecostal movement have pointed out that some of its covenant communities have patterned themselves after the Bruderhof.[51] Critics might validly attack the groups' belief system and they might rightly ask whether the ends justify the means. If, however, both of these matters were granted, it could be shown that—sociologically and psychologically, at least—the processes described here are, in fact, highly effective mechanisms for achieving the desired ends of conversion and commitment. The processes may even be necessary for the continued existence of such intense groups. At the same time, Catholic pentecostals should not be too sanguine that alleged abuses, such as the "breakthrough ministry" (which employed exactly what Lifton calls the "cult of confession"), are merely exceptional cases. Rather, such extremes are inherent in the very ideals of the movement and made real possibilities by the regular practices of the sectarian core.

The idealization of the sectarian core within Catholic pentecostalism is one of intense commitment. It encompasses an ideal of order and authority that is embodied in a theocratic stratification system, but extends beyond the immediate scope of the prayer group itself to define roles and relationships in the family, as well. The organization of the core group also incorporates a number of commitment mechanisms to enhance the total integration of the individual into the group. Such total commitment is perceived as desirable, not only because of the goodness of the group's beliefs and practices, but also because of the evils of the world outside. The sectarian mode is, thus, the response of the group to its minority status relative to the threatening dominant world view.

Catholic Pentecostals as a Cognitive Minority

A group which resists the world view of the rest of society must serve as its own support for the plausibility structure undergirding the reality of its belief system. Any group, including an institutional church, which resists in important ways the dominant world view can be considered a "cognitive minority,"[52] an appelation that applies to pentecostal Catholics, both relative to the larger church and also to the rest of American society in general. Some pentecostal beliefs are dramatically dissonant. Consider, for example, how different it is in this society for people to believe that God literally performs miracles in their everyday lives (healing them, getting them jobs, and countless "holy coincidences"), that God's power can be directed to accomplishing things they want and need through the power of prayer, that God speaks regularly to them through the voices of others, and that both the Spirit of God and evil spirits are active in the world and can possess the individual with all their power. These beliefs are clearly dissonant from those of many people in Western society, including most Christians.

Catholic pentecostalism, therefore, has many characteristics of cognitive deviance and, as such, requires certain social-psychological adjustments by its members. Its sectarian structure is understandable, because the maintenance of such cognitive deviance requires the support of a close-knit group of fellow believers.[53] As developed in the preceding discussion, this form of organization is termed a "sect," but the sect should be understood as a form of sociation which even some established churches are now beginning to resemble. Non-religious groups can also be sectarian in the maintenance of cognitive dissonance.[54] The heavy emphasis of charismatic Catholics on community can be understood in this context: Whatever its spiritual significance, the religious community serves the necessary function of supporting a cognitively deviant conception of reality. The more the individual seeks to believe fully and practice this separate reality, the more important the group support becomes.

The content of interaction in the group is important for maintaining this dissonant world view. According to Berger and Luckmann, "the conversational apparatus maintains reality by 'talking through' various elements of experience and allocating them a definite place in the real world."[55] The analysis of witnessing shows how this conversation operates in the larger group; in the context of the core group, this "talking through" occurs more frequently and more deeply. Conversation with significant others is stronger reality-confirmation than other conversation in the individual's social situation. Members of a dissonant group come to serve as significant others for each other. Often members, especially highly involved members, find that they have cut off or reduced (sometimes deliberately, more often not) their ties with their previous significant others—spouses, parents, friends. This severance functions to reduce the problems of dissonance, eliminating some sources of conflict between their former and new selves. A problem commonly expressed by many women in the movement is the sense of hurt and hostility of their non-pentecostal husbands. Some of this conflict can be explained by the wives' proselytizing, their assertion of their preferences for how to spend their time, and perhaps the husbands' envy of their wives' newfound satisfaction and meaning. One especially important source of conflict, however, is that many husbands correctly sense that they have been displaced as their wives' foremost significant other.

Not only former significant others, but also other non-believers in one's everyday world constitute a threat to the dissonant belief system. One stance toward all of these "others" is to try to convert them. This is effective, not only because believers want others to share their happy condition, but also because if the others convert they are no longer threats to belief.[56] If proselytizing is not successful or practicable, believers often protect their dissonant belief system by withdrawing. In this sense, pentecostal Catholics need their group in the same sense as do traditional sectarians—as a way of holding the world at arm's length, so to speak.

Thus the sectarian form of social organization of the Catholic pentecostal movement can be seen as related to its status as a cognitive minority. The prayer group structures itself in order to preserve its distinctive belief system in the face of dissonance with the rest of the society. This would be the case regardless of the specific content of the dissonant beliefs. On the other hand, Catholic pentecostals espouse specific beliefs which themselves promote a sectarian mode. In particular, their ideals of authority, community, and order contribute to a sectarian form of social organization.

The movement does not fit neatly into either the categories of sect or cult; rather it has levels of involvement, some of which are more cult-like, and some of which are more sect-like. The viability of both the sectarian and cultic forms of this and similar movements points to larger issues about the place of religion in society. The sectarian form is related to the decreased salience of religious explanations and religious motivations in the everyday life of members of the dominant society. Certain types of religiosity, even if they have many adherents, find themselves with the status of cognitive minorities and must organize themselves accordingly. At the same time, the cultic form points to the lack of power of religious groups to define and control a deviant version of reality; diverse belief systems compete in a market-like arena where the individual is free to synthesize an eclectic version of truth.

Nine—
Conclusion

An analysis of the Catholic pentecostal movement is helpful for understanding religiosity and group movements in contemporary Western society. More importantly, such an analysis reveals much about the whole society and the place of the individual in it. The latter theme is central to the sociology of religion. This concluding chapter locates the interpretation of the Catholic pentecostal and similar religious movements squarely within the discussion of these broader theoretical perspectives.

First, this chapter examines Catholic pentecostals' claim to be counter-acting secularization. The initial step in such an analysis is to distinguish the different meanings and uses of the word "secularization." The secularization hypothesis is a controversial one among sociologists; however, a serious approach to the claims of the movement (as well as of many sociologists and journalists) requires some use of this term. Second, certain trends in the direction of the movement are described and discussed; evaluation is made not in terms of the desirability of these trends, but rather in terms of their probable impact on society, the church, and the lives of movement members. The specific issue of whether or not the Catholic pentecostal movement is a significant influence for real change in American society is discussed in some detail. Some aspects of the movement hold potential for influencing the society; other aspects seriously inhibit such influence.

The final part of this chapter locates the significance of recent religious movements within a larger societal problem of legitimation. In particular, the underlying legitimations of society and self have become problematic. Also related are such issues as the basis of societal integration, legitimation of normative and motivational structures in society, legitimation of the individual's self (identity) and, concomitantly, the individual's sense of order and meaning. Such issues are not peculiar to American society, but are rather related to institutional structures and modes of consciousness characteristic of modern societies regardless of their socio-political stance. Thus the diverse religious and quasi-religious group movements of contemporary societies are responding not only to the concrete personal and shared biographical experiences (described in Chapter 3) that may have propelled them into existence as a group; but also, indirectly, they address a broader and more fundamental issue of the basis of order and legitimacy in modern societies.

Impact of the Movement on the Church and the Larger Society

An early and continual claim of members of the Catholic pentecostal movement has been that they are countering the extensive secularity of modern society. This claim is important both as an indicator of the movement's intended thrust and as a possible impact on society. Can and does the movement counter-act secularization? Before such a question can be addressed, however, it is necessary to explore the differences and convergences between the pentecostals' and the sociologists' use of the concept of "secularization."

When Catholic pentecostals decry secularization, they typically mean that their Christian religion is not pervasive and powerful in society. For example, if a non-Christian religion emerged powerfully in the United States (imagine, for instance, a national theocracy of Hare Krisna, with schoolchildren chanting their mantras, and meditation breaks on the GM assembly lines), this would not be viewed by pentecostals as "de-secularization." When Catholic pentecostals bemoan the lack of religion in other spheres of life (the work world, education, family), they mean the lack of fundamental Christian religion. For instance, a major statement issued in 1977 by the leaders of the movement, and addressed to the U.S. Catholic bishops, called for the evangelization of church members who were merely nominal Christians ("baptized pagans"). It decried the influence of secularity within the church itself and called for the recognition of several pentecostal principles to overcome these forces: specifically, reliance on Scripture as ultimate authority, recognition of prophecy, and attention to spiritual warfare with the forces of Evil.[1]

Similarly, interviews with respondents produced an image of "secularization" which was nearly identical with "de-Christianization." The most frequent concern identified with "secularization" was the weakness of Christian norms in guiding behavior. Examples given included: permissiveness of parents, "gay" liberation, widespread pornography, drugs and rock music, abortion, pre-marital and extra-marital sexual activity, and restriction of prayer in public schools. Less frequently, members cited: that religion does not "carry over" into business dealings, that politics are morally corrupt, and that communism is making inroads into American institutions. Thus to Catholic pentecostals, the most salient evidence of secularization of society is Christianity's loss of control over the norms of private life; secondarily, secularization implies Christianity's lack of control in public spheres such as business, politics, and education.

Another component of the pentecostal definition of secularization is the individual's loss of meaning and sense of identity. For example, one woman said, "There's just so many in society today—not just young people but adults too—that have no sense of where they're going or what the meaning of life is. They've got nothing in their lives that tells them who they are or where they should be heading—no direction and no meaning. It's sad. Now that kind of emptiness, that's the worst of it [secular society]." According to pentecostals, the solution to problems of meaning and identity cannot be found outside Christianity. During one prayer meeting, for example, a man recounted his son's "search for identity." The problem began when the son left parochial high school and entered a state college. The witnessing tale recounted the boy's vain search for answers in philosophy and psychology courses, probable experimentation with drugs, TM and Silva Mind Control, and most recently exploring Subud. The speaker concluded with an emphasis on the inadequacy of non-Christian solutions to his son's search: the boy could "find himself" only in Jesus.

Another less-frequently mentioned sense of secularization refers to ways of thinking about the world. For example, one woman exclaimed to the interviewer:

> When I say "I was blind, but now I see"—like in the song— I really mean it. For instance, you probably see things in a secular way of seeing. You call God's providence "mere coincidence." A miracle just looks like "an accident of nature." Secular society just sees the surface of things and takes that as though it was reality. That way of seeing misses the real forces behind events—the power of God. And evil and sin, too. . . . I mean, denying the real forces behind the surface leads to denying the forces of evil and the reality of sin. So, like, secular society hasn't got a chance against . . . it's a victim of Satan . . . the people in society are victims, because they can't see the forces that are really behind it all.

Thus secularization refers to the inability or unwillingness of the society to perceive and interpret everyday reality in terms of a realm that transcends that everyday reality. Specifically, secular consciousness does not allow for a God who is a direct force in the sphere of everyday life.[2]

Use of the concept of secularization by Catholic pentecostals converges with some sociological uses of the idea. The main point of disparity is that when Catholic pentecostals assert the lack of religion in modern society, they are generally equating religion with a very specific historical and institutional form of religion. By contrast, sociologists attempt to define religion more broadly, such that the rise of one religion with the simultaneous decline of another would not be considered an instance of secularization. Although there are several social processes which may be linked with each other, it is useful to treat them as more or less discrete in order to evaluate the secularization hypothesis and the pentecostal movement's claims to counter the process. Aspects of sociological theories of change correspond surprisingly closely to some of the uses of the idea of secularization by respondents in this study.

Four social developments appear to be crucial to a sociological discussion of secularization: (1) institutional differentiation and specialization and the segregation of religion in the "private sphere"; (2) pluralism and the undermining of the religious legitimation of the society's normative structure; (3) privatization of the self and de-legitimation of many social sources of identity; (4) dominance of a cognitive style which precludes non-rational elements of explanation and discourages reference to a transcendental realm in the experiencing of oneself and one's world. Rather than argue whether or not the general term, "secularization," applies, an examination of the above aspects may provide more acceptable points of departure for theorizing about social change and the condition of religion. Both those theorists who utilize the secularization hypothesis[3] and those who disagree with it[4] could agree upon the existence of several of these social developments. They would not, however, agree that, taken together, these developments constitute an identifiable trend for all modern and modernizing societies, nor that these distinct developments necessarily pointed to the decline of religion; some sociologists would say that they pointed rather to the decline of only a particular institutional form of religion, with religious functions still being performed in other guises.

Institutional Specialization and the Segregation of Religion in the "Private Sphere"

One set of explanations of the place of religion in contemporary society begins with the extent of institutional specialization. Accordingly, the various functions performed in society have become increasingly compartmentalized into differentiated institutional forms. Institutions (such as religion and family) which had formerly pervaded all social life are relegated to their own separate compartments, increasingly irrelevant to other institutional settings. Indeed, especially in the economic sphere (and by extension, the politico-legal spheres), the very grounds of operation—based on functional rationality—are inimical to religious modes of thought and action.[5] These institutions in modern societies (not only capitalist ones) are organized according to a means-ends rationality, in which questions of efficient functioning, cost-effectiveness, and bureaucratic specialization of tasks, are relevant. Within the framework of this functional rationality, issues such as meaning, morality, personal feelings, or even social benefit are virtually irrelevant, and are relegated to other spheres of human life.[6]

This differentiation is directly linked with the process of privatization of religion.[7] Certain institutions, such as economic, political, educational, and legal ones, have become increasingly segregated from the institutions of the private sphere of the individual's life (family, religion, leisure activities). As a result, religion is not only less relevant to the operation of institutions of the public sphere, but it is also less able to provide the individual with motivation and meaning for those spheres. Privatization also reduces the inevitability of religion; religious beliefs, norms, and practices become voluntary and non-serious.

Pluralism and the Problem of Legitimating Norms

Pluralism refers to the societal tolerance of competing versions of truth. Such a stance enables complex, heterogeneous societies to function effectively; in America, pluralism has even been converted into a civic virtue. At the same time, however, pluralism results in the relativization of norms and values. The particular choice one makes among the various competing versions of truth appears to be purely voluntary and arbitrary; thus norms and values are undermined.[8] It is not only the norms themselves that have become problematic; the critical issues are: On what grounds can operative norms be legitimated? Are there any common bases for moral judgment? Increasingly the courts are being called upon to create legitimations for judgment in the absence of cultural consensus.[9]

Privatization and Legitimation of Self

Privatization refers to the extent to which the individual finds sources of identity and meaning only in the private sphere. The concomitants of personal identity are a sense of order, an interpretation of reality, a system of meaning, and the integration of oneself into a larger community.[10] The individual finds fewer sources of identity in the public sphere, partly because the order of this sphere is functional rationality and notions such as "meaning" are irrelevant. The "privatization of the self"[11] creates problems that may be reflected in the widespread quest for holistic world views (such as expressed by many contemporary religious movements, communal-agrarian groups, many alternative health movements, some strands of parapsychology, and so on). On the other hand, such "privatization of self" also promotes some of the personal freedoms enjoyed by many in modern society (for example, the extent to which one's reference groups are not imposed by kin or neighborhood but are more freely chosen). Nevertheless, such a process does result in a problem of legitimating oneself; identity becomes problematic. The legitimations providing order, interpretation of reality, meaning, and community, have been undermined. Ironically, one of the results has been the enhancement of a rather naked form of individualism—"Do your own thing."[12]

Cognitive Style and Transcendence

The cognitive style appropriate to modern bureaucratic structures in the public sphere and utilized in modern science, medicine, law, and so on, is not amenable to that of religion, which embodies ir-rational, non-linear thinking, reference to a transcendent, empirically non-verifiable realm, and which allows that undifferentiated "experiencing" is a valid way of "knowing." The impact of the cognitive style of modern institutions has filtered down to everyday life (albeit, not consistently or pervasively). As a result, not only is one's everyday knowledge more restricted to this-worldly items, but indeed this world itself is transformed. Gellner states, "The very idiom in which the world is characterized becomes distinct, not just from the idiom in which we might have spoken of the elfs [sic], but also from the way in which we think of ourselves and of each other."[13] He suggests that these processes relegate other modes of cognition (for example, fantasy, play, religion) to the status of non-serious, to be practiced in private life as "frills." The dominant mode of cognition, however, still applies to those areas that "really matter," such as business, health, technology, government.[14]

Considering only the above four developments (rather than attempting to generalize about "secularization" as an all-encompassing process), what potential is there that a religious movement, such as the Catholic pentecostal movement, can successfully "re-sacralize" society? Such re-sacralization need not resemble Christianity; Robbins and Anthony suggest that dualistic religions (such as Christianity) are less suited to the task than monistic religions (such as certain Oriental religions).[15] Nevertheless, the difficulties in re-sacralization lie less in the content of belief and practice than in the social structures within which such a movement for change must operate. Movements such as Catholic pentecostalism are going counter, not merely to modern society, but to important aspects of modernity itself.

Although one cannot make any firm predictions about the future of modern society, the structure of society suggests that the two particular developments described above are not likely to be reversed by religious movements: the structure of institutions of the public sphere and the cognitive style of "functional rationality." Movements such as Catholic pentecostalism are not likely to change the institutional structure, both because they lack power over the operations of this sphere, and because there are strong vested interests in the continued operation of these structures. In contrast to some other religious movements in contemporary society, members of the Catholic pentecostal movement are characteristically *not* counter-cultural; they are generally upright citizens, responsible performers of their jobs, and providers of a comfortable middle-class existence for their families. Modern society, with its segregation of leisure time and its high standard of living, has made possible the very type of movement which Catholic pentecostals enjoy. For example, modern society has provided the leisure for men and especially for women to spend many hours away from work and home each week at prayer meetings, share groups, or in the performance of tasks for their prayer group. Modern transportation networks have made possible, not only extensive travel to frequent prayer meetings, but also huge national and international pentecostal gatherings. Modern communications media are heavily used by the movement; for example, one prayer group leader quipped, "After you get baptized in the Spirit, the next thing you need to get is a tape-cassette player." Yet, at root, these social and material provisions are part of the world decried by much movement literature; the re-sacralization that Catholic pentecostals desire is not fully compatible with the maintenance of the structure of the institutions upon which these provisions hinge.

Functional rationality, as a bureaucratic principle and as a cognitive style, is also not likely to be reversed. It is firmly grounded in the way institutions function in this society; it is implicit in the thought-action patterns of most people—including the pentecostals themselves. Yet their search for holism creates some interesting tensions between their "ways of knowing" in different settings. The above chapters on healing illustrate these tensions. On one hand, members want the scientific/rational approach of doctors; on the other hand, they believe that nonrational ways of knowing (for example, discernment) are effective.

Although members of such religious groups appreciate nonrational styles of cognition in certain aspects of life, they desire and utilize rational modes in other aspects.[16] They would be upset if the airplane in which they were riding were piloted by a person in a trance, if the job for which they had applied were allotted by divination, if the judge for their court case were not interested in rational evidence but intuited the resulting decision. Thus there is an interesting tension between believing that the supernatural realm does impinge on the events of everyday life (including safe arrival from a journey, getting jobs, and winning court cases) and, on the other hand, the overwhelming lack of certainty as to whether any given situation is so influenced (that is, "of the Lord").

A further example of the general acceptance of functional rationality by Catholic pentecostals can be seen in the nexus between their faith and their work-world. In the course of this research, several places of work were visited. One was a small printing business owned by a prayer group member and employing exclusively other prayer-group members (four full-time and two part-time). Although workers gathered to pray together at the beginning and ending of the day and certain work routines were flexible to allow for religious activities, the business operated generally as other businesses. The bookkeeper did not call on the Lord to tally columns; the printers did not rely on discernment to repair their presses; the stockroom did not count on miracles to replenish the stock. When the manager fired a worker for inefficiency, he did so "in good conscience," because the woman knew he "still loved her in the Lord." The manager cited a few instances in which he prayed over business decisions, but the results of these prayers never contradicted the functionally rational alternatives (for example, he received guidance in prayer to replace an old press with a more efficient one), so it is not possible to observe the impact of "alternate ways of knowing" in his business. In general, Catholic pentecostals interviewed did not anticipate that knowledge obtained through prayer would contradict ordinary guidelines of life in society, except in certain special cases such as trials of faith.

Catholic pentecostal spirituality is highly amenable to the separation of public and private spheres. Pentecostal piety goes to the marketplace, but it is largely hidden. As one woman explained, "It's my own little secret, and it keeps me going." A man witnessed, "I need that prayer each morning to get my batteries charged. You know, the business world can be a real zoo." Such piety is relevant to the believer's everyday life in the public sphere in that it provides motivation ("I get stuck doing a lot of dirty work there, but I just offer it all up in love to Jesus"); legitimation ("I can't stand my boss, but we must be obedient to the ones the Lord sets over us"); and an effective emotional stance ("I used to get so nervous and anxious that I'd make lots of mistakes, but now I can relax and get on with the work, because I know Jesus is taking care of it all"). In other words, in the public sphere, pentecostal spirituality enables believers to function more effectively in a world in which they do not feel at home. But interaction in the public sphere is defined as far less important than key aspects of the private spheres: personal devotion, family life, and the prayer group. Loss of freedom and self-determination in the public sphere are compensated by the production of a sense of freedom in the private sphere. In essence, the pentecostal movement among Catholics represents the celebration and enhancement of the privatization of religion. As suggested in Chapter 8, this celebration may increase the plausibility of religion for those participating in the enclave of the movement. It does not, however, substantially alter the social-structural aspects of secularization.

Much, indeed most, of the Catholic pentecostal movement's thrust for change is directed toward the individual believer; secondarily, it is directed toward the Catholic church. Thirdly, and least importantly, it aims to change the society. Thus the key change sought is the re-Christianization of the life of the individual, church, and society, as discussed above. The eventual impact of the movement in all three of these areas depends largely upon its relationship with the larger society.

To what extent can and does the Catholic pentecostal movement have an impact on large-scale issues defined as social problems, such as poverty, racism, or oppression? These issues highlight the pentecostals' enjoyment of privatized religion. As suggested in Chapter 2, persons of greatly disparate persuasions on social issues are very comfortable together in the movement, because their socio-political beliefs are largely irrelevant to their pentecostalism. The privatization of religion enhances the segregation of these "opinions" on social issues from the sphere of religious experience and meaning, making possible a sense of community grounded in a single point of commonality—pentecostal experience. This structural aspect of the movement, together with its adamantly voluntaristic theology, makes it highly unlikely that the movement will produce any significant effort for socio-economic change, at least in developed countries.[17] Theodicies provided by the Catholic pentecostal belief system legitimate members' middle-class comforts and allow them to express their concern for less comfortable members of society by prayer. The result of these theodicies is that Catholic pentecostals are generally not only oblivious to social-structural sources of problems, including their problem of secularization, but they are even inured to thinking about structural issues.[18]

Not only does the movement fail to tackle effectively structural changes in the larger society, but indeed it serves largely to integrate its members into that dominant society. Its members become more satisfactory factory workers, housewives, secretaries, and students.[19] The values promoted by the movement—submission, orderliness, peace of mind, pleasant interpersonal relationships—are all helpful in coping with and adapting to the demands of institutions of the larger society.[20] Unlike certain youth culture religious movements, however, Catholic pentecostalism has attracted relatively few members who were strongly alienated from the dominant culture before joining the movement; few members were "into" the counter-culture of the 1960s, and very few were socio-political activists. If members were never really very alienated from the dominant society, why then is this integrative function so strongly evident? A plausible explanation lies not so much in the biographies of the members recruited, but in the quality of life in societal institutions. One hypothesis is that important human needs, such as the expression of one's feelings and the sense of belonging to a community, are not being met in the public sphere due to the very nature of the functionally rational institutions of this sphere.[21]

Another integrative aspect of religious movements such as Catholic pentecostalism relates to a sense of power. The belief system does not challenge the power of the existing institutions of the dominant society. Rather, as the individual's power and freedom in the public sphere are diminished (due largely to the nature of modern bureaucratic institutions), such movements produce a sense of power and an experience of freedom in private life. This is not to say that the privatized sense of power and freedom are not real; the power experienced in healing or the sense of freedom when speaking in tongues, for example, are very real and meaningful to Catholic pentecostals. Nevertheless, such privatized power and freedom are utterly irrelevant to the public institutions. The pentecostal experience can compensate for a lack of power and freedom in the institutions of the larger society and, indirectly, make it less likely that such individuals will want to challenge those institutions.

The less-integrative aspects of Catholic pentecostalism are largely in the private sphere—conflict within families, shifting allegiance out of competing voluntary organizations, divisions within parishes, and so on. Furthermore, the integrative effects are not necessarily permanent.[22] What happens when the individual leaves the movement or when the prayer group folds? For example, one young man who had left an intensive prayer community found himself unable to make decisions for himself, because he had relied so heavily on his group leaders' guidance in making the "right" decisions. A woman, who had tried successfully for three years to meet the pentecostal ideal of the submissive housewife, was literally unable to function when her husband left her without support. These illustrations suggest that, while pentecostal beliefs and practices generally support societal norms and values and serve to integrate members into society, certain values and practices may be highly dysfunctional.

The Catholic pentecostal movement and similar religious movements may, however, be transformative of aspects of the private sphere. In spite of some of the divisiveness they engender, the long-term impact may be to shore up weakened institutions such as family and community. The less sectarian prayer groups have greater potential for this outcome, because they remain more integrated with their residential community and do not exaggerate their differences from other members of that community (for example, they are less purist or totalistic than more sectarian groups). The effect of this transformation could be the creation of "mediating structures"[23] which acknowledge the expressive and communal needs of individuals, while representing them more powerfully to the public sphere. The pentecostal healing ministry, for example, might become such a mediating structure in those groups that serve beyond the immediate membership. This development might wrest some of the control and power currently held by public sphere institutions, such as hospitals and the medical profession; it might enhance the curing-caring functions of the church, family and community.

Most Catholic pentecostal ministries, however, are largely self-serving; they do not extend beyond the prayer group or movement activities. These relationships are, thus, unlikely to produce such mediating structures. Nevertheless, these movements do have the potential for such small and middle-scale transformations, because they can promote an experience of community, they can create new middle-level leadership roles for their members, and they generate a sense of power to accomplish things that would not otherwise be attempted. Certain aspects of the Catholic pentecostal belief system, however, limit the likelihood and effectiveness of these transformations. For example, the movement reduces members' sense of responsibility and consciousness of themselves—individually and collectively—as actors and agents.

The Future of the Catholic Pentecostal Movement

No firm projections about the future of the movement can be drawn because much depends upon events and changes in the larger society and not merely upon the character and direction of the movement itself. All movements are bound to change in time; the Catholic pentecostal movement has already undergone considerable change since its inception in the 1960s. All movements come to an end. It would be too narrow to call such an end "death," because the end of some movements consists of transcending or outmoding themselves.[24] For example, the women's suffrage movement ended when women were granted the vote, but spawned later feminist movements. The following projections about the future of Catholic pentecostalism are based on certain distinct trends that have developed (and are documented throughout this book). Two very different patterns of allegiance to Catholic pentecostalism were described in Chapter 8: a cultic type and a sectarian type. These two types are representative of the different directions the movement is taking.

The sectarian type is characterized by totalistic allegiance, opposition to the larger society, internal elitism, purism, and emphasis on order and authority. The central organization of the movement, most covenant communities, and many ordinary prayer groups—both large and small—are clearly moving toward an increasingly sectarian pattern of organization and allegiance. As noted in the preceding chapter, many groups have both sectarian cores and a cultic fringe. Among the more sectarian membership, there is an increased sense of opposition toward the rest of society, as highlighted by prophecies and teachings of national leaders. At the same time, this segment of the movement emphasizes purism in belief and practice—clearly fitting Weber's "religious virtuosi."[25] This purism is accompanied by a routinized form of interaction among members, which is increasingly characterized by authoritarian organization and internal stratification according to the virtues promoted by the belief system. Although these patterns, taken together, increase the likelihood of a split within the movement between the more sectarian and more cultic-type members,[26] thus far the more sectarian segment has constrained itself somewhat because of its avowed intent to become the dominant pattern of religiosity within the whole church. Such members cannot risk cutting off less sectarian members so long as that faction adheres to the goal of total renewal. Thus far, the sectarian aspect has been manifest within the movement in the form of communalism, stratification, and segregation of core group activities.

Historically, the sectarian religious impulse has been expressed either in a break from the parent group or in the encapsulation of the impulse in the form of a religious Order. As suggested in the preceding chapter, the Catholic pentecostal movement is not very likely to break away from the Catholic church. This is not because the schismatic tendency is absent, but rather because the larger church has neither the will nor the power to effectively eject a disobedient minority.[27] The potential for a break is clearly present within the movement itself, implicit in the distinctive sources of authority within the movement. Indeed, the willingness to disobey church authorities in order to practice pentecostalism is generally one difference between sectarian and cultic modes of allegiance. Pentecostalism is *the* central feature of the sectarian Catholic pentecostal's religious life; every aspect of living is perceived and ordered according to the pentecostal world view. Thus being forbidden any important part of pentecostal practice would precipitate a personal crisis. By contrast, the cultic adherent holds pentecostal beliefs and practices as merely one way among many. If that way were blocked, others could readily take its place.

There is growing evidence that continued participation in the Catholic pentecostal movement increases the willingness of the individual to disobey church authorities were they to forbid pentecostalism within the church. In the early stages of this research, most non-student members interviewed indicated that they would so obey (albeit, reluctantly).[28] By later stages of the research (1976, 1977) these same members were generally unwilling to give up their pentecostal beliefs and practices under any circumstances. By contrast, relatively new members (those who had belonged approximately one year or less) were more willing to obey church authorities.[29]

Not only has the church less power to effectively eject dissident minorities, but also it lacks some of its earlier power to control them by encapsulation; the Catholic pentecostal movement has been largely accommodating, not coerced, in its encapsulation. Historically, dissident minorities who remained within the church were encapsulated in the form of the religious Order.[30] There are many parallels between the Catholic pentecostal movement and numerous historical Orders. This movement appears to be somewhat different, because it includes both men and women together, married and single, and adults with their childen, and overlaps existing Religious and clergy-laity distinctions. These differences should not be over-emphasized. Each resolution of problems created by the "new" demographic composition of this movement has brought the organization ever closer to that of the classical Order. The movement's increasing emphasis on authority and obedience along clearly stratified lines addresses many of the problems of gender, age, and "vocation" distinctions in the groups; this emphasis directly parallels similar developments in historical Orders.[31] Thus a strong possibility for the future direction of this segment of the Catholic pentecostal movement is the formation of a modern form of an Order of religious virtuosi.

The cultic type, by contrast, is characterized by a segmented, non-totalistic kind of allegiance, together with a looser, voluntaristic association with fellow believers. Although most prayer groups have representatives of both patterns of membership, ordinary unspecialized prayer groups are more likely to consist of this type of member than are covenant communities, prayer groups of Religious, or campus groups. Competing commitments of "ordinary" prayer group members typically preclude religious totalism, whereas many more intensive and purist groups screen out cultic style adherents. The direction of the more cult-like segment of the movement appears to be characterized by routinization, cooptation, and replacement. Charismatic spirituality becomes routinized into a form of devotionalism, comparable to pre-Vatican II devotionalism. As religious experience becomes safe, orderly, controlled, and encapsulated, it ceases to threaten the *status quo* of the individual member, the church, or society. While routinization itself is not inimical to the goal of renewal of the whole church, the accompanying fundamental compromises are. Not only is the fervor dulled by routinization, but also the content of the message is transformed into something less specific, less demanding, less critical. The effects of routinization on the content of prophecies (see Chapter 4) demonstrates this transformation.[32]

Cooptation implies the opposite of renewal. Instead of the new movement gaining control in the old institution and changing it from within, the old institution gains control over the new movement, allowing movement members to feel important and effective while ultimately undermining the movement's impact for change. For example, one prayer group visited (but not researched specifically in this study) boasted of its impact on its local parish. The pastor was a member of the core of the prayer group and gave them "full cooperation"—the use of church facilities for meetings, his participation in their occasional liturgies, announcement of prayer meetings and other activities in the church bulletin. The group was pleased that several members of the parish council were "Spirit-filled," and that their members were active in parish work, such as choir, First-Friday observances, fundraising, Mass Lectors and Eucharistic Ministers, and so on. Aside from their enthusiastic labors, however, these church members were indistinguishable from non-pentecostal active church members. Furthermore, the pastor had given up none of his authority or decision-making prerogatives (for example, the parish council had no real powers); he merely gained workers who *felt* important.

Not all ordinary prayer groups have been coopted to this extreme, but the potential remains a strong one. Important variables that account for a different relationship between local church authorities and the group include: the early development of lay leadership, the willingness of the church authorities to share real power, the awareness of group members of power and other structural issues and their sophistication in being able to deal with these issues, the ability of the group members to expand their notions of ways of serving the church.[33]

The third development among cultic-style adherents is "replacement." This refers to the extent to which non-totalistic adherence to beliefs and practices of pentecostalism can more readily be replaced by adherence to various other beliefs and practices. The segmented, eclectic assortment of beliefs of cult-like members is highly fluid. For example, one member said, "I've kind of dropped out of prayer meeting. I still go once in a while, I can still enjoy a good prayer meeting, but I get just as much out of watching Oral Roberts on TV. . . . I find I watch a lot of religion shows on TV lately. You get a lot out of it and don't have the struggles of getting a babysitter and having to drive out after dark and all." These respondents illustrate how readily a cultic-style adherence to one belief and practice can be supplanted by another. Although the replacement currently observed does not appear to be in any single direction, it could be hypothesized that another movement which addressed the same kinds of needs might capture the adherence of many cultic-style Catholic pentecostals.

Even though the ordinary prayer groups will probably prove to be more ephemeral than the more intensive groups, such as covenant communities, they will probably have greater long-term impact. Even after a prayer group is routinized, coopted or faded away, its influence is apparent. One interesting impact is the very experience of a community of believers. Several members attested to the change in their relationships with all others in their parish and community after they had gained a sense of what community might mean. This experience is directly related to another impact—the location of oneself in a community (that is, the nexus of identity and belonging). Another very important impact of many prayer groups is the multifold personal experience of loving, caring, and healing. For example, one prayer minister exclaimed, "Even if [our prayer group] folds tomorrow, I and several others are going to keep on visiting and praying with the sick in this community. I know how much it meant to me to have the love and prayers of others when I was so down, and I'm going to keep on spreading the love and care I received." There are also some very practical learning experiences that may have a long-term impact. For example, many members have gained leadership experience and interpersonal skills that may carry over into other areas of parish and community life. Even mistakes or unpleasant events within the movement may be important learning experiences. For example, one woman said:

> I was very active then . . . head of the Book ministry. . . .
> Our [core] group was planning a retreat for the rest of the
> group, and they [certain leaders] were planning this partic-
> ular exercise, but I didn't like the idea. Some people could
> get hurt—you know, their personal feelings and all. So I op-
> posed the plan and tried to get some others to speak up.
> Before the next planning meeting, ———— took me aside and
> told me that they had discerned that I was disruptive and
> that the planning was "in the Lord." He asked me to go
> along with their plan, in obedience. Well, I didn't believe
> it was "in the Lord," but I kept quiet, because I didn't want
> to cause any conflict . . . but people were hurt—real bad . . .
> and several never came back to prayer meeting . . . I left the
> group shortly after that and never regretted it. But I thank
> that experience for one thing—I've become much more
> assertive and not afraid of conflict, at least not where people's
> feelings—including my own feelings—are concerned.

Another long term (although difficult to measure) impact is that of
spiritual experiences. It is probable that the enjoyment of a spiritual
experience in one setting would lead to seeking further such experiences. It might also make the individual more open to the creative
use of imagination and fantasy. Because the influence of spiritual experiences is more individual, the impact of a large number of people
having had such experiences is difficult to estimate; it is also difficult
to tell whether these pentecostal experiences are substantially different
from earlier such experiences (for example, a special moment on re-
treat, or during prayers in some earlier form of devotion). Nevertheless, the potential impact of specifically religious experiences needs
to be recognized.

Order and Legitimation in Modern Society

The appropriate theoretical focus for understanding
such religious movements in contemporary society does not stop with
the notion of secularization; the more crucial theoretical concern is
the implications of this development for two functions historically
addressed by religion: (1) the legitimation and integration of society,
and (2) the legitimation of the individual. As modern society becomes
highly differentiated and pluralistic, what norms, values, or beliefs
can possibly serve as the common moral bond of the whole society?
In other words, do the processes of modernization that bear on secularization also result ultimately in the total disintegration of the whole
society?

The relationship between modernization, individualism, and social
integration was a central concern for Durkheim, Weber, and other

classical theorists.[34] Modern functionalist successors to Durkheim argue that religion is that which fulfills certain functions (expresses collective sentiments, allows an individual to transcend him or herself, forms and maintains the identity of the individual or group, and so forth).[35] Since these functions are basic to the human social condition, there will always arise what Durkheim called "cults" to meet these needs, even though the historical institutional forms of religion may die out. Durkheim states:

> There can be no society which does not feel the need of upholding and reaffirming at regular intervals the collective sentiments and the collective ideas which make its unity and its personality. . . . If we find a little difficulty today in imagining what these feasts and ceremonies of the future could consist in, it is because we are going through a stage of transition and moral mediocrity. The great things of the past which filled our fathers with enthusiasm do not excite the same ardour in us, either because they have come into common usage to such an extent that we are unconscious of them or else because they no longer answer to our actual aspirations; but as yet there is nothing to replace them. . . . In a word, the old gods are growing old or already dead, and others are not yet born. . . . It is life itself, and not a dead past which can produce a living cult.[36]

Some interpretations of the modern upsurge of religious fervor suggest that these diverse sects and cults are fulfilling Durkheim's predictions.[37] While it may be true that some of these movements are peculiarly suited to modern society, none of these sects or cults is capable of effecting societal integration. Indeed, it could be argued that the attempt to impose such a general normative order would be greatly dysfunctional.[38] The contemporary plethora of highly diverse, generally privatized religious movements may reflect the overall disintegration of American society.[39]

Although there is analytical value in exploring the extent to which various other modern developments (psychotherapy, football, political sects, rock music) constitute functional equivalents to certain aspects of traditional religion, the modern situation is qualitatively different. There is no single, unifying set of functional equivalents, nor any that are capable of establishing the normative basis for evaluating action in the public sphere. The current sociological discussion about the existence and scope of American "civil religion" addresses the same problematic issues of this development.[40]

Given these differences, how is integration of modern societies possible? What is the basis of legitimation for motivation and order in such societies? Fenn argues that cultural integration (beliefs, values, norms) is neither possible nor necessary under present conditions.

According to his analysis, legitimacy depends, rather, upon the capacity of the society to meet certain popular demands—especially, high levels of consumption. At the societal level, then, issues of legitimacy are reduced to a lower level of generality; duly established priorities, effectiveness and propriety become the operative criteria.[41] Religion remains alive and important—but only in the private sphere.

Thus it is possible for modern society to be integrated at a societal level without consensus on beliefs, values, or norms. But is this integration plausible on a continuing basis? Several internal qualities appear to undermine its legitimacy. First, the sources of legitimacy of modern society are desperately fragile. Major disruptions in economic production or distribution, such as the "energy crisis," would result in the dramatic collapse of legitimacy of a society relying on high levels of consumption. Other international economic factors—often out of the full control of any nation—are equally threatening.[42] Indeed, it might be hypothesized that many recent movements are a response to the very precariousness of the current basis of integration of society. This hypothesis would also account for the widespread appeal of authoritarian resolutions.

Second, the integration of society based upon functional rationality in the public sphere implies that the public sphere can and does operate on a unified neutral principle. Certain structural changes, such as re-politicization of the economy (that is, the concept of the economy as the result of human manipulation) may, indeed, increase the disjunction of institutions of the public sphere.[43] A similar difficulty appears in the realm of law and psychiatry, where the attempt to apply normative legitimations at a lower level of generality (for example, the medical model) is breaking down.

Third, individual satisfaction and sources of motivation—both located almost exclusively in the private sphere—are undermined by certain changes in the social structure. Habermas suggests that these changes are not avoidable; that the present socio-cultural system is based upon a privatistic syndrome (civil-familial-vocational) that is being non-renewably dismantled. Furthermore, he argues, the core components of the ideology which supports modern societal arrangements are undermined by changes in the social structure. Key motivational components, such as possessive individualism and achievement orientation, have become diminished, because they cease to correspond with the actual results of the individual's actions in the system. In other words, the present strength of the private sphere is already declining; it is predicated upon elements which are remnants of a cultural tradition for which the present social structure can create no functional alternatives.[44] If the private sphere is relied upon to provide the motivation for the individual's contribution to, and cooperation with, public institutions, then such weaknesses in the private sphere threaten to undermine the operation of the entire system.

The weakness of private sphere institutions has implications, not only for the integration of the society, but also for the legitimation of the individual. What do these developments imply about the location of identity in modern society? Several authors have linked the individual's problems of legitimating one's social identity with the capacity of modern society for integration.[45] Habermas proposes that the identity of the self is a symbolic structure which increasingly must find its support outside the central structures of society.[46]

The necessity of legitimating oneself is itself linked to the historical process of "disenchantment," or de-mystification, of the world. As Weber pointed out, only in the disengagement of the supernatural from everyday life did the modern concept of individualism become possible.[47] Accordingly, the Protestant Ethic developed in a transition from a collectivity-monitored legitimation of persons to a more voluntary form of self-legitimation (one important historical product of which was the Protestant sect). Weber's thesis about the Protestant Ethic is not merely a commentary upon a discrete historical religious form, but is rather directed to understanding certain thrusts in the dominant society. In other words, the social impact of the Protestant Ethic in modern society is felt by all members of society (including Catholics and pentecostals) because it is the legacy of modernity. In this context, the concern of Catholic pentecostals interviewed in this study about "where I stand before God" becomes understandable. The effect of privatization and disenchantment of the social world is that important aspects of identity—meaning and self-worth—become problematic.

Robertson argues that the rise of contemporary religious movements, especially those which represent a "new pietism," may be, not merely compensatory responses, but important forms for effecting a new integration of individualism-in-relation-to-the-world.[48] The new pietism is uniquely suited to the task of legitimating the modern individual, because of its synthesis of asceticism and mysticism (in the Weberian sense of these words). Such movements, accordingly, have the potential to force society itself to adapt to a "right to identity."[49] In several respects, the Catholic pentecostal movement corresponds to the type Robertson has called the "new pietism"; it enables its members to withdraw in a limited way from the world, yet operate more effectively in that world. Robertson's speculation is an interesting possibility, but as yet there is very little data to support his prospect of an insistence on a "right to identity," relative to the major institutions of the public sphere. It is somewhat difficult to imagine what the new individualism-in-relation-to-the-world might be like; it may be as remote from the ideals of the movements that spawn it as the old integration was from the Protestant sects.

Conclusion

The sociological significance of the Catholic pentecostal movement and similar religious and quasi-religious movements in contemporary society lies in what these developments imply about the relationship of the individual to society in the modern condition. Four aspects of secularization are particularly relevant to this condition: (1) institutional differentiation and specialization and the segregation of religion in the private sphere, (2) pluralism and the undermining of religious legitimation of the normative structure of the larger society, (3) privatization of the self and de-legitimation of many social sources of identity, and (4) dominance of a cognitive style that precludes non-rational elements of explanation and discourages the reference to a transcendental realm in the experiencing of oneself and one's world. These four aspects correspond to concerns of movement members themselves, except that their criticism is not only of the loss of influence of religion in general, but more particularly of Christianity.

The potential of any religious movement to effectively influence society on these four aspects is varied. There is little likelihood that religion, from its weakened stance in the private sphere, can effect significant changes in the mode of operation of the public sphere; institutional differentiation and functional rationality are implicit in modern economic functions, and by extension in political and legal functions, as well. In fact, few modern religious movements actually seek such a radically different mode in the public sphere; they are dependent upon existing patterns of consumption. Such movements are, also, not likely to effect a reversal of pluralism by a re-establishment of a Christian hegemony. By their mutual support, members can be personally strengthened against normative relativism, but they are not able to change modern society's growing pluralism.

The other two aspects of secularization are somewhat more amenable to the impact of a religious movement such as Catholic pentecostalism. Such groups do have the potential to strengthen institutions of the private sphere and to re-create sources for the legitimation of self. Indeed, the very experience of conversion is one such source; being "born again" is one way of establishing one's self-worth. Nevertheless, most of these sources are located in the private sphere (and are carried invisibly into the public sphere, relevant only to the individual's personal motivation and meaning). They are, therefore, voluntaristic and less-than-inevitable. Also, these movements may re-affirm the value of non-rational modes of cognition, but these are likely to remain segregated from public-sphere operations. For example, it may become socially acceptable to withdraw in meditation daily to calm oneself, but meditation is not likely to become the cognitive style by which businesses or laboratories are operated.

The future of the Catholic pentecostal movement itself is, of course, fluid and open to many changes. Two directions seem probable, based upon current developments within the movement. One is that the segment of membership which is generally more sectarian appears to be becoming even more so; the possible outcome of this development is the creation of a peculiarly modern form of religious Order. The sectarian segment is not likely to be cut off from the larger church because the church lacks the power to eject it. The other, more cult-like segment, is highly vulnerable to cooptation, routinization, and replacement; there is much evidence that these processes have already blunted the power and fervor of the movement. Nevertheless, because cultic adherents are less withdrawn from the dominant society, they are also more likely to have some impact within it, so long as they also retain some of their distinctiveness. For example, groups which have expanded their sense of community to their larger residential community beyond the immediate prayer group seem to be having some impact.

The larger interpretive framework within which such movements should be understood is the classical sociological issue of the relationship of the individual to the society. Several observers suggest that the precariousness of the legitimation structures of the society and the self has precipitated a crisis situation. The old structures are not adequate to the new social situation; new modes of legitimation are not yet evident. This critical situation has implications both for societal integration and for the very identities of members of the society. Whether new religious movements are merely lame reactionary responses to this crisis or whether they may presage a new legitimation structure by promoting a new mode of individual-to-society relationship is not clear. There are many qualities of Catholic pentecostalism—its authoritarianism, re-mystification, disinterest in structural issues in changing society, among others—that make it unlikely to effect such a synthesis. Perhaps some sociologist as remote in time from the present legitimation transition as Weber was from the Protestant Reformation will be able to clearly delineate the long-term impact of such a contemporary religious movement as Catholic pentecostalism.

Notes

CHAPTER ONE
1. Kevin Ranaghan and Dorothy Ranaghan, *Catholic Pentecostals* (New York: Paulist, 1969), p. 189.
2. Secularization, as a social process, is neutral; it should not be confused with secularism, which implies a positive evaluation and embracement of secularity.
3. Peter L. Berger, *A Rumor of Angels: Modern Society and the Rediscovery of the Supernatural* (Garden City, N.Y.: Doubleday, 1969), p. 7.
4. Nils Bloch-Hoell, *The Pentecostal Movement: Its Origin, Development and Distinctive Character* (Oslo: Universitets-forlaget, 1964); Walter J. Hollenweger, *The Pentecostals: The Charismatic Movement in the Churches* (Minneapolis: Augsburg Publishing House, 1972); Richard Quebedeaux, *The New Charismatics: The Origins, Development, and Significance of Neo-Pentecostalism* (Garden City, N.Y.: Doubleday, 1976).
5. See especially Cecil D. Bradfield, *Neo-Pentecostalism: A Sociological Assessment* (Washington, D.C.: University Presses of America, 1979), and Douglas McGaw, *A Tale of Two Congregations: Commitment and Social Structure in a Charismatic Mainline Church* (Hartford, Conn.: Hartford Seminary Foundation, 1980; McGaw, "Meaning and Belonging in a Charismatic Congregation: An Investigation into Sources of Neo-pentecostal Success," *Review of Religious Research* 21, no. 3 (1980): 284–301.
6. Ranaghan and Ranaghan, *Catholic Pentecostals*, 1969.
7. In 1975, CRS was a $1.7 million business (*National Catholic Reporter*, Sept. 12, 1975).
8. *National Catholic Reporter*, June 23, 1972, June 22, 1973, June 6, 1975, June 18, 1976, Aug. 12, 1977, June 30, 1978, June 20, 1980.

9. *New York Times*, May 14, 1978.

10. *New York Times*, Sept. 8, 1974; *Newsweek*, June 16, 1975.

11. Published by the movement's Communication Center and distributed by CRS; regional directories have recently become available from groups coordinating regional conferences. Note that some groups choose not to list themselves; others listed are defunct. Membership figures cited in the national and regional directories tend to be considerably higher than average attendance (since membership lists are kept with the intent of keeping in touch with people, including persons no longer attending).

12. *National Catholic Reporter*, July 5, 1974.

13. *National Catholic Reporter*, March 10, 1972, April 19, 1974, Nov. 30, 1973; *New York Times*, June 28, 1974.

14. See, for example, Anne Parsons, "The Pentecostal Immigrants: A Study of an Ethnic Central City Church," *Journal for the Scientific Study of Religion* 4 (1965): 183–197.

15. See also Meredith B. McGuire, *Religion: The Social Context* (Belmont, Calif.: Wadsworth, 1981), pp. 229–244.

16. See, for example, Thomas Luckmann's analysis in *The Invisible Religion: The Problem of Religion in Modern Society* (New York: Macmillan, 1967).

17. Meredith B. McGuire, "Toward a Sociological Interpretation of the 'Underground Church' Movement," *Review of Religious Research* 14, no. 1 (1972): 41–47.

18. The two main written sources when the study was begun were Edward D. O'Connor, *The Pentecostal Movement in the Catholic Church* (Notre Dame, Ind.: Ave Maria Press, 1971), and Ranaghan and Ranaghan, *Catholic Pentecostals*, 1969. See also issues of *The New Covenant* and a recent publication, *Catholic Charismatic*, which represents a different faction of the movement.

19. Joseph Fichter, *The Catholic Cult of the Paraclete* (New York: Sheed and Ward, 1975).

20. For sources on pentecostalism and neo-pentecostalism in other cultures, see: Leda Abbelle Catucci, "Catholic Neo-pentecostals: Salvation through Irrationalism," *La Critica Sociologica* 43 (1977): 39–46; Albert Doutreloux and Colette Degive, "Perspective Anthropologique sur un mouvement religieux actual," *Social Compass* 25, no. 1 (1978): 43–54; Cornelia B. Flora, *Pentecostalism in Colombia: Baptism by Fire and Spirit* (Rutherford, N.J.: Fairleigh Dickinson University Press, 1976); André Godin, "Moi perdu ou moi retrouvé dans l'experiénce charismatique: perlexité des psychologues," *Religion and Social Change: Actes de 13th Conference Internationale de Sociologie Religieuse* (Lille, France: CISR, 1975), pp. 310–336; Gustavo Guizzardi, "New Religious Phenomena in Italy: Towards a Post-Catholic Era?" (presented to the Sociology of Religion Research Committee, World Congress of Sociology, Toronto, Aug., 1974); Christian L'alive D'Epinay, *Haven of the Masses: Study of the Pentecostal Movement in Chile* (London: Lutterworth, 1969); D'Epinay, *Religion, Dynamique Sociale et Depéndance: Le protestantism en Argentine et au Chile* (Paris, Mouton: 1975); M. J. Maciote, "Neo-pentecostali e carismatici," *La Critica Sociologica*

43 (1977): 17–38; Enzo Pace, "Charismatics and the Political Presence of Catholics: The Italian Case," *Social Compass* 25, no. 1 (1978): 85–99; M. T. V. Reidy and James Richardson, "Neo-Pentecostalism in New Zealand," *Australia and New Zealand Journal of Sociology* 14, no. 3 (1978): 222–230; Paul Reny and Jean Paul Rouleau, "Charismatiques et Socio-politiques dans l'Eglise catholique au Quebec," *Social Compass* 25, no. 1 (1978): 125–143; Pedro A. Ribeiro de Oliveira, "Le renouveau charis-matique au Bresil," *Social Compass* 25, no. 1 (1978): 37–42; James Richard-son and M. T. V. Reidy, "Neo-Pentecostalism in Ireland: A Comparison with the American Experience," *Social Studies: The Irish Journal of Sociology* 5, no. 34 (1977): pp. 243–261; Jean Seguy, "Pentecotisme et Neo-Pente-cotisme: Pour une Interpretation Macro-Sociologique," *The Contemporary Metamorphosis of Religion?: Actes de 12th Conference Internationale de So-ciologie Religieuse* (Lille, France: CISR, 1973), pp. 271–283; Seguy, "Sit-uation Sociohistorique du Pentecotisme," *Lumiere et Vie* 125 (1975): 35–59; J. Tennekes, "The Pentecostal Movement in Chile: An Expression of Social Protest," *Sociologische Gids* 17, no. 6 (1970): 480–487; Emilio Willems, *Followers of the New Faith: Culture Change and the Rise of Protestantism in Brazil and Chile* (Nashville: Vanderbilt University Press, 1967).

21. Thomas Luckmann, "Comments on the Laeyendecker et al. Research Pro-posal," *Actes de 12th Conference Internationale de Sociologie Religieuse* (Lille, France: CISR, 1973), pp. 63–68.

22. Joseph Ryan, "Ethnoscience and Problems of Method in the Social Scientific Study of Religion," *Sociological Analysis* 39, no. 3 (1978): 241–249. Also, Del Hymes, "The Ethnography of Speaking," in *Anthropology and Human Behavior*, ed. T. Gladwin and W. C. Sturtevant (Washington, D.C.: Anthropological Society of Washington, D.C., 1962).

23. Clifford Geertz, "From the Native's Point of View: On the Nature of Anthro-pological Understanding," *Bulletin of the American Academy of Arts and Sciences* 28, no. 1 (1974): 26–45; David M. Schneider, "Notes toward a Theory of Culture," in *Meaning in Anthropology*, ed. Basso and Selby (Albuquerque: University of New Mexico, 1976), pp. 197–220; Aaron V. Cicourel, *Cognitive Sociology* (New York: Free Press, 1973); Robert S. Ellwood, Jr., "Emergent Religion in America: An Historical Perspective," in *Understanding the New Religions*, ed. J. Needleman and G. Baker (New York: Seabury, 1978), pp. 267–284.

24. Johannes Fabian, "Genres in an Emerging Tradition: An Anthropological Approach to Religious Communication," in *Changing Perspectives in the Scientific Study of Religion*, ed. Alan W. Eister (New York: Wiley, 1974), pp. 249–272. On the concept of intersubjectivity, see Alfred Schutz, *Collected Papers II: Studies in Social Theory* (The Hague: Martinus Nijhoff, 1964), esp. pp. 20–63.

25. John A. Saliba, "The New Ethnography and the Study of Religion," *Journal for the Scientific Study of Religion* 13, no. 2 (1974): 145–159.

26. Jack D. Douglas, *Research on Deviance* (New York: Random House, 1972), p. 28.

27. Meredith B. McGuire, "The Social Context of Prophecy: Word Gifts of the

Spirit Among Catholic Pentecostals," *Review of Religious Research* 18, no. 2 (1977): 134–147. Understandably, some members had their own interpretation of this—namely, that the researcher was "intellectualizing" everything and had to "let go" and just believe.

28. James T. Richardson et al., *Organized Miracles: A Study of a Contemporary Youth Movement* (New Brunswick, N.J.: Transaction Press, 1978).

29. Gary Schwartz, *Sect Ideologies and Social Status* (Chicago: University of Chicago, 1970), p. 242.

30. Thomas Robbins, Dick Anthony, and Thomas Curtis, "The Limits of Symbolic Realism: Problems of Empathic Field Observation in a Sectarian Context," *Journal for the Scientific Study of Religion* 12, no. 3 (1973): 249–271.

CHAPTER TWO

1. For example, a national survey found that only 36 percent of Roman Catholic respondents were "absolutely sure there is a devil"—a figure comparable with that of moderate Protestants, such as Methodists and Presbyterians. Rodney Stark and Charles Y. Glock, *American Piety: The Nature of Religious Commitment* (Berkeley: University of California Press, 1968), p. 38.

2. Joseph Fichter, *The Catholic Cult of the Paraclete* (New York: Sheed and Ward, 1975), p. 44.

3. Milton Rokeach, *The Open and Closed Mind* (New York: Basic, 1960), p. 33.

4. This synopsis of the Catholic Pentecostal belief system is drawn from Edward D. O'Connor, *The Pentecostal Movement in the Catholic Church* (Notre Dame, Ind.: Ave Maria Press, 1971), and Kevin Ranaghan and Dorothy Ranaghan, *Catholic Pentecostals* (New York: Paulist, 1969). These early sources are relatively cautious theologically; other sources (for example, articles in *New Covenant* and the movement's instructional tape-cassettes) are less so.

5. O'Connor, *Pentecostal Movement*, 1971, p. 135.

6. Cf., Luther Gerlach and Virginia Hine, "Five Factors Crucial to the Growth and Spread of a Modern Religious Movement," *Journal for the Scientific Study of Religion* 7, no. 1 (1968): 34.

7. James Beckford, *The Trumpet of Prophecy: A Sociological Study of Jehovah's Witnesses* (New York: Halsted, 1975), p. 196.

8. Quoted in John R. Thompson, "La Participation Catholique dons le Mouvement du renouveau Charismatique," *Social Compass*, 21, no. 3 (1974): 343.

9. Peter L. Berger, *The Sacred Canopy: Elements of a Sociological Theory of Religion* (Garden City, N.Y.: Doubleday, 1967), p. 111. The term "disenchantment of the world" Berger borrows from Weber.

10. Fichter, *Catholic Cult*, 1975, p. 71.

11. Peter Freund uses this concept to interpret miracles perceived by the "premies" (disciples) following the Guru Maharaj Ji, "Documenting Experiences: Telling and Retelling as Mediation," presented to the American Sociological Association (New York, Aug., 1976).

12. Cf., William Samarin, "Glossolalist Folk Linguistics" (presented to the

Research Committee on Sociolinguistics, World Congress for Sociology, Toronto, Aug., 1974).

13. Cf., Edward J. Moody's theories about the rise of contemporary witchcraft belief, in "Magical Therapy: An Anthropological Investigation of Contemporary Satanism," in *Religious Movements in Contemporary America*, eds. Irving I. Zaretsky and Mark P. Leone (Princeton: Princeton Univ. Press, 1974), pp. 355–382.

14. O'Connor, *Pentecostal Movement*, 1971, pp. 79–80. See also the entire issue of *New Covenant*, April, 1974, on "Confronting the Reality of Satan."

15. Luther P. Gerlach and Virginia H. Hine, *People, Power, Change: Movements of Social Transformation* (New York: Bobbs-Merrill, 1970), p. 174.

16. Fichter, *Catholic Cult*, 1975, p. 132. Compare Richard Bord and Joseph Faulkner, "Religiosity and Secular Attitudes: The Case of Catholic Pentecostals," *Journal for the Scientific Study of Religion* 14, no. 3 (1975): 257–270. They found a fairly strong dualistic perspective and belief that evil forces abound. See also W. J. Samarin, *Tongues of Men and Angels* (New York: Macmillan, 1973), pp. 171–172. He found that Evangelical neo-pentecostals increased belief in tongues, healing, and demons. Belief in demons increased more dramatically than any other belief.

17. James Richardson, Robert Simmonds, and Mary Harder, "Thought Reform and Jesus Movement," *Youth and Society* 4, no. 2 (1972): 197; Thomas Robbins et al., "The Last Civil Religion: The Unification Church of the Reverend Sun Myung Moon," *Sociological Analysis* 37, no. 2 (1976): 111–125.

18. Compare John Lofland and Rodney Stark, "Becoming a World-Saver: A Theory of Conversion to a Deviant Perspective," in *Religion in Sociological Perspective*, ed. C. Glock (Belmont, Calif.: Wadsworth, 1973), p. 36.

19. Randy Cirner, "Deliverance," *New Covenant*, April, 1974, pp. 4–7, and May, 1974, pp. 22–24.

20. Compare the sense of "conspiracy" among the Jehovah's Witnesses Beckford, *Trumpet of Prophecy*, 1975, p. 198, and the John Birch Society in A. Westin, "The John Birch Society," in *The Radical Right*, ed. David Bell (Garden City, N.Y.: Doubleday, 1964), p. 243. The John Birch Society, for example, sees Communists at the heart of events everywhere, even seemingly remote events such as: "trouble in the South over integration," the closing of American banks in 1933, and the Federal Reserve System. See also Michael Barkun's discussion of "conspiracy thinking" in millennial movements, in *Disaster and the Millennium* (New Haven, Conn.: Yale University Press, 1974), p. 145. Compare the social sources of paranoia in Gustav Ichheiser, *Appearances and Reality* (San Francisco: Jossey-Bass, 1970).

21. Andrew Weil, *The Natural Mind: A New Way of Looking at Drugs and the Higher Consciousness* (Boston: Houghton-Mifflin, 1973), pp. 178–179.

22. Berger, *Sacred Canopy*, 1967, p. 58; Max Weber, *The Sociology of Religion*, trans. Ephraim Fischoffs (Boston: Beacon, 1964), pp. 138–150.

23. Cf., Rokeach, *Open and Closed Mind*, 1960, p. 69, and Robbins et al., "The Last Civil Religion," 1976, on ethical dualism and absolutism.

24. *Finding New Life in the Spirit* (Notre Dame, Ind.: Charismatic Renewal Services, 1972), pp. 28–29.

25. Compare Philip Slater, *Microcosm: Structural, Psychological and Religious Evolution in Groups* (New York: Wiley, 1966).

26. Fichter, *Catholic Cult*, 1975, p. 308.

27. Francis J. Connell, *Baltimore Catechism*, no. 3 (New York: Benziger, 1943), pp. 24–26.

28. O'Connor, *Pentecostal Movement*, 1971, p. 267.

29. Jay P. Dolan, *Catholic Revivalism: The American Experience, 1830–1900* (Notre Dame, Ind.: University of Notre Dame Press, 1978), pp. 185–203.

30. Reported by "Charismatics Warned God's Wrath Coming," *National Catholic Reporter*, June 20, 1980.

31. Fichter, *Catholic Cult*, 1975, p. 88. Note that Fichter's categories of "liberal," "moderate," and "conservative" are derived from an index measuring attitudes on the Church's role in social change; these are not measures of political or theological stances.

32. Bruce Yocum, "Prophecy," *New Covenant* (Aug., 1973), p. 22.

33. Several strong prophecies spoke of imminent darkness and desolation, a time of trial. See *National Catholic Reporter*, June 6, 1975, p. 13.

34. See, for example, the entire September, 1972, issue of *New Covenant*, and especially Michael Scanlan, "Preparing for Difficult Times," *New Covenant* (September, 1976), p. 4.

35. Berger, *Sacred Canopy*, 1967, p. 69.

36. Compare William McPherson, "Ideology in the Jesus Movement" (presented to the Society for the Scientific Study of Religion, Milwaukee, Oct., 1975); James Richardson, "Causes and Consequences of the Jesus Movement in the U.S.," *Acts of the C.I.S.R.* (1973), p. 398; and James Richardson, Mary Harder, and Robert Simmonds, *Organized Miracles: A Sociological Study of a Jesus Movement Organization* (New Brunswick, N.J.: Transaction, 1979).

37. Fichter, *Catholic Cult*, 1975, p. 92; see also Fichter, "Liberal and Conservative Catholic Pentecostals," *Social Compass* 21, no. 3 (1974): 303–310.

38. Fichter, *Catholic Cult*, 1975, p. 87.

39. See, for example, Peter Worsley, *The Trumpet Shall Sound: A Study of Cargo Cults in Melanesia* (New York: Schocken, 1968); also Barkun, *Disaster and the Millennium* (Boston: Beacon, 1974).

40. Gustavo Guizzardi, "New Religious Phenomena in Italy: Towards a Post-Catholic Era?" (presented to the Research Committee on Sociology of Religion, World Congress of Sociology, Toronto, Aug., 1974).

41. Francis McNutt, "Pentecostals and Social Justice," *New Covenant* (November, 1972), pp. 4–6.

42. Compare Fichter, *Catholic Cult*, 1975, p. 90.

43. Max Weber, *The Theory of Social and Economic Organization*, trans. A. M. Henderson and T. Parsons (New York: Oxford University Press, 1947), pp. 358–359.

44. Michael Hill, *The Religious Order: A Study of Virtuoso Religion and Its Legitimation in the Nineteenth Century Church of England* (London: Heinemann, 1973), p. 3.

45. Max Weber, *The Sociology of Religion*, trans. E. Fischoff (Boston: Beacon, 1963), pp. 163–165.
46. Emile Durkheim, *The Elementary Forms of the Religious Life*, trans. J. W. Swain (New York: Free Press, 1965), pp. 253, 257.
47. Ibid., p. 240.
48. Cf., Frances Westley, "Searching for Surrender: A Catholic Charismatic Renewal Group's Attempt to Become Glossolalic," *American Behavioral Scientist* 20, no. 6 (1977): 925–940.
49. The social power of the group is often objectified as some transcendent power, such as the Deity, the State, the King, the Party, the Corporation; cf., Edward Shils, *Center and Periphery: Essays in Macrosociology* (Chicago: University of Chicago Press, 1975), pp. 256–275. This objectification enables individual members to deflect personal responsibility for their decisions and actions.
50. Benjamin Zablocki, *Alienation and Charisma: A Study of Contemporary American Communes* (New York: Free Press, 1980), p. 10.
51. Cf., Shils, *Center and Periphery*, p. 263.
52. Johannes Fabian, *Jamaa: A Charismatic Movement in Katanga* (Evanston, Ill.: Northwestern University Press, 1971), p. 187; see also Shils, *Center and Periphery*, p. 127.
53. Ibid., p. 7.
54. Randall Collins, "On the Microfoundations of Macrosociology," *American Journal of Sociology* 86, no. 5 (1981): 984–1014.
55. Rosabeth M. Kanter, *Commitment and Community: Communes and Utopias in Sociological Perspective* (Cambridge, Mass.: Harvard University Press, 1972), pp. 113–116.
56. Ibid., pp. 116–125.

CHAPTER THREE
1. This description is corroborated by Joseph Fichter, *The Catholic Cult of the Paraclete* (New York: Sheed and Ward, 1975), p. 65, and Michael I. Harrison, "Sources of Recruitment to Catholic Pentecostalism," *Journal for the Scientific Study of Religion* 13, no. 1 (1974): 49–64.
2. Peter L. Berger and Thomas Luckmann, *Social Construction of Reality: A Treatise in the Sociology of Knowledge* (Garden City, N.Y.: Doubleday, 1966), pp. 157ff. A detailed discussion of the processes of conversion and commitment is given in Meredith B. McGuire, *Religion: The Social Context* (Belmont, Calif.: Wadsworth, 1981).
3. This new "way of seeing" is part of the reason why some psychologists suggest that mystical experiences are related to conversion. Walter H. Clark, "The Influence of Religious Experience," in *Religious Experience: Its Nature and Function in the Human Psyche*, ed. W. H. Clark et al. (Springfield, Ill.: Thomas, 1973), pp. 41–59.
4. R. Kenneth Jones, "Some Epistemological Considerations of Paradigm Shifts: Basic Steps towards a Formulated Model of Alternation," *Sociological Review* 25 (1977): 253–271.
5. Berger and Luckmann, *Social Construction of Reality*, 1966, pp. 144–147.

6. Jones, "Epistemological Considerations," 1977, pp. 255–259; see also R. Kenneth Jones, "Paradigm Shifts and Identity Theory: Alternation as a Form of Identity Management," in *Identity and Religion: International Cross-Cultural Approaches*, ed. Hans Mol (London: Sage International Sociology, 1978), pp. 59–82.

7. Takie Sugiyama Lebra, "Millenarian Movements and Resocialization," *American Behavioral Scientist* 16, no. 2 (1972): 200.

8. Kenneth Burke, *A Rhetoric of Motives* (Englewood Cliffs, N.J.: Prentice-Hall, 1953), Peter Freund, "A Conceptual Framework for the Analysis of Conversion," Ph.D. dissertation, New School for Social Research, 1969. Compare these same rhetorics in non-religious sects; Jones, "Paradigm Shifts," 1978, and R. Kenneth Jones, "Some Sectarian Characteristics of Therapeutic Groups," in *Sectarianism: Analyses of Religious and Non-religious Sects*, ed. R. Wallis (London: Peter Owen, 1975), pp. 190–210, and Roger O'Toole, "'Underground' Traditions in the Study of Sectarianism: Non-religious Uses of the Concept 'Sect'," *Journal for the Scientific Study of Religion* 15, no. 2 (1976): 145–156.

9. See James Beckford, "Accounting for Conversion," *British Journal of Sociology* 29, no. 2 (1978): 249–262.

10. Berger and Luckmann, *Social Construction of Reality*, 1966, pp. 157–163. See also James Richardson and Mary Stewart, "Conversion Process Models and the Jesus Movement," *American Behavioral Scientist* 20, no. 6 (1977): 819–838.

11. David F. Gordon, "The Jesus People: Identity Synthesis," *Urban Life and Culture* 3, no. 2 (1974): 159–178; Thomas Robbins and Dick Anthony, "Getting Straight with Meher Baba: A Study of Mysticism, Drug Rehabilitation and Post-adolescent Role Conflict," *Journal for the Scientific Study of Religion* 11, no. 2 (1972): 122–140; David Glanz and Michael J. Harrison, "Varieties of Identity Transformation: The Case of Newly Orthodox Jews," *The Jewish Journal of Sociology* 20, no. 2 (1978): 129–141, and Richard Travisano, "Alternation and Conversion as Qualitatively Different Transformations," in *Social Psychology Through Symbolic Interaction*, ed. G. P. Stone and H. A. Farberman (Waltham, Mass.: Ginn Blarsdell, 1970), pp. 594–606.

12. Cf., Ronald Wimberly et al., "Conversion in a Billy Graham Crusade: Spontaneous Event or Ritual Performance," *Sociological Quarterly* 16, no. 2 (1975): 162–170, and Hans Zetterberg, "The Religious Conversion as a Change of Social Roles," *Sociology and Social Research* 36, no. 1 (1952): 159–166.

13. Berger and Luckmann, *Social Construction of Reality*, 1966, p. 149.

14. Beckford, "Accounting for Conversion," 1978; Max Heirich, "Change of Heart: A Test of Some Widely Held Theories about Religious Conversion," *American Journal of Sociology* 83, no. 3 (1977): 653–680.

15. Cf. Alan R. Tippet, "The Phenomenology of Worship, Conversion, and Brotherhood," in *Religious Experience: Its Nature and Function in the Human Psyche*, eds. W. Clark et al. (Springfield, Ill.: Thomas, 1973), pp. 92–109.

16. Peter McHugh, "Social Disintegration as a Requisite of Resocialization," *Social Forces* 44, no. 3 (1966): 362. On the "crisis of moral meanings," compare Jack Douglas, "Deviance and Order in a Pluralistic Society," in *Theoretical Sociology*, ed. J. C. McKinney and E. A. Tiryakian (New York: Appleton-Century-Crofts, 1970), pp. 368–401. See also Michael Barkun, *Disaster and the Millennium* (New Haven, Conn.: Yale University Press, 1974); Jones "Epistemological Considerations," 1977, "Paradigm Shifts," 1978; John Lofland, *Doomsday Cult: A Study of Conversion, Proselytization and Maintenance of Faith* (Englewood Cliffs, N.J.: Prentice-Hall, 1966); Neil Smelser, *Theory of Collective Behavior* (New York: Free Press, 1963); Anthony Wallace, "Mazeway Disintegration: The Individual's Perception of Socio-cultural Disorganization," *Human Organization* 16, no. 2 (1957): 23–27, and "Revitalization Movements," *American Anthropologist* 58, no. 2 (1956): 264–281. Richardson et al. emphasize the cumulative effects of individual experiences of ambiguity and stress. James Richardson et al., *Organized Miracles: A Study of a Contemporary Youth Movement*, New Brunswick, N.J.: Transaction Press, N.J. (1978).

17. Robert W. Balch and David Taylor, "Seekers and Saucers: The Role of the Cultic Milieu in Joining a UFO Cult," *American Behavioral Scientist* 20, no. 6 (1977): 839–960; Roger Straus, "Changing Oneself: Seekers and the Creative Transformation of Life Experience," in *Doing Social Life*, ed. J. Lofland (New York: Wiley, 1976), pp. 252–272.

18. Marty sees this function of providing a sense of identity and community ties as one of the main attractions of the charismatic movement; Martin E. Marty, *A Nation of Behavers* (Chicago: University of Chicago Press, 1976), p. 108; also, Kenneth McGuire, "People, Prayer and Promise: An Anthropological Analysis of a Catholic Charismatic Covenant Community," Ph.D. dissertation, Ohio State University, 1976. On ethnicity and religious belonging, see Andrew M. Greeley, *Unsecular Man* (New York: Schocken, 1972).

19. Berger, 1967, *Sacred Canopy*, pp. 140ff.

20. Meredith B. McGuire, "Toward a Sociological Interpretation of the 'Underground Church' Movement," *Review of Religious Research* 14, no. 1 (1972): 41–47, and "An Interpretive Comparison of Elements of the Pentecostal and Underground Church Movements in American Catholicism," *Sociological Analysis* 35, no. 1 (1974): 57–65.

21. For example, Kevin Ranaghan and Dorothy Ranaghan, *Catholic Pentecostals* (New York: Paulist, 1969), pp. 80, 239; Edward D. O'Connor, *The Pentecostal Movement in the Catholic Church* (Notre Dame, Ind.: Ave Maria Press, 1971), pp. 35, 147; Kilian McDonnell, *Catholic Pentecostalism: Problems in Evaluation* (Pecos, N.M.: Dove, 1970), p. 51.

22. Cf. Michael Harrison, "Sources of Recruitment," 1974.

23. Benedict J. Mawn, "Testing the Spirits: An Empirical Search for the Socio-Cultural Situational Roots of Catholic Pentecostal Religious Experience," Ph.D. dissertation, Boston University, 1975. See Ranaghan and Ranaghan, *Catholic Pentecostals*, 1969, pp. 12, 18, for a similar description of malaise and "crisis of faith." This is perhaps related to the importance of

the knowledge that one is saved, as in O'Connor, *The Pentecostal Movement*, 1971, p. 245.

24. *New York Times*, December 3, 1973.

25. Thomas Robbins et al., "The Last Civil Religion: The Unification Church of the Reverend Sun Myung Moon," *Sociological Analysis* 37, no. 2 (1976): 111–125; see also, Stanley Aronowitz, *False Promises: The Shaping of American Working Class Consciousness* (New York: McGraw-Hill, 1973).

26. Evan Vlachos, "Apocalyptic Strains and the Potential for Utopian Movements in the United States" (presented to the Society for the Scientific Study of Religion, Milwaukee, Oct., 1975).

27. Harrison, "Sources of Recruitment," 1974, pp. 60–62; Arthur Greil, "Previous Disposition and Conversion to Perspectives of Social and Religious Movements," *Sociological Analysis* 38, no. 2 (1977): 115–125.

28. On the effects of prior socialization, see also Charles Harper, "Spirit Filled Catholics—Some Biographical Comparisons," *Social Compass* 21, no. 3 (1974): 318. See also Hans Toch, *The "Social Psychology of Social Movements* (New York: Bobbs-Merrill, 1965).

29. McGuire, "Pentecostal and Underground Church Movements," 1974; Harrison, "Sources of Recruitment," 1974. Cursillo appears to have been a significant early source of recruitment to Catholic pentecostalism, but of decreasing importance as the pentecostal movement gained its own momentum. In 1974, Fichter found that 37 percent of the "veteran" members and 19 percent of the "new" members had previously participated in Cursillo retreats, *Catholic Cult*, 1975, p. 75.

30. William J. Samarin, "Religious Motives in Religious Movements," *International Yearbook for the Sociology of Religion*, vol. 8 (1973): 173.

31. Harrison, "Sources of Recruitment," 1974, and "Preparation for Life in the Spirit," *Urban Life and Culture* 2, no. 4 (1974): 387–414; Heirich, "Change of Heart," 1977; Rodney Stark and William Sims Bainbridge, "Networks of Faith: Interpersonal Bonds and Recruitment to Cults and Sects," *American Journal of Sociology* 85, no. 6 (1980): 1376–1395.

32. Luther Gerlach and Virginia Hine, "Five Factors Crucial to the Growth and Spread of a Modern Religious Movement," *Journal for the Scientific Study of Religion* 7, no. 1 (1968): 23.

33. James Beckford, *The Trumpet of Prophecy: A Sociological Study of Jehovah's Witnesses* (New York: Wiley, 1975), p. 178.

34. Only the larger groups had these formal induction procedures, whereas smaller groups used informal induction methods. Since about 1975, very small groups are supposed to send recruits to Life in the Spirit seminars at nearby larger groups that have a trained (and approved) "teaching ministry."

35. Word of God Community, *The Life in the Spirit Seminars: Team Manual* (Notre Dame, Ind.: Charismatic Renewal Publications, 1973), p. 105.

36. Ibid., pp. 106, 107.

37. Luther P. Gerlach and Virginia H. Hine, *People, Power and Change: Movements of Social Transformation* (New York: Bobbs-Merrill, 1970), p. 111.

38. John Lofland and Rodney Stark, "Becoming a Worldsaver: A Theory of

Conversion to a Deviant Perspective," in *Religion in Sociological Perspective*, ed. C. Glock (Belmont, Calif.: Wadsworth, 1973), p. 41.

39. Peter L. Berger, *The Sacred Canopy: Elements of a Sociological Theory of Religion* (Garden City, N.Y.: Doubleday, 1967), p. 51.

40. Harrison, "Preparation for Life in the Spirit," 1974, and "Sources of Recruitment," 1974.

41. For a discussion of proselyting and the maintenance of belief, see Leon Festinger, Henry W. Riecken, and Stanley Schachter, *When Prophecy Fails: A Social and Psychological Study of a Modern Group that Predicted the Destruction of the World* (New York: Harper and Row, 1956). For concrete examples of problems experienced by Catholic pentecostals, see Sue Manney, "Alone in the Spirit," *New Covenant* (Oct., 1973), pp. 17–19.

42. Straus, "Changing Oneself," 1976, p. 266.

43. Howard S. Becker, "Notes on the Concept of Commitment," *American Journal of Sociology* 66, no. 1 (1960): 32–40. Cf., Thomas Burns and J. Stephen Smith, "The Symbolism of Becoming in the Sunday Morning Worship Service of an Urban Black Holiness Church," *Anthropological Quarterly* 51, no. 3 (1978): 185–204.

44. Virginia Hine, "Bridge-burners: Commitment and Participation in a Religious Movement," *Sociological Analysis* 31 (Summer) 1970, p. 63.

45. Harrison, "Preparation for Life in the Spirit," 1974, p. 405.

46. Lebra, "Millenarian Movements," 1972, pp. 207–210.

47. Cf., Rosabeth M. Kanter, *Commitment and Community: Communes and Utopias in Sociological Perspective* (Cambridge, Mass.: Harvard University Press, 1972).

48. Harrison, "Preparation for Life in the Spirit," 1974, p. 391.

49. *Team Manual*, 1973; participants' booklet, *Finding New Life in the Spirit* (Notre Dame, Ind.: Charismatic Renewal Services, 1972); both have been revised and reprinted several times since initial publication.

50. James Richardson, personal communication.

51. These observations are corroborated by Adams Lovekin and H. Newton Malony, "Religious Glossolalia: A Longitudinal Study of Personality Changes," *Journal for the Scientific Study of Religion* 16, no. 4 (1977): 383–393. Their study also suggests that it is not receiving the gift of tongues *per se* but rather the experience of the close-knit seminar group that accounts for "positive" personality changes observed.

52. This preliminary attendance information differs from Harrison's observations of four weeks or less; the difference is probably due to the increased formalization of the induction process since his 1969 study, "Preparation for Life in the Spirit," 1974, p. 391.

53. These themes are consistent with the recommended seminar format, *Team Manual*, 1973, p. 87.

54. Note the parallels with how other powerful figures (for example, doctors and lawyers) coach their clients in the use of acceptable vocabularies, Thomas Scheff, "Negotiating Reality: Notes on Power in the Assessment of Responsibility," *Social Problems* 16, no. 1 (1968): 3–17.

55. On witnessing as an assertion of status in the group, see Johannes Fabian,

237   *Notes*

Jamaa: A Charismatic Movement in Katanga (Evanston, Ill.: Northwestern University Press, 1971), p. 179.

56. Testimony can be viewed as a performance, success in which validates performers' claims to a status in the group; cf., J. Stephen Kroll-Smith, "Testimony as Performance: The Relationship of an Expressive Event to the Belief System of a Holiness Sect," *Journal for the Scientific Study of Religion* 19, no. 1 (1980): 16–25.

57. Harrison's data shows that 80 percent of members of a prayer group report having "talked with people about Christ several times a week or more"; however, his figures do not permit comparison of frequency of witnessing with frequency of glossolalia, Michael I. Harrison, "The Maintenance of Enthusiasm: Involvement in a New Religious Movement," *Sociological Analysis* 36, no. 2 (1975): 150–160.

Fichter, *Catholic Cult*, 1975, p. 62, reports that all of his respondents had received baptism in the Spirit, and 86 percent had received the gift of tongues. Unfortunately, Fichter's questionnaire did not distinguish between tongues as a "prayer-gift" (which is private), and tongues used for prophecy (which is public). Also, his data include no figures on witnessing and other public or semi-public acts.

Cf., also, Beckford's analysis of Jehovah's Witnesses' requirement of a demonstration talk as a testimony of faith, followed by public proselyting, in *Trumpet of Prophecy*, 1975, p. 186.

58. Irving I. Zaretsky, "In the Beginning was the Word: The Relationship of Language to Social Organization in Spiritualist Churches," in *Religious Movements in Contemporary America*, ed. Irving I. Zaretsky and Mark P. Leone (Princeton, N.J.: Princeton University Press, 1974), p. 202.

59. Cf., Lee R. Cooper, "'Publish' or Perish: Negro Jehovah's Witnesses' Adaptation in the Ghetto," in *Religious Movements*, 1974, ed. Zaretsky and Leone, pp. 700–721, and William Shaffir, "Witnessing as Identity Consolidation: The Case of the Lubavitcher Chassidim," in *Identity and Religion*, ed. H. Mol (London: Sage International), pp. 39–57.

60. Berger and Luckmann, *Social Construction of Reality*, 1966, pp. 151ff; see also, Bryan Taylor, "Conversion and Cognition," *Social Compass* 13, no. 1 (1976): 5–22.

61. Only the parts in quotation marks are verbatim.

62. Luther P. Gerlach and Virginia H. Hine, *Lifeway Leap* (Minneapolis: University of Minnesota Press, 1973), p. 184.

63. Festinger et al., *When Prophecy Fails*, 1956.

64. For Catholic pentecostals, as well as other developing movements, the ideology is articulated in a continuing process in which witnessing plays an important part. Since language is dependent on a "shared, intersubjective temporality," the very articulation of an ideology is a "communicative event"; Johannes Fabian, "Genres in an Emerging Tradition: An Anthropological Approach to Religious Communication," in *Changing Perspectives in the Scientific Study of Religion*, ed. A. Eister (New York: Wiley, 1974), p. 253.

65. Erving Goffman, *Frame Analysis: An Essay on the Organization of Experience* (New York: Harper and Row, 1974), pp. 504, 559.

66. Peter Freund, "Documenting Experiences: Telling and Retelling as Mediation" (presented to the American Sociological Association, New York, Aug., 1976).

CHAPTER FOUR

1. Jim Cavnar, *Participating in Prayer Meetings* (Ann Arbor: Word of Life Press, 1974), p. 5. See also, Edward D. O'Connor, *The Pentecostal Movement in the Catholic Church* (Notre Dame, Ind.: Ave Maria Press, 1971), p. 112.
2. This analysis is based primarily on observations in numerous prayer groups in the research "sample" and visited elsewhere. The formats, however, are sufficiently uniform that they are represented in numerous Catholic pentecostal books and manuals. These descriptions of prayer meetings are corroborated by observations by Ralph Lane, Jr., "Catholic Charismatic Renewal," in *The New Religious Consciousness*, ed. Charles Y. Glock and Robert N. Bellah (Berkeley: University of California Press, 1976), pp. 162–179, and Frances R. Westley, "Searching for Surrender: A Catholic Charismatic Renewal Group's Attempt to Become Glossolalic," *American Behavioral Scientist* 20, no. 6 (1977): 925–940.
3. Kilian McDonnell, *Catholic Pentecostalism: Problems in Evaluation* (Pecos, N.M.: Dove, 1970); see also, O'Connor, *Pentecostal Movement*, 1971, pp. 121, 226.
4. Cf., Bryan Wilson's observations in "The Pentecostalist Minister: Role Conflicts and Status Contradictions," *American Journal of Sociology* 64, no. 5 (1959): 498.
5. Compare Samarin's description of prophecy among Protestant pentecostals; W. M. Samarin, *Tongues of Men and Angels* (New York: Macmillan, 1972).
6. Harrison observed a similar pattern, that most prophecies and interpretations of tongues were given by group leaders, Michael I. Harrison, "The Maintenance of Enthusiasm: Involvement in a New Religious Movement," *Sociological Analysis* 36, no. 2 (1975): 154, 155.
7. See Samarin, *Tongues of Men and Angels*, 1972, p. 56.
8. Cavnar, *Participation in Prayer Meetings*, 1974, pp. 37–47.
9. Cf., J. Stephen Kroll-Smith, "Testimony as Performance: The Relationship of an Expressive Event to the Belief System of a Holiness Sect," *Journal for the Scientific Study of Religion* 19, no. 1 (1980): 16–25; Richard Bauman, "Verbal Art as Performance," *American Anthropologist* 77, no. 2 (1975): 290–312.
10. Cf., Irving I. Zaretsky, "In the Beginning was the Word: The Relationship of Language to Social Organization in Spiritualist Churches," in *Religious Movements in Contemporary America*, ed. I. Zaretsky and M. Leone (Princeton, N.J.: Princeton University Press, 1974), p. 192.
11. The use of the masculine pronoun here and elsewhere in this chapter is deliberate because leaders were rarely female. Several groups studied felt strongly that women should never hold positions of authority over men.
12. William Samarin, "Protestant Preachers in the Prophetic Line," *International Yearbook for the Sociology of Religion* 8 (1973): 256.

13. Lane, "Catholic Charismatic Renewal," 1976, p. 169.
14. Harrison also noted the movement's tendency toward routinization of forms of worship and greater stratification, in "Maintenance of Enthusiasm," 1976: 159.
15. Cf., Samarin, "Protestant Preachers," 1973, p. 255.
16. John Thompson, "Intellectuals and Charismatic Renewal Among Catholics: Defining Charismatic Experience as 'Catholic'" (presented to the Society for the Scientific Study of Religion, Chicago, Oct., 1977).
17. Compare Shibutani's discussion of the construction of a common "definition of the situation" in the reception of rumor, Tamotsu Shibutani, *Improvised News: A Sociological Study of Rumor* (Indianapolis: Bobbs-Merrill, 1966).
18. The unifying force of this co-production of meanings is similar to Schutz's concept of "growing older together," in being able to take shared meanings for granted, Alfred Schutz, *Collected Papers II: Studies in Social Theory* (The Hague: Martinus Nijhoff, 1964), p. 33.
19. Cf. Shibutani, *Improvised News*, 1966, pp. 15–16.
20. Samarin, "Protestant Preachers," 1973, p. 254.
21. Kevin Ranaghan and Dorothy Ranaghan, *Catholic Pentecostals* (New York: Paulist, 1969), p. 173.
22. Wilson described this interpretation as a "relatively new development" among Protestant pentecostals in 1959, in "Pentecostalist Minister," 1959, p. 498.
23. Emilio Willems, "Validation of Authority in Pentecostal Sects of Chile and Brazil," *Journal for the Scientific Study of Religion* 6, no. 2 (1967): 253.
24. This observation is corroborated by Chordas, who suggests that this "radicalization of charisma" is itself a product of a rhetorical dynamic within the pentecostal system of discourse. He suggests that some (but not all) prayer groups create, through their regular production of prophecy and other "divine" speech, an ever escalating spiral of more radical and symbolically charged formulations. The nature of pentecostal modes of speaking and hearing is such that, once one accepts the underlying cognitive framework and the vocabulary which expresses it, literally anything is believable if it comes about in the expected course of "revelation" (see Chapter 5). Although Chordas does not explicitly develop interpretations of why some groups develop this "radicalization," his description corroborates my observation that it is correlated with a sectarian orientation (see Chapter 8).
25. Samarin, *Tongues of Men and Angels*, 1972, p. 171.
26. Ranaghan and Ranaghan, *Catholic Pentecostals*, 1969, p. 128.
27. Samarin gives several instances of such invalidation among Protestant pentecostals in *Tongues of Men and Angels*, 1972, p. 166.
28. Ibid.
29. Goffman describes similar audience co-participation in the success of the performance, Erving Goffman, *Presentation of Self in Everyday Life* (Garden City, N.Y.: Doubleday, 1959), pp. 77ff.
30. These meetings of discernment were not open to the observer (or to other

members of the prayer group, for that matter), but the descriptions given here were obtained from respondents who were members of the core group.

31. Compare with Wilson's observation that the role of discerner in Protestant pentecostal churches is often that of the minister *qua* minister, "Pentecostalist Minister," 1959, p. 498. Another study documents the use of tongues and discernment in intra-group power plays, Andrew Walker and James S. Atherton, "An Eastern Pentecostal Convention: The Successful Management of a 'Time of Sharing'," *Sociological Review* 19, no. 3 (1971): 367–387.

32. Cavnar, *Participating in Prayer Meetings*, 1974, pp. 23–25.

33. Samarin, "Protestant Preachers," 1973, p. 255; compare also, Walker and Atherton, "An Eastern Pentecostal Convention," 1971, p. 387.

34. Westley, "Searching for Surrender," 1977.

35. Samarin, *Tongues of Men and Angels*, 1972, p. 56.

36. Berger, applying Weber's concept of "disenchantment of the world," suggests that secularization is characterized by the loss of three concomitants of the sacred—mystery, miracle, and magic. Similarly, attempts to counteract forces of secularization frequently employ a re-mystification of everyday reality, Peter L. Berger, *The Sacred Canopy: Elements of a Sociological Theory of Religion* (Garden City, N.Y.: Doubleday, 1967), p. 111.

CHAPTER FIVE

1. The term "states" is also misleading; it misses the idea of the fluidity and process-like qualities of alternate realities. The classic exception to these generalizations is, of course, James and his school. James described multiple worlds or sub-universes each of which is real after its own fashion, while it is attended to, and the reality lapses with the attention. William James, *Principles of Psychology*, vol. 2 (New York: Dover, 1950), p. 293.

2. See, for example, Erika Bourguignon, *A Crosscultural Study of Dissociational States* (Columbus, Ohio: The Ohio State University Research Foundation, 1968).

3. Deborah Offenbacher, "Alternate Realities: The New Consciousness and the Oversocialized Conception of Man" (presented to the Eastern Sociological Association, Boston, April, 1976).

4. Alfred Schutz, *Collected Papers I: The Problem of Social Reality* (The Hague: Martinus Nijhoff, 1962), p. 232.

5. Erving Goffman, *Frame Analysis: An Essay on the Organization of Experience* (New York: Harper and Row, 1974).

6. Useful material on these aspects may be drawn from Arthur J. Deikman, "Biomodal Consciousness," pp. 67–86; and "Deautomatization and the Mystic Experience," pp. 216–233, in *The Nature of Human Consciousness: A Book of Readings*, ed. R. E. Ornstein (New York: Viking, 1973); Roland Fischer, "Cartography of Inner Space," in *Hallucinations: Behavior, Experience and Theory*, ed. R. K. Siegel and L. J. West (New York: Wiley,

1975), pp. 197–239; Ernest Hartmann, "The Psycho-physiology of Free Will: An Example of Verticle Research," in *Psychoanalysis: A General Psychology*, ed. R. Lowenstein et al. (New York: International University Presses, 1966); Robert E. Ornstein, *The Psychology of Consciousness*, 2d. ed. (New York: Harcourt, Brace, Jovanovich, 1977); Julian Silverman, "A Paradigm for the Study of Altered States of Consciousness," *British Journal of Psychiatry* 114 (1968): 1201–1218.

7. Deborah Offenbacher, personal communication. Silverman also employs a continuum of "attentional styles" along five parameters: sensitivity, intensity modulation, information-search, differentiation, distractibility, in "Altered States of Consciousness," 1968, p. 1203.

8. The nature of the "shock" is unclear. Schutz suggests that it is a partition of attention. It is probable that the partition has simultaneously social, psychological, and physiological dimensions. For example, research on trance and possession shows that these "states" have not only psychological and physiological qualities, but also social. For instance, Bourguignon found cases of children learning possession-appropriate behavior in play situations; Erika Bourguignon, "The Self, the Behavioral Environment, and the Theory of Spirit Possession," in *Context and Meaning in Cultural Anthropology*, ed. M. Spiro (New York: Free Press, 1965), p. 47.

9. Edward D. O'Connor, *The Pentecostal Movement in the Catholic Church* (Notre Dame, Ind.: Ave Maria Press, 1971), p. 126. An early 1960s study of Italian Catholics converted to Protestant pentecostalism showed little or no trance or possession, Anne Parsons, *Belief, Magic and Anomie: Essays in Psychosocial Anthropology* (New York: Free Press, 1969), p. 265. Lewis states emphatically that spirit possession does not necessarily involve trance. In fact, he points out that researchers who try to define the phenomenon in terms of its physiological or psychological correlates are likely to be misled, since possession is "a cultural evaluation of a person's condition"—not the symptoms of the condition itself, I. M. Lewis, *Ecstatic Religion: An Anthropological Study of Spirit Possession and Shamanism* (Baltimore: Penguin, 1971), pp. 45–46. Compare also, Bourguignon, "The Self," 1965, pp. 40–41.

10. W. J. Samarin, *Tongues of Men and Angels* (New York: Macmillan, 1972), p. 2. Samarin's findings are corroborated by Nils Holm, "Ritualistic Pattern and Sound Structure of Glossolalia in Material Collected in the Swedish-Speaking Parts of Finland," *Temenos: Studies in Comparative Religion* 11 (1975): 43–60, and "Functions of Glossolalia in the Pentecostal Movement," *Psychological Studies on Religious Man*, ed. T. Kallstad (Uppsala, Sweden: Uppsala University Publications, 1978), pp. 141–158.

11. James R. Jaquith, "Toward a Typology of Formal Communicative Behavior: Glossolalia," *Anthropological Linguistics* 9, no. 8 (1967): 1–8.

12. This finding is corroborated by my own experience. At the time of this phase of the study, my daughter (then age three) often played with nonsense syllables, stringing together long chants or songs of meaningless sounds. Her lack of self-consciousness seemed to be the key to producing such extensive glossolalia in her play. Having heard tongues

spoken in the prayer groups studied for several months, I tried to do it at home. I found that if I could suspend my attention to my own vocalizations I could continue speaking in tongues for quite a while. As soon as I paid attention to my "words," I lost the thread of glossolalic utterances. Experienced tongue-speakers, however, can sometimes remember some of their "words"—especially the combination of sounds they usually use to start their glossolalic utterances.

13. Samarin, *Tongues of Men and Angels*, 1972, p. 253.

14. O'Connor, *Pentecostal Movement*, 1971, pp. 123–125.

15. See also, Samarin, "Glossolalist Folk Linguistics" (presented to Socio-linguistics Research Committee, World Congress for Sociology, Toronto, Aug., 1974). On the meaningfulness of glossolalia to pentecostals, see Morton T. Kelsey, *Tongue Speaking* (Garden City, N.Y.: Doubleday, 1964); Kilian McDonnell, *Charismatic Renewal and the Churches* (New York: Seabury, 1976); John L. Sheriff, *They Speak With Other Tongues* (New York: Pyramid, 1964).

16. Samarin, *Tongues of Men and Angels*, 1972, pp. 197–211; see also, Samarin, "Forms and Functions of Nonsense Language," *Linguistics* 50 (1969): 70–74.

17. Virginia Hine, "Bridge-burners: Commitment and Participation in a Religious Movement," *Sociological Analysis* 31, no. 2 (1970): 61–66. See Chapter 3 above for critical discussion of the commitment process.

18. Lewis, *Ecstatic Religion*, 1971.

19. O'Connor, *Pentecostal Movement*, 1971, p. 127; Word of God Community, *The Life in the Spirit Seminars: Team Manual* (Notre Dame, Ind.: Charismatic Renewal Publications, 1973), p. 150. This discussion applies only to personal glossolalic prayer. Glossolalic prophecy, like prophecy in the vernacular, is a public act and requires special anointing.

20. E. Mansell Pattison, "Behavioral Science Research on the Nature of Glossolalia," *Journal of the American Scientific Affiliation* 20 (1968): 73–86.

21. See also Lewis, *Ecstatic Religion*, 1971, who suggests that possession shamanism is also self-assertion.

22. Samarin, *Tongues of Men and Angels*, 1972, p. 203.

23. O'Connor, *Pentecostal Movement*, 1971, pp. 126–127.

24. Religious speaking by Catholic pentecostals could be considered related to dissociation only if "dissociation" were defined extremely broadly to include all kinds of involvements away from the sphere of everyday life. By this definition, then, all spheres here considered as "modified reality" would be dissociation. By such a broad definition, dissociation would then include ordinary "hard-thinking" and ordinary prayer in the vernacular. Goodman, one of the foremost proponents of the "trance-produced" interpretation of glossolalia tries to hedge her theory by broadening the definition this way: Felicitas D. Goodman, *Speaking in Tongues: A Cross-Cultural Study of Glossolalia* (Chicago: University of Chicago Press, 1972), and "Not Speaking in Tongues" (presented to the Sociolinguistics Research Committee, World Congress of Sociology, Toronto, Aug., 1974).

25. Erika Bourguignon, "Cross-Cultural Perspectives on the Religious Uses of

Altered States of Consciousness," *Religious Movements in Contemporary America*, ed. Irving I. Zaretsky and Mark P. Leone (Princeton: Princeton University Press, 1974), pp. 228–243. Arnold Ludwig, "Altered States of Consciousness," in *Trance and Possession States*, ed. R. Prince (Montreal: R. M. Bucke Memorial Society, 1968), pp. 69–165.

26. Hart Pavelsky and H. Newton Malony, "The Physiological Correlates of Glossolalia" (presented to the Society for the Scientific Study of Religion, Milwaukee, Oct., 1975).

27. For good critical reviews of this literature, see Virginia Hine, "Pentecostal Glossolalia: Toward a Functional Interpretation," *Journal for the Scientific Study of Religion* 8, no. 2 (1969): 211–226; James Richardson, "Psychological Interpretations of Glossolalia: A Re-examination of Research," *Journal for the Scientific Study of Religion* 12, no. 2 (1973): 199–207.

28. Adams Lovekin and H. Newton Malony, "Religious Glossolalia: A Longitudinal Study of Personality Changes," *Journal for the Scientific Study of Religion* 16, no. 4 (1977): 383–393; E. Mansell Pattison, "Ideological Support for the Marginal Middle-Class," in *Religious Movements*, ed. Zaretsky and Leone, 1974, pp. 418–455; Samarin, *Tongues of Men and Angels*, 1972, p. 210; O'Connor, *Pentecostal Movement*, 1971, p. 125; John P. Kildahl, *The Psychology of Speaking in Tongues* (New York: Harper and Row, 1972), p. 81; and Richard Hutch, "The Personal Ritual of Glossolalia," *Journal for the Scientific Study of Religion* 19, no. 3 (1980): 255–266.

29. Kildahl, *Psychology of Speaking*, 1972.

30. Goffman, *Frame Analysis*, 1975, pp. 514, 522, 534.

31. Peter L. Berger and Thomas Luckmann, *Social Construction of Reality: A Treatise in the Sociology of Knowledge* (Garden City, N.Y.: Doubleday, 1966), p. 75.

32. Cited by Peter L. Berger, "Languages of Murder," *Worldview* 15, no. 1 (1972): 13.

33. See Samarin, "Nonsense Language," 1969 and 1975, p. 129ff. for comparison of the function of freedom in glossolalia with other naturally occurring nonsense speech.

34. It is possible to extend this perspective even further, to non-religious forms of anomalous speech. For example, this interpretation suggests that it might be fruitful to analyze schizoid speech, not as a symptom *per se* of pathology, but as an expression or understandable outcome of an altered relationship between speakers and their speech. This suggested parallel does not imply that religious speaking is pathological; on the contrary, it implies that other anomalous speech may be less than pathological. If there is a psychological problem, it lies in the altered relationship of the speaker to the speech and not in the form of speech itself. This parallel is speculative, but may prove fruitful as a point of departure for further analysis.

35. Cf., Regina A. Holloman, "Ritual Opening and Individual Transformation: Rites of Passage at Esalen," *American Anthropologist* 76, no. 2 (1974): 265–280; and Frances Westley, "Searching for Surrender: A Catholic Charismatic Renewal Group's Attempt to Become Glossolalic," *American Behavioral Scientist* 20, no. 6 (1977): 925–940.

36. Similarly vague messages are given by Spiritualist mediums, cf., Irving Zaretsky, "In the Beginning was the Word: The Relationship of Language to Social Organization in Spiritualist Churches," in *Religious Movements*, Zaretsky and Leone, eds., 1974, pp. 166–232.

37. James Cavnar, *Participating in Prayer Meetings* (Ann Arbor: Word of Life Press, 1974).

38. Samarin, *Tongues of Men and Angels*, 1972, p. 163.

39. Zaretsky and Leone, *Religious Movements*, 1974, p. 185.

40. Erving Goffman, *Presentation of Self in Everyday Life* (Garden City, N.Y.: Doubleday, 1959), pp. 208–212.

41. This is comparable to what Garfinkel calls "membershipping." The social group validates the individual's communicated experiences as real; Harold Garfinkel, *Studies in Ethnomethodology* (Englewood Cliffs, N.J.: Prentice-Hall, 1967), p. 79.

42. For prophecy, the norms were far stricter, and more attention was paid to competency and quality of performance. See Samarin, *Tongues of Men and Angels*, 1972, p. 74.

43. Cf., Janice Demarest, "A Sociolinguistic Study of Christian Science Oral Testimonies" (presented to the Society for the Scientific Study of Religion, Milwaukee, Oct., 1975).

44. Cf., *Tongues of Men and Angels*, Samarin, 1972, p. 165. In this context he cites Ayer, "No matter what a person says (or "says") at that time is 'understandable' and in a sense 'verifiable'," A. J. Ayer, ed., *The Concept of a Person* (New York: St. Martin's Press, 1963), p. 51.

45. Alfred Schutz, *Collected Papers III: Studies in Phenomenological Philosophy* (The Hague: Martinus Nijhoff, 1966), pp. 72, 77; cf. also, Peter L. Berger and Thomas Luckmann, "Sociology of Religion and Sociology of Knowledge," *Sociology and Social Research* 47, no. 4 (1963): 421–422.

CHAPTER SIX

1. See, for example, Morton Kelsey, *Healing and Christianity* (New York: Harper and Row, 1973).

2. Peter L. Berger, *The Sacred Canopy: Elements of a Sociological Theory of Religion* (Garden City, N.Y.: Doubleday, 1967), pp. 53ff.

3. Much of what is described in these chapters also applies to other religious and quasi-religious groups involved in healing practices, but conclusions here are focused on the pentecostal Catholic context and special uses of healing.

4. Francis MacNutt, *The Power to Heal* (Notre Dame, Ind.: Ave Maria Press, 1977), p. 103.

5. Horacio Fabrega, Jr., *Disease and Social Behavior: An Elementary Exposition* (Cambridge, Mass.: MIT, 1974), p. 95.

6. Eliot Freidson, *Profession of Medicine: A Study of the Sociology of Applied Knowledge* (New York: Dodd, Mead, 1970).

7. Arthur M. Kleinman, "Some Issues for a Comparative Study of Medical Healing," *International Journal of Social Psychiatry* 19, no. 3/4 (1973): 160.

8. Allan Young, "Some Implications of Medical Beliefs and Practices for Social Anthropology," *American Anthropologist* 78, no. 1 (1976): 5–24.

9. For example, studies by Bernard Grad, "Healing by the Laying on of Hands: Review of Experiments and Implications," *Pastoral Psychology* 11 (1970): 19–26.

10. For example, Louis Rose, *Faith Healing* (Harmondsworth, Middlesex: Penguin, 1970).

11. Kenneth Calestro, "Psychotherapy, Faith Healing, and Suggestion," *International Journal of Psychiatry* 10, no. 1 (1972): 83–113; T. J. Chordas and S. J. Gross, "Healing of Memories: Psychotherapeutic Ritual Among Catholic Pentecostals," *Journal of Pastoral Care* 30 (1976): 245–257; Jerome D. Frank, *Persuasion and Healing: A Comparative Study of Psychotherapy* (New York: Schocken, 1973); Michael Owen Jones, *Why Faith Healing,* Canadian Centre for Folk Culture Studies, Paper #3 (Ottawa: National Museum of Man, National Museum of Canada, Dec., 1972); Ari Kiev, ed., *Magic, Faith and Healing: Studies in Primitive Psychiatry Today* (New York: Free Press, 1964); I. Lubchansky et al., "Puerto Rican Spiritualists View Mental Illness: The Faith Healer as a Paraprofessional," *American Journal of Pyschiatry* 127 (1970): 312–321; Raymond Prince, "Fundamental Differences of Psychoanalysis and Faith Healing," *International Journal of Psychiatry* 10, no. 1 (1972): 115–128; L. H. Rogler and A. B. Hollingshead, "The Puerto Rican Spiritualist as Psychiatrist," *American Journal of Sociology* 67 (1961): 17–21; E. Fuller Torrey, *The Mind Game: Witchdoctors and Psychiatrists* (New York: Emerson Hall, 1972), and "Spiritualists and Shamans as Psychotherapist: An Account of Original Anthropological Sin," in *Religious Movements in Contemporary America,* ed. Irving I. Zaretsky and Mark P. Leone (Princeton, N.J.: Princeton University, 1974), pp. 330–337.

12. Vincent Crapanzano and Vivian Garrison, eds., *Case Studies in Spirit Possession* (New York: Wiley, 1977); I. M. Lewis, *Ecstatic Religion: An Anthropological Study of Spirit Possession and Shamanism* (Baltimore: Penguin, 1971); V. W. Turner, *The Drums of Affliction: A Study of Religious Processes Among the Ndembu of Zambia* (Oxford: Clarendon Press and the International African Institute, 1968): especially pp. 25–51.

13. Vivian Garrison, "Sectarianism and Psychosocial Adjustment: A Controlled Comparison of Puerto Rican Pentecostals and Catholics," in Zaretsky and Leone, *Religious Movements,* 1974, pp. 298–329; Alan Harwood, *Rx: Spiritualist as Needed; A Study of a Puerto Rican Community Mental Health Resource* (New York: Wiley-Interscience, 1977); June Macklin, "Belief, Ritual and Healing: New England Spiritualism and Mexican-American Spiritism Compared," Zaretsky and Leone, *Religious Movements,* 1974, pp. 383–417.

14. See especially, E. Mansell Pattison, "Faith Healing: A Study of Personality and Function," *Journal of Nervous and Mental Disease* 157, no. 6 (1973): 397–409; also, "Ideological Support for the Marginal Middle Class: Faith Healing and Glossolalia," in Zaretsky and Leone, *Religious Movements,* 1974, pp. 418–458; and Gillian Allen and Roy Wallis, "Pentecostalists as

a Medical Minority," *Marginal Medicine*, ed. Roy Wallis and Peter Morley (New York: Free Press, 1976), pp. 110–137.

15. Freidson, *Profession of Medicine*, 1970, pp. 286 ff.
16. Wallis and Morley, *Marginal Medicine*, 1976.
17. Raymond Prince, "Psychoanalysis and Faith Healing," 1972.
18. Kevin Ranaghan and Dorothy Ranaghan, *Catholic Pentecostals* (New York: Paulist, 1969), p. 217; Edward D. O'Connor, *The Pentecostal Movement in the Catholic Church* (Notre Dame, Ind.: Ave Maria Press, 1971), pp. 162–163.
19. *National Catholic Reporter*, July 5, 1974. Harrell points out that the faith healing aspect of Catholic pentecostalism drew directly on the guidance of independent revivalists more than on classical pentecostalism *per se*; David E. Harrell, Jr., *All Things Are Possible: The Healing and Charismatic Revivals in Modern America* (Bloomington, Ind.: Indiana University Press, 1975).
20. Francis MacNutt, *Healing* (Notre Dame, Ind.: Ave Maria, 1974) and MacNutt, *Power to Heal*, 1977. Father MacNutt's prominence in the movement came under fire in 1980 when he decided to leave the priesthood and get married. The internal controversy which ensued illustrates the difficulty of a movement's reliance on highly authoritative figures whose legitimacy may subsequently be debunked or undermined (see *National Catholic Reporter*, Feb. 15, 1980, and letters to the editor in subsequent issues).
21. See especially *New Covenant*, 1974–1975.
22. The term "healing ministry" is sometimes used to refer to the ministry of the individual who has received a specialized "gift of healing." The more general usage of the concept, however, refers to a team of core group members who conduct a prayer group's healing services (public and private). Often it is used synonymously with the yet-broader term, "prayer ministry"—a team of core groups members who serve the prayer group by praying with individual members for special needs of all sorts.
23. Pattison, "Faith Healing," 1973, pp. 418ff.
24. See MacNutt, *Healing*, 1974, pp. 125ff., for a similar description.
25. Fabrega, *Disease and Social Behavior*, 1974, p. 81.
26. Young, "Implications of Medical Beliefs," 1976.
27. Cf., Thomas Scheff, "Negotiating Reality: Notes on Power in the Assessment of Responsibility," *Social Problems* 16, no. 1 (1968): 3–17, and Michael Balint, *The Doctor, His Patient and the Illness* (New York: International University Presses, 1964), pp. 21ff.
28. There are strong parallels with the social functions of divination, although the underlying belief system is very different; cf., George K. Park, "Divination and Its Social Contexts," *Journal of the Royal Anthropological Institute*, 93 (1963), pp. 195–209; Turner, *Drums of Affliction*, 1968.
29. MacNutt, *Healing*, 1974, pp. 162ff.
30. Joseph Fichter, *The Catholic Cult of the Paraclete* (New York: Sheed and Ward, 1975), p. 128.
31. Compare Rosabeth M. Kanter, *Commitment and Community: Communes and*

Utopias in Sociological Perspective (Cambridge, Mass.: Harvard University Press, 1972), pp. 61ff.

32. This "official" form of exorcism is also practiced and encouraged by the movement, and several instances of this "official" type were reported to me by priests engaged in the deliverance ministry. For a more detailed description, see MacNutt, *Healing*, 1974, pp. 208–231, and Randy Cirner, "Deliverance," *New Covenant*, April, 1974, pp. 4–7, and May, 1974, pp. 22–25. See Fichter, *Catholic Cult*, 1975, p. 134, for an assessment of the early stages of this phenomenon. See also the *New York Times*, November 29, 1974.

33. Cf. Emile Durkheim's discussion of the "negative cult," *The Elementary Forms of the Religious Life* (New York: Collier, 1965), pp. 337ff.

34. See MacNutt, *Healing*, 1974, p. 131. Lawrence LeShan, studying healing in another quasi-religious context, concurs that the faith of the healer is more important than the faith of the person prayed for, in *The Medium, the Mystic and the Physicist* (New York: Ballantine, 1975).

35. Frank, *Persuasion and Healing*, 1973, p. 73, and Calestro, "Psychotherapy," 1972, both link this factor with the ability of the healer to evoke the patient's expectancy of help.

36. The concept of "soaking prayer" is somewhat more complex as presented by MacNutt (he borrows the term from faith healer Tommy Tyson). In this usage, "soaking prayer" refers to an often prolonged prayer which emphasizes touching—sometimes long after the words of the prayer for healing are ended; sometimes glossolalia is used when ordinary prayer is exhausted. It is especially recommended as a prayer approach for severe or chronic conditions requiring extensive or repeated sessions of prayer. See MacNutt, *Power to Heal*, 1977, pp. 35–55.

37. Dennis Linn and Matthew Linn, *Healing of Memories* (Paramus, N.J.: Paulist, 1974).

38. Michael Scanlan, *Inner Healing* (Paramus, N.J.: Paulist, 1974), pp. 44ff.

39. Not verbatim, but close. Note that these techniques are largely learned from the Protestant healer, Agnes Sanford; see *New Covenant*, May, 1974, pp. 3–10.

40. Cf., Berger, *Sacred Canopy*, 1967, pp. 40–41, on religious ritual.

41. Kleinman, "Medical Healing," 1973, p. 162.

42. Erving Goffman, *Asylums: Essays on the Social Situation of Mental Patients and Other Inmates* (Garden City, N.Y.: Doubleday, 1961), especially pp. 321ff, also Erving Goffman, *Presentation of Self in Everyday Life* (Garden City, N.Y.: Doubleday, 1959), p. 165.

43. MacNutt, *Healing*, 1974, p. 145.

44. See Leonard B. Glick, "Medicine as an Ethnographic Category: The Gimi of the New Guinea Highlands," *Ethnology* 6, no. 1 (1967): 31–56.

45. W. J. Samarin's study of non-Catholic pentecostals found a belief that glossolalia was especially effective in healing and exorcism, in *Tongues of Men and Angels* (New York: Macmillan, 1972), p. 154. Catholic pentecostals studied also believed it to be useful, especially when one is not certain how to focus the prayer.

46. Cf., Wallis and Morley, *Marginal Medicine*, 1976, p. 69.
47. Much psychotherapy does indeed embody a quasi-religious ideology, and, as such, it is probably correctly perceived by Catholic pentecostals as a competing belief system, Peter Berger, "Toward a Sociological Understanding of Psychoanalysis," *Social Research* 32, no. 1 (1965): 26–41.
48. Pattison, "Faith Healing," 1974; cf., Fabrega, *Disease and Social Behavior*, 1974; Young, "Medical Beliefs and Practices," 1976.
49. Young, "Medical Beliefs and Practices," 1976, p. 13.
50. Cf. Scheff, "Negotiating Reality," 1968.
51. MacNutt, *Healing*, 1974, p. 162.
52. MacNutt, *Power to Heal*, 1977, p. 129.
53. Cf., Young, "Medical Beliefs and Practices," 1976.
54. Due to a malfunction of the tape recorder, this quotation is not verbatim.
55. Luckmann, *The Invisible Religion: The Problem of Religion in Modern Society* (New York: Macmillan, 1967); Arthur Kleinman, "The Failure of Western Medicine," *Human Nature* 2 (1978): 63–68.
56. MacNutt, *Power to Heal*, 1977, p. 149, develops a similar—although far more sophisticated—explanation. His explanations are notably different from those of persons interviewed, however, in his emphasis on social and political, as well as purely individualistic suffering.
57. Berger, *Sacred Canopy*, 1967, pp. 53–56.
58. The definition of death is also socially constructed; even the dominant medical system applies the definition differently according to the social situation; cf., David Sudnow, *Passing On: The Social Organization of Dying* (Englewood Cliffs, N.J.: Prentice-Hall, 1967); Barney G. Glaser and Anselm L. Strauss, *Awareness of Dying* (Chicago: Aldine, 1965).
59. This is also asserted in much of the movement's literature; cf., MacNutt, *Power to Heal*, 1977, p. 155.
60. Frank, *Persuasion and Healing*, 1973, pp. 327ff.
61. See, however, Thomas S. Kuhn's argument that scientific knowledge, too, is based on a self-sustaining paradigm which is highly resistant to disconfirmation, in *The Structure of Scientific Revolutions* (Chicago: University of Chicago Press, 1970).
62. Fabrega, *Disease and Social Behavior*, 1974; Freidson, *Profession of Medicine*, 1970; Kleinman, "Medical Healing," 1973.
63. MacNutt distinguishes eleven reasons why people are not healed; his explanations that were not used by the groups studied include: the social environment prevents healing from taking place (again, note the contrast between MacNutt's social emphasis and the groups' individualistic one); not using the natural means of preserving health; refusal to see medicine as a way God heals; and a different person should be the instrument of healing (this legitimation applies to ministries such as MacNutt's in which individual healers are believed to have received special "gifts of healing"); see MacNutt, *Healing*, 1974, pp. 249ff.
64. Marcia Millman, *The Unkindest Cut: Life in the Back Rooms of Medicine* (New York: William Morrow, 1978).

CHAPTER SEVEN

1. Horacio Fabrega, Jr., *Disease and Social Behavior: An Elementary Exposition* (Cambridge, Mass.: MIT Press, 1974); Peter L. Berger and Thomas Luckmann, *Social Construction of Reality: A Treatise in the Sociology of Knowledge* (Garden City, N.Y.: Doubleday, 1966); Arthur Kleinman, *Patients and Healers in the Context of Culture: An Exploration of the Borderline between Anthropology, Medicine, and Psychiatry* (Berkeley: University of California, 1980).

2. Talcott Parsons, "Definitions of Health and Illness in Light of American Values and Social Structure," *Patients, Physicians, and Illness: A Source Book in Behavioral Science and Health*, ed. E. Garthy Jaco (New York: Macmillan, 1972), pp. 107–127.

3. Eliot Freidson, *Profession of Medicine: A Study of the Sociology of Applied Knowledge* (New York: Dodd, Mead, 1970), p. 239.

4. Judith Lorber, "Deviance as Performance: The Case of Illness," *Social Problems* 14, no. 3 (1967): 302–310.

5. Howard S. Becker, *Outsiders: Studies in the Sociology of Deviance* (New York: Free Press, 1963); Erving Goffman, *Stigma: Notes on the Management of Spoiled Identity* (Englewood Cliffs, N.J.: Spectrum, 1963); Andrew Twaddle, "Illness and Deviance," *Social Science and Medicine* 7, no. 3 (1973): 751–762.

6. Freidson, *Profession of Medicine*, 1970, p. 208.

7. Diagnostic actions may be compared, to a limited extent, with divination; the diviner analyzes the sources of deviance, sanctioning some and exculpating others; cf., George K. Park, "Divination and Its Social Contexts," *Journal of the Royal Anthropological Institute* 93 (1963): 195–209, and V. W. Turner, *The Drums of Affliction: A Study of Religious Processes Among the Ndembu of Zambia* (Oxford: Clarendon Press and The International African Institute, 1968), pp. 25–51. The imputation of responsibility then implies an appropriate course of therapeutic action. Allan Young, "Internalizing and Externalizing Medical Belief Systems: An Ethopian Example," *Social Science and Medicine* 10, no. 1 (1976): 147.

8. Becker, *Outsiders*, 1963, pp. 147–163.

9. Freidson, *Profession of Medicine*, 1970, p. 361. See also, Jerome D. Frank, *Persuasion and Healing: A Comparative Study of Psychotherapy* (New York: Schocken, 1973), p. 8.

10. Z. A. Medvedev and R. A. Medvedev, *A Question of Madness* (New York: Knopf, 1971). Similar uses of medical definitions for political purposes in the U.S. are exemplified by the treatment of Ezra Pound and General James Walker (cited in Freidson, *Profession of Medicine*, 1970, p. 246). Social control functions of religious "therapy" are discussed by Brian S. Turner, "Confession and Social Structure," *The Annual Review of the Social Sciences of Religion* 1 (1977): 29–58. Turner suggests that in the analysis of practices such as confession, Marxist and structural–functionalist interpretations dovetail. Although this social control function is most obvious in examples drawn from "mental illness," similar *moral* imperatives can be seen, for example, in the 1977 court order that par-

ents of a child suffering from leukemia submit the child to professionally prescribed chemotherapy, rather than a less unpleasant—but also less respectable—naturopathic therapy.

11. Peter L. Berger, "Towards a Sociological Understanding of Psychoanalysis," *Social Research* 32, no. 1 (1965): 26–41. See also Murray Edelman, "The Political Language of the Helping Professions," *Politics and Society*, 4, no. 3 (1974): 295–310.

12. The Catholic pentecostals' status as a "cognitive minority" (see Chapter 8) sometimes results in the labelling of the group's behavior as "deviant." There is, indeed, a tendency among sociologists and psychologists to presume that membership in enthusiastic movements is itself evidence of pathology. This attitude is comparable to the common sense view that it is unnatural for anyone to believe that strongly in anything. In contemporary society, strongly religious groups, such as Jesus People, Moonists, Hare Krishnas, and pentecostals are viewed as "kooks," "freaks," "weirdoes." While the application of such labels demonstrates the normative non-religiousness of the larger society, scientific study of such behavior should remain more objective. Observations during this research suggest that, while the groups may attract a disproportionate number of people with problems, overall there was very little pathological behavior observed. Religious behaviors often assumed to evidence pathology (for example, glossolalia, prophecy, faith healing) are, on the contrary, understandable as fulfilling many rich and meaningful functions within the group, given their distinctive belief system.

13. Cf., William James on the "religion of healthy mindedness" in which doubt, fear, worry, etc., are against the norm, *Varieties of Religious Experience* (New York: New American Library, 1958), p. 88.

14. Unlike the bureaucratized system of the larger society, however, these labels are far less likely to be made public or to be the basis of long-term stigma.

15. Allan Young, "Some Implications of Medical Beliefs and Practices for Social Anthropology," *American Anthropologist* 78, no. 1 (1976): 5–24. See also, Claude Levi-Strauss, *Structural Anthropology* (Garden City, N.Y.: Doubleday, 1967), especially pp. 181–201, and Turner, *Drums of Affliction*, 1968, for similar emphasis on the significance of symbolization in healing.

16. Erving Goffman, *Asylums: Essays on the Social Situation of Mental Patients and Other Inmates* (Garden City, N.Y.: Doubleday, 1961), especially pp. 13–74; E. Fuller Torrey, *The Mind Game: Witchdoctors and Psychiatrists*, (New York: Emerson Hall, 1972), p. 64; Turner "Confession and Social Structure," 1977.

Kiev suggests that traditional therapies differ from Western psychotherapy on this matter: traditional therapies reintegrating the individual in the community and reaffirming the values of the group, and Western psychotherapy, by contrast, promoting the growth and development of the individual and the liberation of the individual as a person; Ari Kiev, "Magic, Faith, and Healing in Modern Psychiatry," *Religious Systems and Psychotherapy*, ed. Richard H. Cox (Springfield, Ill.: Thomas, 1973), pp. 225–235. Although individualism is a major value of Western society, this statement should be interpreted as somewhat of an idealization because the practical definition of the "well-adjusted" person implies the affirmation of societal values and the integration of the individual into some larger community (as is amply demonstrated by psychotherapy's treatment of women's problems with their socially prescribed roles). Perhaps the major real difference is that Western society, with its surface pluralism, offers more possible settings into which the individual may become "adjusted."

17. Linda Scicutella Mai, "The Re-Emergence of Body Symbolism in the Catholic Charismatic Renewal" (presented to the Society for the Scientific Study of Religion, Hartford, Conn., Oct., 1978).

18. Victor Turner, "Metaphors of Anti-Structure in Religious Culture," *Changing Perspectives in the Scientific Study of Religion*, ed. Allan Eister (New York: Wiley, 1974), pp. 63–84.

19. Berger, "Sociological Understanding," 1965.

20. George Kosicki, "The Healing Power of the Eucharist," *New Covenant*, July, 1974, p. 14.

21. Turner, *Drums of Affliction*, 1968.

22. Mary Douglas, *Natural Symbols: Explorations in Cosmology* (New York: Pantheon, 1970); and Mary Douglas, *Purity and Danger: An Analysis of Concepts of Pollution and Taboo* (London: Routledge and Kegan Paul, 1966); Mai, "Body Symbolism," 1978.

23. See also, Yonina Talmon, "Millenarian Movements," *Archives Europeanes des Sociologie* 7, no. 2 (1966): 173.

24. Douglas, *Purity and Danger*, 1966; Mai, "Body Symbolism," 1978; Francis Westley, "Purification and Healing Rituals in New Religious Groups" (presented to the Society for the Scientific Study of Religion, Chicago, Oct., 1977).

25. Berger and Luckmann, *Social Construction of Reality*, 1966, pp. 50–51.

26. Cf., Abner Cohen, *Two-Dimensional Man: An Essay on the Anthropology of Power and Symbolism in Complex Society* (Berkeley: University of California Press, 1974), p. 134.

27. This quotation is nearly verbatim.

28. Emile Durkheim, *The Elementary Forms of the Religious Life* (New York: Collier, 1965), p. 260. It is interesting that some of the specific examples of such collective representations cited by Durkheim are body symbols, such as blood.

29. Young, "Medical Belief Systems," 1976, p. 149, points out that evil spirits are typically the personification of the inverse of group norms. For example, in describing the "deliverance ministry" of Catholic pentecostals, MacNutt says that demons usually identify themselves by the title of a particular vice, such as anger, jealousy, lust, etc., Francis MacNutt, *Healing* (Notre Dame, Ind.: Ave Maria Press, 1974), p. 227.

30. Cf. Ari Kiev, ed., *Magic, Faith and Healing: Studies in Primitive Psychiatry Today* (New York: Free Press, 1964), p. 8; Arthur Kleinman, "Some Issues for a Comparative Study of Medical Healing," *International Journal*

of *Social Psychiatry* 19, no. 3/4 (1973): 162; Levi-Strauss, *Structural Anthropology*, 1967, p. 199; Edward Moody, "Magical Therapy: An Anthropological Investigation of Contemporary Satanism," in *Religious Movements in Contemporary America*, ed. Irving I. Zaretsky and Mark P. Leone (Princeton, N.J.: Princeton University, 1974), p. 381; E. M. Pattison et al., "Faith Healing: A Study of Personality and Function," *Joural of Nervous and Mental Disease*, 157, no. 6 (1973): 405; and Young, "Medical Belief Systems," 1976: 13.

31. E. M. Pattison, "Ideological Support for the Marginal Middle-Class: Faith Healing and Glossolalia," in *Religious Movements*, Zaretsky and Leone, 1974, p. 452.

32. Kleinman, "Comparative Study," 1973, p. 160.

33. Numerous researchers have noted that supposedly purely physical experiences, such as pain, are also culturally shaped and come to represent a number of possible meanings. See David Mechanic, "Response Factors in Illness: The Study of Illness Behavior," in *Patients, Physicians and Illness*, 1972, pp. 128–140; T. S. Szasz, *Pain and Pleasure: A Study of Bodily Feelings* (New York: Basic, 1957); and B. Berthold Wolff and Sarah Langley, "Cultural Factors and the Response to Pain: A Review," *American Anthropologist* 70, no. 3 (1968): 494–501.

34. Young, "Medical Belief Systems," 1976, p. 8.

35. H. Waitzkin and J. D. Stoeckle, "The Communication of Information about Illness," in *Advances in Psychosomatic Medicine: Psychosocial Aspects of Physical Illness*, ed. Z. Lipowski (Basel: Karger, 1972), pp. 180–215.

36. Kenneth Calestro, "Psychotherapy, Faith Healing, and Suggestion," *International Journal of Psychiatry*, 10, no. 1 (1972): 101.

37. Pattison, "Faith Healing," 1973: 403, and Pattison, "Ideological Support," 1974.

38. The purpose of comparing pentecostal behavior with shamanism is not to denigrate faith healing or to attach a pejorative interpretation, but rather to suggest that the phenomenon is related to a larger class of practices and may be better understood by comparing and contrasting it with other practices in that larger class.

    See Mircea Eliade, *Shamanism: Archaic Techniques of Ecstasy*, trans. Willard R. Trask (New York: Pantheon, 1964); Kiev, *Magic, Faith and Healing*, 1964; David Landy, *Culture, Disease, and Healing: Studies in Medical Anthropology* (New York: Macmillan, 1977); I. M. Lewis, *Ecstatic Religion: An Anthropological Study of Spirit Possession and Shamanism* (Baltimore: Penguin, 1971); Elmer S. Miller, "Shamans, Power Symbols and Change in Argentine Toba Culture," *American Ethnologist* 2, no. 3 (1975): 477–496, and Julian Silverman, "Shamans and Acute Schizophrenia," *American Anthropologist* 69, no. 1 (1967): 21–31.

39. Mircea Eliade, *Myths, Dreams, and Mysteries: The Encounter Between Contemporary Faiths and Archaic Realities* (New York: Harper and Row, 1943), p. 77.

40. Silverman, "Shamans and Schizophrenia," 1967, p. 23; see also critiques by D. Handelman, "Shamanizing on an Empty Stomach," *American An-*

thropologist 70, no. 2 (1968): 353–356, and J. H. Weakland, "Shamans, Schizophrenia, and Scientific Unity," *American Anthropologist* 70, no. 2 (1968); 356.

41. Silverman, "Shamans and Schizophrenia," 1967.
42. Lewis, *Ecstatic Religion*, 1971, p. 203.
43. Miller, "Shamans," 1975, p. 483.
44. Ibid., p. 479.
45. Durkheim, *Elementary Forms*, 1965.
46. Leonard B. Glick, "Medicine as an Ethnographic Category: The Gimi of the New Guinea Highlands," *Ethnology* 6, no. 1 (1967): 31–56.
47. Francis MacNutt, *The Power to Heal* (Notre Dame, Ind.: Ave Maria Press, 1977), p. 143.
48. Kiev, *Magic, Faith and Healing*, 1964, p. 8.
49. Lewis, *Ecstatic Religion*, 1971, p. 203.
50. Cf. E. Mansell Pattison, "Exorcism and Psychotherapy: A Case of Collaboration," in Cox, *Religious Systems*, 1973, pp. 284–295.
51. Frank, *Persuasion and Healing*, 1973, p. 75; cf. William James, *Varieties of Religious Experience*, 1958, p. 100. It is possible that what researchers call the "placebo effect" may be the individual's response to this society's peculiar symbolization of empowerment. In other words, while a chemically inert pill is not real medicine, the sense of power the individual gains by that symbol is real. This symbolic empowerment may have concrete physical and psychological effects.
52. Frank, *Persuasion and Healing*, 1973; Lawrence Le Shan, *The Medium, The Mystic, and The Physicist* (New York: Ballantine, 1975).
53. Fabrega, *Disease and Social Behavior*, 1974; D. Hayes-Bautista and D. Haveston, "Holistic Health Care," *Social Policy* 7, no. 5 (1977): 7–13.
54. David Graham, "Health, Disease and the Mind-Body Problem: Linguistic Parallelism," *Psychosomatic Medicine*, 20, no. 1 (1967): 52–71. Graham suggests that the mind-body dualism may be due merely to a linguistic parallelism by which the same phenomenon is conceived differently; if this is the case, would it also extend to the spiritual realm, admitting the appropriateness of that alternative for interpreting the phenomenon of illness?
55. Fabrega, *Disease and Social Behavior*, 1974.
56. See, for example, W. F. Kiely, "Coping with Severe Illness," in Lipowski, *Advances in Psychosomatic Medicine*, 1972, pp. 105–118; and Harold G. Wolff, "A Concept of Disease in Man," *Psychosomatic Medicine* 24 (1962): 25–30.
57. Suggested by Peter Freund, personal communication.
58. Gerald Caplan and Marie Killilea, eds., *Support Systems and Mutual Help: Multi-disciplinary Explorations* (New York: Gruen and Stratton, 1976); Sidney Cobb, "Social Support as a Moderator of Life Stress," *Psychosomatic Medicine* 38, no. 5 (1976): 300–314; Lowell S. Levin, Alfred Katz, and Erik Holst, *Self-Care: Lay Initiatives in Health* (New York: Prodist, 1976).
59. O. Von Mering and L. W. Early, "Major Changes in the Western Environment," *Archives in General Psychiatry* 13, no. 3 (1965): 195–201.

60. A. H. Schmale, "Giving Up as a Final Common Pathway to Changes in Health," in *Advances in Psychosomatic Medicine*, ed. Z. Lipowski, 1972, pp. 20–40.

61. Cf., Lewis, *Ecstatic Religion*, 1971, p. 203.

62. Margaret Gold, "A Crisis of Identity: The Case of Medical Sociology," *Journal of Health and Social Behavior* 18, no. 2 (1977): 160–168.

63. Goffman, *Asylums*, 1961, especially pp. 323–386; Thomas S. Szasz, *The Myth of Mental Illness: Foundations of a Theory of Personal Conduct* (New York: Harper and Row, 1964).

64. Freidson, *Profession of Medicine*, 1970; Fabrega, *Disease and Social Behavior*, 1974.

65. Cf., however, Thomas Scheff, "Negotiating Reality: Notes on Power in the Assessment of Responsibility," *Social Problems* 16, no. 1 (1968): 3–17.

66. Walter Wardwell, "Orthodoxy and Heterodoxy in Medical Practice," *Social Science and Medicine* 6, no. 3 (1972): 759–763. See also Young, "Medical Belief Systems," 1976, on the relationship between this consolidation and the professionalization of medical specialists.

67. Cf., Geoffrey Nelson, "The Concept of Cult," *Sociological Review* 16, no. 3 (1968): 351–362; Roy Wallis, *The Road to Total Freedom: A Sociological Analysis of Scientology* (New York: Columbia, 1977).

68. Young, "Medical Belief Systems," 1976, pp. 18–19.

CHAPTER EIGHT

1. These concepts are used somewhat differently from other authors' applications; for a detailed discussion of the concepts, "church," "sect," "denomination," "cult," see Meredith B. McGuire, *Religion: The Social Context* (Belmont, Calif.: Wadsworth, 1981), Chapter 5. As used here, these concepts do not refer to the content of beliefs; cf. Wallis' apt critique of definitions by Glock and Stark, *Religion and Society in Tension* (Chicago: Rand McNally, 1965) in Wallis, *The Road to Total Freedom: A Sociological Analysis of Scientology* (New York: Columbia, 1977), p. 13.

2. John Moore, "The Catholic Pentecostal Movement," in *A Sociological Yearbook of Religion in Britain*, ed. M. Hill (London: SCM Press, 1973), pp. 73–90; Geoffrey K. Nelson, "The Concept of Cult," *Sociological Review* 16, no. 3 (1968): 354; Howard Becker, *Systematic Sociology* (New York: Wiley, 1932), pp. 627–628; David Martin, *Pacifism* (London: Routledge and Kegan Paul, 1965), p. 194.

3. Wallis, *Road to Total Freedom*, 1977, pp. 14–15. See also Colin Campbell, "Clarifying the Cult," *British Journal of Sociology* 28, no. 3 (1977): 375–388, and John A. Jackson and Ray Jobling, "Towards an Analysis of Contemporary Cults," in *A Sociological Yearbook of Religion in Britain*, ed. D. Martin, vol. 1 (London: SCM Press, 1968), pp. 94–105.

4. Roy Wallis, "Ideology, Authority, and the Development of Cultic Movements," *Social Research* 41, no. 2 (1974): 304. See also Robert Balch and David Taylor, "Seekers and Saucers: The Role of the Cultic Milieu in Joining a UFO Cult," *American Behavioral Scientist* 20, no. 6 (1977): 839–860, and Roger Straus, "Changing Oneself: Seekers and the Creative

Transformation of Life Experience," *Doing Social Life*, ed. J. Lofland (New York: Wiley, 1976), pp. 252–272.

5. Wallis, *Road to Total Freedom*, 1977, p. 17.

6. Wallis, "Ideology," 1974, p. 305.

7. Peter L. Berger, *The Sacred Canopy: Elements of a Sociological Theory of Religion* (Garden City, N.Y.: Doubleday, 1967), p. 163.

8. Wallis, *Road to Total Freedom*, 1977, pp. 16–17. James Richardson, too, focuses on patterns of authority in his distinction between cult and sect, "From Cult to Sect: Creative Electicism in New Religious Movements," *Pacific Sociological Review* 22, no. 2 (1979): 139–166. Richardson, however, emphasizes the oppositional quality of cults, James Richardson, "An Oppositional and General Conceptualization of Cult," *Annual Review of the Social Sciences of Religion*, vol. 2 (The Hague: Mouton, 1980).

9. This model, while basically consistent with Wallis', emphasizes the concomitant forms of personal allegiance that relate to the patterns of authority; see McGuire, *Religion: The Social Context*, 1981.

10. Joseph Fichter, *The Catholic Cult of the Paraclete* (New York: Sheed and Ward, 1975), p. 106. Moore, "Catholic Pentecostal Movement," 1973, p. 81, applies Nelson's concept of "centralized cult." Cf. also Cecil D. Bradfield's study of non-Catholic neo-pentecostals, "Our Kind of People," (presented to the Association for the Sociology of Religion, New York, Aug., 1976). Similarly, Hegy suggests that pentecostal activities may be a cultic form of group devotion within the larger church; Pierre Hegy, "Images of God and Man in a Catholic Charismatic Renewal Community," *Social Compass* 25, no. 1 (1978): 7–21. See also C. Lincoln Johnson and Andrew J. Weigart, "An Emerging Faithstyle: A Research Note on the Catholic Charismatic Renewal," *Sociological Analysis* 39 no. 2 (1978): 165–172. In this sense prayer groups would be comparable to the social organization of Novenas, Marian devotions, and Sodalities in pre-Vatican II usage; historical examples of sect-like social organization within the church also exist (for example, monasticism). See Wach's concept of "ecclesiolae in ecclesia," Joachim Wach, *Sociology of Religion* (Chicago: University of Chicago Press, 1944), pp. 173ff. The sectarian core of the charismatic movement may, indeed, be moving toward the social organization and orientation of the Order; see Michael Hill, *The Religious Order: A Study of Virtuoso Religion and Its Legitimation in the Nineteenth-Century Church of England* (London: Heinemann, 1973).

11. Rick Casey, *National Catholic Reporter*, Sept. 12, 1975.

12. *New Covenant*, April, 1975, p. 18; March, 1977, p. 4; April, 1977, p. 18.

13. Michael Harrison, "The Maintenance of Enthusiasm: Involvement in a New Religious Movement," *Sociological Analysis* 36, no. 2 (1975): 150–157, also, "Dimensions of Involvement in Social Movements," *Sociological Focus* 10, no. 4 (1977): 353–366. Weber observes that "all intensive religiosity has a tendency toward a sort of status stratification." The same criteria which distinguish religious virtuosi from the masses also delineate "levels" of virtuosi. See Max Weber, "The Social Psychology of the World Religions," in *From Max Weber: Essays in Sociology*, trans. Hans H. Gerth and C. Wright Mills (New York: Oxford, 1946), p. 287.

14. Ernst Troeltsch, *The Social Teaching of the Christian Churches*, vol. 1 (New York: Harper and Row, 1960), especially pp. 331ff.

15. Berger, *Sacred Canopy*, 1967, p. 163.

16. Michael Scanlan, *New Covenant*, September, 1976, p. 6.

17. Moore, "Catholic Pentecostal Movement," 1973, p. 89, notes that, while they are forced to tolerate independent groups, the traditional religions frequently make a virtue of this necessity. This kind of "open-minded-ness" may characterize the Catholic hierarchy's reaction to Catholic pentecostalism.

18. Colin Campbell, "The Cult, the Cultic Milieu, and Secularization," *Sociological Yearbook of Religion in Britain*, ed. M. Hill, vol. 5 (London: SCM Press, 1973), p. 135. See also, Colin Campbell, "The Secret Religion of the Educated Classes," *Sociological Analysis* 39, no. 2 (1978): 146–156; Frances Westley, "The Cult of Man: Durkheim's Predictions and New Religious Movements," *Sociological Analysis* 39, no. 2 (1978): 135–145.

19. Thomas Luckmann, *The Invisible Religion: The Problem of Religion in Modern Society* (New York: Macmillan, 1967), p. 105.

20. Luckmann, *Invisible Religion*, 1967, pp. 98–106; see also Luckmann's and other authors' analyses in *The Culture of Unbelief: Studies and Proceedings from the First International Symposium on Belief, Rome, March 22–27, 1969* ed. Rocco Caporale and Antonio Grumelli (Berkeley: University of California Press, 1971).

21. See J. Massyngberde Ford, *Which Way for Catholic Pentecostals?* (New York: Harper and Row, 1976), also, various articles in *National Catholic Reporter*, especially a series by Rick Casey, Aug. and Sept., 1975. In recent years, there has been a major split in the movement between groups favoring the sectarian mode (following the Ann Arbor/Notre Dame leadership) and those preferring the cultic mode. The latter faction has developed its own leadership and media, although not as extensively and aggressively as the former. See Ralph Lane, Jr., "The Catholic Charismatic Renewal Movement in the United States: A Reconsideration," *Social Compass* 25, no. 1 (1978): 7–21.

22. "Holy War," *Newsweek*, June 16, 1975, pp. 48, 49; see also, *National Catholic Reporter*, Aug. 29, 1975.

23. Harrison, "Maintenance of Enthusiasm," 1975.

24. John Connor, "Covenant Communities: A New Sign of Hope," *New Covenant*, April, 1972, p. 2; Jim Cavnar, "Nonresidential Households," *New Covenant*, Nov., 1975, p. 18.

25. Mary Reddy, "A Gate: Through Which Many May Pass to Jesus," *New Covenant*, March, 1972, p. 10.

26. Harrison, "Maintenance of Enthusiasm," 1975, p. 150.

27. The obvious parallel with Catholic religious Orders is also influential, but this model offers little aid for a lay community with married and single members of both genders. For Catholic pentecostals who had been or still were members of Orders, the traditional style of religious community required much revision to be adapted to their new religiosity.

28. *New Covenant*, Dec., 1972, p. 25.

29. *New Covenant*, July, 1973, p. 4.

30. Bert Ghezzi, "Love and Order," *New Covenant*, Dec., 1973, pp. 12, 13.
31. Steve Clark, "What is Christian Community," *New Covenant* (Nov., 1974), p. 5.
32. Ghezzi, "Love and Order," 1973, p. 15.
33. Ralph Martin, "Headship and Submission" (Charismatic Renewal Cassettes, 1975).
34. Steve Clark interview, "Authority in Christian Communities," *New Covenant* Dec. 1974, p. 24.
35. Martin, "Headship and Submission," 1975.
36. Francis MacNutt, "Pentecostals and Social Justice: A Problem and a Hope," *New Covenant*, Nov., 1972, p. 5.
37. Kevin and Dorothy Ranaghan, Charismatic Renewal Cassettes, n.d.
38. Cf., the even more caste-stratified system of the Bruderhof in Benjamin Zablocki, *The Joyful Community* (Baltimore: Penguin, 1971), the Hassidim (Jerome Mintz, "Brooklyn's Hassidim," *Natural History* 86 (1977): 46–59; Solomon Poll, *The Hassidic Community in Williamsburg: A Study in the Sociology of Religion* (New York: Schocken, 1969); and Jesus People, James Richardson, Mary Harder, and Robert Simmonds, *Organized Miracles: A Sociological Study of a Jesus Movement Organization* (New Brunswick, N.J.: Transaction, 1979). There is some dissatisfaction with this subjugation of women in some communities of Catholic pentecostals, and this issue is one of the key reasons for a recent split in the national federation of their covenanted communities.
39. Sue Manney, "Alone in the Spirit," *New Covenant*, Oct., 1973, pp. 17–19.
40. Barbara Morgan, "As God Sees Us," *New Covenant*, June, 1976, p. 8.
41. Barbara Morgan, "Family Life," *New Covenant*, May, 1973, p. 4; see also, Gary and Barbara Morgan, "God is Changing Our Family," *New Covenant*, Dec., 1971, p. 15; and Bob and Sharon Morris, "Freeing the Child," *New Covenant*, Feb., 1974, p. 24.
42. Brick Bradford, "Divine Order in Christian Marriage," *New Covenant*, Jan., 1974 and Feb., 1974, p. 19.
43. See Harder, Richardson, and Simmonds for an analysis of a similar structure in a Jesus People commune, "Life Style: Courtship, Marriage and Family in a Changing Jesus Movement Organization," *International Review of Modern Sociology* 6, no. 1 (1976): 155–172. See also Jon Wagner, "Male Supremacy: Its Role in a Contemporary Commune and Its Structural Alternatives," *International Review of Modern Sociology* 6, no. 1 (1976): 173–180; and Mary W. Harder, "Sex Roles in the Jesus Movement," *Social Compass* 21, no. 3 (1974): 345–353.
44. Lewis A. Coser, *Greedy Institutions: Patterns of Undivided Commitment* (New York: Free Press, 1974), p. 7.
45. Rosabeth M. Kanter, *Commitment and Community: Communes and Utopias in Sociological Perspective* (Cambridge, Mass.: Harvard University, 1972), pp. 75–125.
46. Robert J. Lifton, *Thought Reform and the Psychology of Totalism* (New York: Norton, 1963).
47. Erving Goffman, *Frame Analysis: An Essay on the Organization of Experience* (New York: Harper and Row, 1974), p. 385.

48. Kanter, *Commitment and Community*, 1972, p. 113.

49. Ibid., p. 116.

50. Lifton, *Thought Reform*, 1963; see, for example, Richardson, Harder, and Simmonds, "Thought Reform and the Jesus Movement," *Youth and Society*, 4, no. 2 (1972): 185–202; Benjamin Zablocki, "Joyful Community," 1971; David Taylor, "Thought Reform and the Unification Church," (presented to the Society for the Scientific Study of Religion, Chicago, Oct., 1977); other authors point out similar practices by the growing anti-cult movement; Anson Shupe et al., "Deprogramming: The New Exorcism," *American Behavioral Scientist* 20, no. 6 (1977): 941–956.

51. Ford, *Which Way for Catholic Pentecostals?* 1976.

52. This concept refers to Berger's (*Sacred Canopy*, 1967, p. 163) adaptation of Festinger's idea of "cognitive dissonance," see Leon Festinger, *A Theory of Cognitive Dissonance* (Palo Alto, Calif.: Stanford University Press, 1957).

53. Berger, *Sacred Canopy*, 1967, pp. 115ff.

54. See R. K. Jones, "Some Sectarian Characteristics of Therapeutic Groups," in *Sectarianism: Analysis of Religious and Non-religious Sects*, ed. R. Wallis (London: Peter Owen, 1975), pp. 190–210; and Roger O'Toole, "Underground Traditions in the Study of Sectarianism: Non-religious Uses of the Concept 'Sect'," *Journal for the Scientific Study of Religion* 15, no. 2 (1976): 145–156.

55. Peter L. Berger and Thomas Luckmann, *The Social Construction of Reality: A Treatise in the Sociology of Knowledge* (Garden City, N.Y.: Doubleday, 1966), p. 151.

56. Leon Festinger, Henry W. Riecken, and Stanley Schachter, *When Prophecy Fails: A Social and Psychological Study of a Modern Group that Predicted the Destruction of the World* (New York: Harper and Row, 1956).

CHAPTER NINE

1. *National Catholic Reporter*, Nov. 25, 1977.

2. Glock argues that the "new religious consciousness" (characteristic mainly of imported Oriental cults and quasi-religious human potential groups) is primarily a reaction against the cognitive style of the dominant society; Charles Glock, "Consciousness Among Contemporary Youth: An Interpretation," in *The New Religious Consciousness*, ed. Charles Y. Glock and Robert N. Bellah (Berkeley: University of California Press, 1976), pp. 353–366.

3. See especially Peter L. Berger, *The Sacred Canopy: Elements of a Sociological Theory of Religion* (Garden City, N.Y.: Doubleday, 1967); Richard K. Fenn, *Toward a Theory of Secularization*, monograph no. 1 (Storrs, Conn.: Society for the Scientific Study of Religion, 1978); Bryan Wilson, *Contemporary Transformations of Religion* (London: Oxford University Press, 1976).

4. See especially Andrew Greeley, *Unsecular Man: The Persistence of Religion* (New York: Schocken, 1972); Thomas Luckmann, *The Invisible Religion: The Problem of Religion in Modern Society* (New York: Macmillan, 1967);

David A. Martin, *The Religious and the Secular: Studies in Secularization* (New York: Schocken, 1969).

5. The concept of "functional rationality" is derived directly from Max Weber's classical statement in *The Protestant Ethic and the Spirit of Capitalism* (New York: Scribner, 1958). This and related themes have been expanded in Luckmann, *Invisible Religion*, 1967; Fenn, *Theory of Secularization*, 1978, and "Toward a New Sociology of Religion," *Journal for the Scientific Study of Religion* 11, no. 1 (1972): 16–32; Daniel Bell, "The Return of the Sacred? The Argument on the Future of Religion," *British Journal of Sociology*, 28, no. 4 (1977): 419–449; and Roland Robertson, "Individualism, Societalism, Worldliness, Universalism: Thematizing Theoretical Sociology of Religion," *Sociological Analysis* 38, no. 4 (1977): 281–308; Roland Robertson, "Theoretical Comments on Religion and Society in Modern America: Weber Revisited" (presented to the IXth World Congress of Sociology, Uppsala, Sweden, Aug., 1978), and "Religious Movements and Modern Societies: Toward a Progressive Problemshift," *Sociological Analysis* 40, no. 4 (1979): 297–314.

6. Note that the churches, too, espouse a bureaucratic model for internal organization; their product may not be functionally rational, but their process is. Various renewal efforts may initially be a reaction against this operative model; however, the Catholic pentecostal movement (at least at the regional and national levels) became rapidly stratified and specialized.

7. Cf. Luckmann, *Invisible Religion*, 1967; Berger, *Sacred Canopy*, 1967; E. Gellner, *Legitimation of Belief* (Cambridge: Cambridge University Press, 1974).

8. Gellner, *Legitimation of Belief*, 1974, p. 48, criticizes the stance of "normative relativism" which implies that there are no universal, independent criteria by which local norms can be judged. See also Peter L. Berger and Thomas Luckmann, "Secularization and Pluralism," *International Yearbook for the Sociology of Religion*, 1966, pp. 73ff.

9. Fenn, "New Sociology of Religion," 1972; *Theory of Secularization*, 1978; also, "Religion and the Legitimation of Social Systems," in *Changing Perspectives in the Scientific Study of Religion*, ed. A. Eister (New York: Wiley, 1974), pp. 143–161; Robert Stauffer, "Civil Religion, Technocracy, and the Private Sphere: Further Comments on Cultural Integration in Advanced Societies," *Journal for the Scientific Study of Religion* 12, no. 4 (1973): 415–426; Jürgen Habermas, *Toward a Rational Society: Student Protest, Science, and Politics*, trans. Jeremy Shapiro (Boston: Beacon, 1970), pp. 112–113.

10. Hans Mol, *Identity and the Sacred* (Agincourt: Book Society of Canada, 1976), pp. 66ff.

11. See also Emil Oestereicher, "The Privatization of the Self in Modern Society" (presented to the Symposium on Narcissism, New York, April, 1978, sponsored by Brooklyn College and The William Alanson White Psychoanalytic Institute). Similar themes are raised in Peter L. Berger, Brigitte Berger, and Hansfried Kellner, *The Homeless Mind* (New York: Vintage-Random, 1973); see also Frederick Bird, "Charisma and Ritual in

New Religious Movements," *Understanding the New Religions*, ed. J. Needleman and G. Baker (New York: Seabury, 1978), pp. 173–189.

12. Individualism as a modern religious theme is discussed by Luckmann, *Invisible Religion*, 1967. Note that individualism in a larger political-philosophical sense, is also related to several of these social developments; see Robertson, "Individualism," 1977.

13. Gellner, *Legitimation of Belief*, 1974, p. 196.

14. Ibid., p. 193.

15. Thomas Robbins and Dick Anthony, "New Religious Movements and the Social System: Integration, Disintegration or Transformation" (presented to the American Sociological Association, New York, Aug., 1976).

16. Cf. Berger et al., 1973, pp. 248, 249.

17. There is mixed evidence in underdeveloped countries that these kinds of movements can be pre-political preparation. See Emilio Willems, *Followers of the New Faith: Cultural Change and the Rise of Protestantism in Brazil and Chile* (Nashville: Vanderbilt, 1967), and Cornelia B. Flora, *Pentecostalism in Colombia: Baptism by Fire and Spirit* (Rutherford, N.J.: Fairleigh Dickinson University Press, 1976), regarding Protestant pentecostalism in Latin America. Bryan Wilson draws a similar point, using African examples, in *Contemporary Transformations*. Counter-evidence, however, is presented in Pedro A. Ribeiro de Oliveira, "Le renouveau charismatique au Brésil," *Social Compass* 25, no. 1 (1978): 37ff; Christian Lalive d'Epinay, *Religion, Dynamique Sociale et Dépendance: Le Protestantisme en Argentine et au Chili* (Paris: Mouton, 1975).

18. Given the extent of privatization of religion in contemporary society, there is some validity in pentecostals' protest that it is sufficient to be "just a religious movement." Nevertheless, to the extent that the movement's concern is re-sacralizing a highly secularized society, its blindness to social structural sources of problems is critical.

19. The exception is the extreme sectarian segment which attempts to remove its members, as much as possible, from the institutions of "the world" (by communal living, self-contained businesses, separate schools, etc.).

20. Cf., Benton Johnson, "Do Holiness Sects Socialize in Dominant Values?" *Social Forces* 39, no. 4 (1961): 309–316; Marion Dearman, "Christ and Conformity: A Study of Pentecostal Values," *Journal for the Scientific Study of Religion*, 13, no. 4 (1974): 437–454; Thomas Robbins, Dick Anthony, and James Richardson, "Theory and Research on Today's New Religions," *Sociological Analysis* 39, no. 2 (1978): 95–122.

21. Thomas Robbins, Dick Anthony, and Thomas Curtis, "Youth Culture Religious Movements: Evaluating the Integrative Hypothesis," *The Sociological Quarterly* 16, no. 1 (1975): 48–64; Robbins et al., "Theory and Research," 1978.

22. James Beckford, "Cults and Cures" (presented to the IXth World Congress of Sociology, Uppsala, Sweden, Aug., 1978).

23. Peter L. Berger and Richard Neuhaus, *To Empower People: The Role of Mediating Structures in Public Policy* (Washington, D.C.: American Enterprise Institute, 1977).

24. Luther Gerlach and Virginia Hine, *People, Power and Change: Movements of Social Transformation* (Indianapolis: Bobbs-Merrill, 1970), p. 196.

25. Max Weber, *The Sociology of Religion*, trans. Ephraim Fischoffs (Boston: Beacon, 1964), pp. 164ff.

26. For example, see Ralph Lane, "The Catholic Charismatic Renewal Movement in the United States: A Reconsideration," *Social Compass* 25, no. 1 (1978): 23–35.

27. This applies, not only to the Catholic pentecostal movement, but also to the "underground church" of the 1960s (cf. Meredith B. McGuire, "Toward a Sociological Interpretation of the Underground Church Movement," *Review of Religious Research* 14, no. 1 [1972]: 41–47) and to the growing Catholic Traditionalist movement.

28. Meredith B. McGuire, "An Interpretive Comparison of Elements of the Pentecostal and Underground Church Movements in American Catholicism," *Sociological Analysis* 35, no. 1 (1974): 57–65.

29. This development is corroborated by recent research by C. Lincoln Johnson and Andrew J. Weigart, "An Emerging Faithstyle: A Research Note on the Catholic Charismatic Renewal," *Sociological Analysis* 39, no. 2 (1978): 165–172.

30. Michael Hill, *The Religious Order: A Study of Virtuoso Religion and its Legitimation in the Nineteenth-Century Church of England* (London: Heinemann, 1973); Ernst Troeltsch, *The Social Teaching of the Christian Churches*, vol. I (New York: Harper and Row, 1960); Weber, *Sociology of Religion*, 1964.

31. Cf., Hill's analysis of the subordination of women's Orders; similarly, resolutions of strife within the Franciscan Order—much admired by many in the Catholic pentecostal movement—parallel the authority-obedience, stratification direction cf., Rosalind B. Brooke, *Early Franciscan Government* (Cambridge: Cambridge University Press, 1959) and Malcolm David Lambert, *Franciscan Poverty* (London: Lutterworth, 1961).

32. Cf. Michael Harrison and John K. Maniha, "The Spirit versus the Letter: Conflict between movements of inspiration and religious institutions" (presented to the Southern Sociological Association, April, 1974); also Roberta Keane, "Transformation of Charisma in a Catholic Pentecostal Community" (presented to the American Sociological Association, San Francisco, Aug., 1975).

33. For example, the healing ministry initially did not fit into existing parish activities. Groups beginning this kind of ministry within the parish setting often gain—at least, temporarily—power, simply because the activity is not easily encapsulated within an existing parish structure.

34. See especially Robertson, "Individualism," 1977.

35. See, for example, Luckmann, *Invisible Religion*, 1967: Mol, *Identity and the Sacred*, 1977; Greeley, *Unsecular Man*, 1972.

36. Emile Durkheim, *The Elementary Forms of the Religious Life* (New York: Collier, 1965), pp. 474–475.

37. See Frances Westley, "The Cult of Man: Durkheim's Predictions and New Religious Movements," *Sociological Analysis* 39, no. 2 (1978): 135–145;

and Colin Campbell, "The Secret Religion of the Educated Classes," *Sociological Analysis* 39, no. 2 (1978): 146–156.

38. Fenn, *Theory of Secularization*, 1972.

39. See especially Robbins and Anthony, "New Religious Movements," 1976.

40. For example, Robert Bellah, "New Religious Consciousness and the Crisis in Modernity," in *The New Religious Consciousness*, ed. Bellah and Glock, 1976, pp. 333–352; Dick Anthony and Thomas Robbins, "The Decline of American Civil Religion and the Development of Authoritarian Nationalism" (presented to the Society for the Scientific Study of Religion, Milwaukee, Oct., 1975), and "The Effect of Detente on the Rise of New Religions: The Unification Church of Rev. Sun Myung Moon," in *Understanding the New Religions*, ed. J. Needleman and G. Baker (New York: Seabury, 1978), pp. 80–100; and Roland Robertson, *Meaning and Change* (Oxford: Basil Blackwell, 1978).

41. Fenn, "New Sociology of Religion," 1972. This arrangement is also highly precarious, as Gouldner points out, Alvin W. Gouldner, *The Dialectic of Ideology and Technology: The Origins, Identity and Future of Ideology* (New York: Seabury, 1976), pp. 252ff.

42. Robert Wuthnow argues that international politico-economic crises are recurrently major factors in developing religious movements, "Religious Movements and the Transitions in World Order," in *Understanding the New Religions*, Needleman and Baker, 1978, pp. 63–79.

43. Jürgen Habermas, *Legitimation Crisis*, trans. Thomas McCarthy (Boston: Beacon, 1975), p. 68. Cf., also, Bell, *Return of the Sacred*, 1977, p. 424, who suggests that societies are radically disjunctive; that is, there is a fundamental antagonism between the norms of the techno-economic realm, the polity, and the culture.

44. Habermas, *Legitimation Crisis*, 1975, p. 77.

45. Cf., Mol, *Identity and the Sacred*, 1976, p. 10; Robertson, *Meaning and Change*, 1978; Robertson, "Theoretical Comments," 1979; Habermas, *Legitimation Crisis*, 1975.

46. Habermas, 1975, *Legitimation Crisis*, p. 128.

47. See Robertson's thorough re-examination of the Weberian thesis in *Meaning and Change*, 1978, "Theoretical Comments," 1979, "Religious Movements," 1979.

48. By Habermas' criteria, movements like Catholic pentecostalism are unsatisfactory resolutions to the legitimation crisis; they are essentially regressive in that they disrupt communicative resolutions. For example, the pentecostal norms of communication (see Chapter 5) and, by extension, the patterns of authority (see Chapter 4), are not compatible with the "fundamental norms of rational speech" which Habermas recommends for overcoming the legitimation crisis (*Legitimation Crisis*, 1975, p. 95).

49. Robertson, "Theoretical Comments," 1978.

Index

Allen, Gillian, 246
Ambiguity, 38, 93–94, 235
Anointing, 111, 118–119
Anomie, 59–60, 176
Anthony, Dick, 22, 210, 230, 234, 261, 263
Aronowitz, Stanley, 236
Atherton, James S., 241
Authority, 31, 43–48, 90–100, 104–105, 115–123, 184–189, 191–199
Autonomy, 190–191

Ba'ale teshuvot, compared, 51
Bainbridge, William Sims, 236
Balch, Robert W., 235, 255
Balint, Michael, 247
Baptism in the Spirit, 28, 38, 61–63, 68–69, 121
Barkun, Michael, 231–232, 235
Bauman, Richard, 239
Becker, Howard S., 62, 237, 250, 255
Beckford, James, 230–231, 234, 236, 238, 261
Bell, Daniel, 260, 263
Bellah, Robert, 263
Berger, Brigitte, 260
Berger, Peter L., 3, 202, 227, 230–235, 237–238, 241, 244–245, 248–252, 256–257, 259–261
Bird, Frederick, 260
Bloch-Hoell, Nils, 227
Body imagery, 167–171

Bord, Richard, 231
Bourguignon, Erika, 241–243
Bradfield, Cecil D., 227, 256
Bradford, Brick, 258
Brainwashing, 61
"Breakthrough ministry," 168, 201
Bridge-burning event, 62–63, 113
Brooke, Rosalind B., 262
Bruderhof, 193, 201
Burke, Kenneth, 234
Burns, Thomas, 237

Calestro, Kenneth, 246, 248, 253
Campbell, Colin, 190, 255, 257, 263
Caplan, Gerald, 254
Casey, Rick, 256–257
Catholic Charismatic, 228 n.18
Catholic Charismatic Renewal. *See* Pentecostalism, among Catholics
Catucci, Leda Abbelle, 228
Cavnar, Jim, 239, 241, 245, 257
Cayce, Edgar, 188
Celibacy, 194
Charisma: pentecostal usage, 44, 240 n.24; routinization of, 93; sociological usage, 43–48
Charisms. *See* Gifts of the Spirit
Chordas, Thomas J., 240, 246
Cicourel, Aaron V., 229
Cirner, Randy, 231, 248
Civil religion, 221

Gerlach, Luther, 230–231, 236, 238, 262
Ghezzi, Bert, 258
Gifts of the Spirit, 28–29, 76–77, 79–85, 91–93, 130–131, 187. *See also* Discernment; Glossolalia; Healing; Interpretation of tongues; Prophecy
Glanz, David, 234
Glaser, Barney, 249
Glick, Leonard B., 248, 254
Glock, Charles Y., 230, 259
Glossolalia (speaking in tongues), 28, 33, 238n.57, 242n.12; and conversion and commitment, 61–63, 68–69; described and defined, 78–84, 112–115; functions of, 103–104, 237n.51; and healing, 138, 248n.36; in prophecy, 94, 96–99, 243n.19; and religious speaking, 115–123
Godin, André, 228
Goffman, Erving, 72, 108–109, 238, 240–241, 244–245, 248, 250–251, 255, 258
Gold, Margaret, 255
Goodman, Felicitas D., 243
Gordon, David F., 234
Gouldner, Alvin W., 263
Grad, Bernard, 246
Graham, David, 254
Greeley, Andrew, 235, 259, 262
Greil, Arthur, 236
Gross, S. J., 246
Guizzardi, Gustavo, 228, 232

Habermas, Jürgen, 222–223, 260, 263
Handelman, D., 253
Harder, Mary, 231–232, 258–259
Hare Krishna, attitudes toward, 28
Harper, Charles, 236
Harrell, David E., 247
Harris, Louis, 57
Harrison, Michael, 62, 188, 233–240, 256–257, 262
Hartmann, Ernest, 242
Harwood, Alan, 246
Haveston, D., 254
Hayes-Bautista, D., 254
Headship, 194–199
Healing, gift of, 15, 130–131, 160, 179–180, 247n.22. *See also* Faith healing
Health, ideal of, 153–155
Hearing religous speaking, 98, 119–123
Hegy, Pierre, 256
Heirich, Max, 234, 236
Hill, Michael, 232, 256, 262
Hine, Virginia, 62, 230–231, 236–238, 243–244, 262
Holism, 133, 154–155, 177, 210
Hollenweger, Walter J., 227

Hollingshead, A. B., 246
Holloman, Regina A., 244
Holm, Nils, 242
Holst, Erik, 254
Hopelessness, 53, 178
Hutch, Richard, 244
Hymes, Del, 229

Ichheiser, Gustav, 231
Individualism, 220–225, 261n.12
Integration, societal, 220–225
Interpretation of tongues, 96–97, 187

Jackson, John A., 255
James, William, 241, 251, 254
Jaquith, James R., 242
Jehovah's Witnesses, compared, 120
Jesus movement, compared, 35, 50–51, 120, 192, 201
Jobling, Ray, 255
Johnson, Benton, 261
Johnson, C. Lincoln, 256, 262
Jones, Michael Owen, 246
Jones, R. Kenneth, 233–235, 259

Kanter, Rosabeth M., 200, 233, 237, 247, 258–259
Katz, Alfred, 254
Keane, Roberta, 262
Kellner, Hansfried, 260
Kelsey, Morton, 243, 245
Kiely, W. F., 254
Kiev, Ari, 246, 251–254
Kildahl, John P., 244
Killilea, Marie, 254
Kleinman, Arthur, 245, 248–250, 252–253
Kosicki, George, 252
Kuhlman, Kathryn, 137, 144, 188
Kuhn, Thomas S., 249

L'alive D'Epinay, Christian, 228, 261
Lambert, Malcolm David, 262
Landy, David, 253
Lane, Ralph, Jr., 239–240, 257, 262
Langley, Sarah, 253
Laying on of hands, 136–137
Lebra, Takie Sugiyama, 62, 234
Legitimation: dualism as, 36–39; of individuals, 209–210, 220–225; and integration of modern society, 220–225, 263n.48; of suffering and death, 155–159; of therapeutic failure, 159–161; and work, 212–213

LeShan, Lawrence, 248, 254
Levin, Lowell S., 254
Levi-Strauss, Claude, 251, 253
Lewis, I. M., 242–243, 246, 253–255
Life in the Spirit seminars, 14–15, 52, 59–
    60, 62–69, 119–120, 187, 236 n.34, 237 n.52
Lifton, Robert, 201, 258–259
Linn, Dennis, 248
Linn, Matthew, 248
Lofland, John, 231, 235–236
Lorber, Judith, 250
Lovekin, Adams, 237, 244
Lubchansky, I., 246
Luckmann, Thomas, 18, 190–191, 202, 228–
    229, 233–234, 238, 244–245, 249–250, 252,
    257, 259–262
Ludwig, Arnold, 244

McDonnell, Kilian, 235, 239, 243
McGaw, Douglas, 227
McGuire, Kenneth, 235
McGuire, Meredith B., 228–230, 233, 235–
    236, 255–256, 262
McHugh, Peter, 235
Maciote, M. J., 228
Macklin, June, 246
MacNutt, Francis, 44, 128, 133, 137, 144,
    149, 232, 245, 247–249, 252, 254, 258
McPherson, William, 232
Magic, 32–34, 136–137, 241 n.36
Mai, Linda Scicutella, 252
Malony, H. Newton, 237, 244
Maniha, John K., 262
Manney, Sue, 237, 258
Marriage Encounter, 58, 142
Martin, David A., 255, 260
Martin, Ralph, 44, 258
Marty, Martin E., 235
Mawn, Benedict J., 55–56, 235
Mechanic, David, 253
Mediating structures, 215
Medical system, dominant: attitude toward,
    141–143, 146–147; comparison with, 126–
    128, 131–132, 160–161, 163–166, 172–179
Medical systems, marginal, 126–128, 142,
    176, 181–182
Mediumship: in communication, 111–112;
    for healing, 175
Medvedev, R. A., 250
Medvedev, Z. A., 250
Meher Baba, compared, 51
Methodology of field research, 10–25
Millenarianism, 39–43, 103, 169, 196,
    232 n.33
Miller, Elmer S., 253–254
Millman, Marcia, 249

Mintz, Jerome, 258
Miracle, 32–34, 241 n.36
Modernization, 220–225
Modified reality, 109–110
Mol, Hans, 260, 262–263
Moody, Edward J., 231, 253
Moore, John, 255–257
Morgan, Barbara, 258
Morgan, Gary, 258
Morley, Peter, 247, 249
Morris, Bob, 258
Morris, Sharon, 258
Mortification of self, 167, 200
Mystery, 32–34, 47, 103, 241 n.36

Nelson, Geoffrey, 255–256
Neuhaus, Richard, 261
New Covenant, 5, 16, 27, 187, 188, 228 n.18,
    230 n.4
Norms: ambiguity of, 91; in cultic and sec-
    tarian adherence, 189; of health, 153–155;
    in communities, 194–199; personification
    of, 252 n.29; of speaking, 69–70, 84–88,
    95–100, 118–123, 245 n.42

Obedience: to church authorities, 217; to
    civil authorities, 42, 196; norms of, 194–
    199. See also Authority; Submission
O'Connor, Edward D., 34, 39, 113–114,
    228, 230–231, 235–236, 239, 242, 244, 247
Oestereicher, Emil, 260
Offenbacher, Deborah, 241–242
Order, 30–48, 53, 171–174, 194–199, 220–
    225
Order, religious, 216–217, 257 n.27, 262 n.31
Ornstein, Robert, 242
O'Toole, Roger, 234, 259

Pace, Enzo, 229
Pain, 253 n.33
Park, George K., 247, 250
Parsons, Anne, 228, 242
Parsons, Talcott, 250
Pattison, E. Mansell, 129, 243–244, 246–
    247, 249, 253–254
Pavelsky, Hart, 244
Pentecostalism: among Catholics, 4–6,
    228 n.11; definition of, 4; among Protes-
    tants, 4, 90–92, 100, 231 n.16
Petitions, 88–90
Placebo, 177, 254 n.51
Plausibility structure, 60–61, 172
Pluralism, 7, 53–58, 181, 189–190, 208–209
Poll, Solomon, 258

Possession, 113, 242 nn.8,9, 243 n.21
Power, 7–8, 30–48, 90–93, 173–182
Powerlessness, 31, 53, 176–179
Praise, 77–85
Prayer groups, types of, 76–77
Prayer meeting, 47–48, 75–93
Prince, Raymond, 246–247
Privatization, 190–191, 208–210, 222–223, 261 n.18
Prophecy, 80–85, 93–105, 110–112, 121
Proselytizing, 42–43
Protestant ethic, 223
Psychopathology, 114, 116–117, 244 n.34, 251 n.12
Psychotheraphy: attitudes toward, 142, 249 n.47; compared with faith healing, 127, 160, 172, 251 n.16

Quebedeaux, Richard, 227

Ranaghan, Dorothy, 227–228, 230, 235, 240, 247, 258
Ranaghan, Kevin, 227–228, 230, 235, 240, 247, 258
Rationality, 208, 210–214, 260 nn.5,6
Recruitment, 59–61, 65
Reddy, Mary, 257
Reidy, M. T. V., 229
Reny, Paul, 229
Resocialization, 37, 60–64, 69–73
Responsibility, 115–123, 164–166, 177, 181, 233 n.49
Resting in the Spirit, 110
Revivalism, Catholic, 40
Revolution by tradition, 44–45
Ribeiro de Oliveira, Pedro A., 229, 261
Richardson, James, 229–232, 234–235, 237, 244, 256, 258–259, 261
Riecken, Henry W., 237, 259
Rituals, of healing, 139–141, 166–167
Robbins, Thomas, 22, 210, 230–231, 234, 236, 261, 263
Roberts, Oral, 136–137, 144
Robertson, Roland, 223–224, 260–263
Rogler, L. H., 246
Rokeach, Milton, 230–231
Roman Catholic church, 54–56, 215–219
Rose, Louis, 246
Rouleau, Jean Paul, 229
Ryan, Joseph, 229

Saliba, John A., 229
Samarin, William, 94, 112–114, 121, 230–231, 236, 239–245, 248

Sanford, Agnes, 248 n.39
Satan, 35–37, 92, 94, 116, 118, 150–152, 173. *See also* Dualism
Scanlan, Michael, 144, 232, 248, 257
Schachter, Stanley, 237, 259
Scheff, Thomas, 237, 247, 249, 255
Schmale, A. H., 255
Schneider, David M., 229
Schutz, Alfred, 108, 122, 229, 240–242, 245
Schwartz, Gary, 22, 230
Scripture, 29, 78–79, 119–120
Second Coming. *See* Millenarianism
Sect and sectarian adherence, 184–191, 202–204, 216–218, 240 n.24
Secularization, 3–4, 8, 190–191, 205–215, 220–225, 227 n.2, 241 n.36
Seekers, 53, 185
Seguy, Jean, 229
Shaffir, William, 238
Shamanism, 112, 173–174
Sheriff, John L., 243
Shibutani, Tamotsu, 94, 240
Shils, Edward, 233
Shupe, Anson, 259
Silence, 81, 83, 103
Silverman, Julian, 242, 253–254
Simmonds, Robert, 231–232, 258–259
Sin, 149–153
Slater, Philip, 232
Smelser, Neil, 235
Smith, J. Stephen, 237, 239
Social activism, 41–43, 54–55, 103, 214
Social control, 181. *See also* Norms
Speaking: authorship of, and responsibility for, 114–123; inspired and ecstatic, 110–115, 240 n.24; speech events, 14. *See also* Glossolalia
Spiritualists, compared, 120–121
Stark, Rodney, 230–231, 236
Stauffer, Robert, 260
Stewart, Mary, 234
Stoeckle, J. D., 253
Stratification, 47, 90–93, 104–155, 179–182, 197, 201, 256 n.13, 260 n.6
Straus, Roger, 235, 237, 255
Strauss, Anselm, 249
Stress, 177, 235 n.16
Submission, 30, 113, 117, 178, 194–199. *See also* Obedience; Surrender
Sudnow, David, 249
Surrender, 101–102, 117
Szasz, Thomas S., 253, 255

Talmon, Yonina, 252
Taylor, Bryan, 238
Taylor, David, 235, 255, 259